T0328435

Over the twentieth century, monetary theory played a crucial role in the evolution of the international monetary system. The severe shocks and monetary gyrations of the interwar years interacted with theoretical developments that superseded the rigid rules of commodity standards and led to the full-fledged conception of monetary policy. The definitive demise of the gold standard then paved the way for monetary reconstruction. Monetary theory was a decisive factor in the design of the reform proposals, in the Bretton Woods negotiations, and in forging the new monetary order. The Bretton Woods system – successful but nevertheless short-lived – suffered from latent inconsistencies, both analytical and institutional, that fatally undermined the foundations of the postwar monetary architecture and brought about the epochal transition from commodity money to fiat money.

Filippo Cesarano is the head of the Historical Research Office of the Bank of Italy. He studied at the University of Rome and the University of Chicago and has been a research Fellow at the Netherlands School of Economics and a visiting scholar at UCLA, Harvard, and the Hoover Institution. As an economist at the Research Department of the Bank of Italy, he has worked in the fields of monetary theory, international economics, and the history of economic analysis. He has published articles in the *American Economic Review, History of Political Economy,* the *Journal of Economic Behavior and Organization,* and the *Journal of International Economics,* among others. He has been a member of the advisory board of the *European Journal of the History of Economic Thought.*

HISTORICAL PERSPECTIVES ON MODERN ECONOMICS

General Editor: Craufurd D. Goodwin, *Duke University*

This series contains original works that challenge and enlighten historians of economics. For the profession as a whole, it promotes better understanding of the origin and content of modern economics.

Other books in the series:

William J. Barber *Designs within Disorder: Franklin D. Roosevelt, the Economists, and the Shaping of American Economic Policy, 1933–1945*

William J. Barber *From New Era to New Deal: Herbert Hoover, the Economists, and American Economic Policy, 1921–1933*

Timothy Davis *Ricardo's Macroeconomics: Money, Trade Cycles, and Growth*

Jerry Evensky *Adam Smith's Moral Philosophy: A Historical and Contemporary Perspective on Markets, Law, Ethics, and Culture*

M. June Flanders *International Monetary Economics, 1870–1960: Between the Classical and the New Classical*

J. Daniel Hammond *Theory and Measurement: Causality Issues in Milton Friedman's Monetary Economics*

Samuel Hollander *The Economics of Karl Marx: Analysis and Application*

Lars Jonung (ed.) *The Stockholm School of Economics Revisited*

Kyn Kim *Equilibrium Business Cycle Theory in Historical Perspective*

Gerald M. Koot *English Historical Economics, 1870–1926: The Rise of Economic History and Mercantilism*

David Laidler *Fabricating the Keynesian Revolution: Studies of the Inter-War Literature on Money, the Cycle, and Unemployment*

Odd Langholm *The Legacy of Scholasticism in Economic Thought: Antecedents of Choice and Power*

Harro Maas *William Stanley Jevons and the Making of Modern Economics*

Philip Mirowski *More Heat Than Light: Economics as Social Physics, Physics as Nature's Economics*

Philip Mirowski (ed.) *Nature Images in Economic Thought: "Markets Read in Tooth and Claw"*

D. E. Moggridge *Harry Johnson: A Life in Economics*

Mary S. Morgan *The History of Econometric Ideas*

Takashi Negishi *Economic Theories in a Non-Walrasian Tradition*

Heath Pearson *Origins of Law and Economics: The Economists' New Science of Law, 1830–1930*

Malcolm Rutherford *Institutions in Economics: The Old and the New Institutionalism*

Esther-Mirjam Sent *The Evolving Rationality of Rational Expectations: An Assessment of Thomas Sargent's Achievements*

Yuichi Shionoya *Schumpeter and the Idea of Social Science*

Juan Gabriel Valdes *Pinochet's Economists: The Chicago School of Economics in Chile*

Karen I. Vaughn *Austrian Economics in America: The Migration of a Tradition*

E. Roy Weintraub *Stabilizing Dynamics: Constructing Economic Knowledge*

MONETARY THEORY
AND BRETTON WOODS

The Construction of an International Monetary Order

FILIPPO CESARANO
Bank of Italy

CAMBRIDGE
UNIVERSITY PRESS

CAMBRIDGE
UNIVERSITY PRESS

32 Avenue of the Americas, New York NY 10013-2473, USA

Cambridge University Press is part of the University of Cambridge.

It furthers the University's mission by disseminating knowledge in the pursuit of education, learning and research at the highest international levels of excellence.

www.cambridge.org
Information on this title: www.cambridge.org/9780521739092

First published 2006
Reprinted 2007
First paperback edition 2009

A catalogue record for this publication is available from the British Library

Library of Congress Cataloguing in Publication data

Cesarano, Filippo.
Monetary theory and Bretton Woods : the construction of an international monetary order / Filippo Cesarano.
p.   cm. – (Historical perspectives on modern economics)
Includes bibliographical references and index.
ISBN-13: 978-0-521-86759-7 (hardback)
ISBN-10: 0-521-86759-2 (hardback)
1. International finance – History   2. Monetary policy – History.   3. United Nations Monetary and Financial Conference (1944 : Bretton Woods, N.H.) – History.   I. Title.
II. Series.
HG3881.C447   2007
332'.042 – dc22

ISBN 978-0-521-86759-7 Hardback
ISBN 978-0-521-73909-2 Paperback

CONTENTS

Contents

PREFACE

Monetary theory has an obvious and recognized role in analyzing monetary systems; it has also been crucial in determining the evolution of those systems. The fulfillment of the issuing function by government, since the early days of coined money, required at least a rudimentary knowledge of the workings of a monetary economy: The state of the art has always influenced the essential features of the monetary mechanism.

The international monetary system introduced at the end of the Second World War is a prime instance of the impact of theory on the institutional framework. The Bretton Woods construction was designed at the drawing board and approved by a formal agreement, and as a consequence the theoretical paradigm was paramount in shaping the new international monetary order. Furthermore, the demise of the short-lived Bretton Woods experience did not just put an end to the postwar monetary reconstruction, but it brought about the generalized diffusion of fiat money, an epoch-making change after 2,500 years of commodity money. These points are closely interrelated, for in the aftermath of the First World War institutions were increasingly influenced by monetary theory, itself developing in response to disruptive shocks. The difficulties of restoring the gold standard stimulated a wide-ranging debate, fueled by the conspicuous imbalances in the major economies and the vicissitudes of the international monetary system. Britain's return to gold in 1925 was followed by most countries, but it proved to be ephemeral. The properties underlying the success of the gold standard had, in fact, been damaged irremediably; the loss of credibility could not be offset by enhanced cooperation because of the altered approach to the monetary mechanism. Then, in the 1930s, the gold standard collapsed, prompting the quest for international monetary reform.

The many factors at work interacted with diverse intensity and timing. Theoretical views of the international monetary system were intertwined with institutional changes, and both were highly diversified. Economists and policymakers displayed a range of positions, while economic developments and changes in monetary arrangements followed different paths in different countries. In the interwar years, the dynamics of these forces were unevenly paced, throwing the international monetary system into disarray. A study of these contrasting elements is therefore essential to an understanding of the origins of the postwar monetary reconstruction, the design of the Bretton Woods architecture, and the latent weaknesses that caused its eventual downfall.

The international monetary order established at Bretton Woods can be viewed as the final stage in the transition from commodity money to fiat money, setting the monetary system on a new foundation. A watershed in monetary history, it was the outcome of a gradual process that spanned the half century after World War I and was propelled by several factors, including, decisively, the theory of money. This work thus focuses on the history of ideas rather than on the history of events, for which it mainly relies on the secondary literature. The theoretical perspective on this critical phase of monetary history has remained largely unexplored, an omission that limits our understanding of the evolution of the international monetary system. This book is an attempt to fill this gap.

ACKNOWLEDGMENTS

I must first express my gratitude to the three anonymous readers, who scrutinized the entire text, for their insightful comments and extremely helpful suggestions. Needless to say, I am solely responsible for any remaining errors.

I have also benefited from years of fruitful exchanges with former teachers, friends, and fellow economists, who have all contributed in various ways to sharpen my knowledge of economic theory and stimulate my research endeavors. With apologies for any unintentional omissions, I would like to thank William Allen, Robert Barro, Cristina Bicchieri, Olivier Blanchard, Mark Blaug, Michael Bordo, Giulio Cifarelli, Robert Clower, Marcello de Cecco, Stefano Fenoaltea, Stanley Fischer, Marc Flandreau, Michele Fratianni, Jacob Frenkel, Benjamin Friedman, Milton Friedman, Frank Hahn, Samuel Hollander, Robert Jones, Pieter Korteweg, David Laidler, Bennett McCallum, Deirdre McCloskey, Ronald McKinnon, Jacques Mélitz, Allan Meltzer, Robert Mundell, Jürg Niehans, Joseph Ostroy, Paul Samuelson, Neil Skaggs, Franco Spinelli, Gianni Toniolo, Giuseppe Tullio, Lawrence White, Jeffrey Williamson, and John Williamson. Craufurd Goodwin, editor of the series in which this volume appears, has always encouraged and supported this project.

I am grateful to the Hoover Institution for its kind hospitality during the summer of 1997, in the early stages of this work.

I also thank Maria Teresa Pandolfi, the librarian of the Bank of Italy, for her help in making some hard-to-find publications available. Giuliana Ferretti and Irene Paris provided assiduous and efficient research assistance. Finally, I am greatly indebted to Daniel Dichter, Brendan Jones, and John Smith for revising my English and, especially, to Roger Meservey for carefully going through the entire manuscript.

The views expressed in this book are the author's own and not necessarily those of the Bank of Italy.

Though everything that follows appears in its current form for the first time in this volume, I have published a number of articles on particular topics since the mid-1990s, and relevant material drawn from them has been incorporated herein, with kind permission of the copyright holders, who are herewith acknowledged: Duke University Press for the articles "On the Effectiveness of Changes in Money Supply: The Puzzle of Mill's View," *History of Political Economy* 28, Fall 1996, and "Keynes's Revindication of Classical Monetary Theory," *History of Political Economy* 35, Fall 2003; Springer Science and Business Media for the article "Currency Areas and Equilibrium," *Open Economies Review* 8, January 1997; Elsevier for the article "Hume's Specie-Flow Mechanism and Classical Monetary Theory: An Alternative Interpretation," *Journal of International Economics* 45, June 1998; Blackwell Publishing for the article "Expectations and Monetary Policy: A Historical Perspective," *Manchester School* 66, September 1998; Emerald Group Publishing for the articles "Providing for the Optimum Quantity of Money," *Journal of Economic Studies* 25, no. 6, 1998, "Competitive Money Supply: The International Monetary System in Perspective," *Journal of Economic Studies* 26, no. 3, 1999, and "Defining Fundamental Disequilibrium: Keynes's

Unheeded Contribution," *Journal of Economic Studies* 30, no. 5, 2003; Duncker & Humblot for the article "Monetary Systems and Monetary Theory," *Kredit und Kapital* 32, no. 2, 1999; Gius. Laterza & Figli for the book *Gli accordi di Bretton Woods. La costruzione di un ordine monetario internazionale*, Rome-Bari, Laterza, 2000.

1 INTRODUCTION

O VER THE COURSE OF THE TWENTIETH CENTURY, THE MONETARY
system underwent an epochal change. Money's link to a commodity was severed, eliminating the basic feature of the system
since the beginning of coinage and producing a break in the evolution of monetary institutions. This transformation was the product
of a gradual process extending from World War I to the suspension of dollar convertibility on 15 August 1971, an act that merely
gave official recognition to a preexisting state of affairs. The transition from the commodity standard to fiat money was driven by the
interplay of the extreme shocks of the interwar period and advances
in monetary theory, which were instrumental in designing the new
monetary arrangements. The study of the Bretton Woods agreements, then, is best viewed in this context, in which economic analysis acquires a central role. Looking at the Bretton Woods architecture from the perspective of the history of economics thus serves
not only to account for the reconstruction of international monetary relations and the key aspects of the reform, but also to shed
light on the rise of fiat money.

1.1. THE BRETTON WOODS ENIGMA

During the quarter-century in which the Bretton Woods system
governed monetary relations, the world economy experienced rapid
and relatively stable growth, especially after the leading European

currencies restored convertibility on 27 December 1958 (Bordo 1993, 12–27). This date divides the life of the system into two equal subperiods. The first began on 18 December 1946 with the launch of the new arrangements and the declaration of par values by thirty-two countries. The second, running until 1971, was the full operational phase. The extremely difficult situation at the end of World War II was dealt with outside the institutions created at Bretton Woods, in that postwar problems were not the responsibility of the International Monetary Fund and the World Bank. To keep from distorting the essential purpose of those institutions, therefore, other instruments were used. In addition to the Marshall Plan, which helped restore stability and growth in Europe, the European Payments Union paved the way to multilateralism, thus facilitating the return of convertibility. Attaining this objective marked the beginning of the full operation of the new institutions, but it also coincided with the first signs of crisis. As early as October 1960, the inflation threat perceived in John F. Kennedy's campaign promise to "get America moving again" (Bordo 1993, 69) pushed the price of gold to $40 an ounce. In 1961, tensions in the London market led to the creation of the Gold Pool to stabilize the price at $35. Furthermore, in order to stem requests to convert dollars into gold, in addition to moral suasion, the Federal Reserve resorted to swap agreements with the other central banks.[1] In short, from the very outset the system revealed weaknesses that raised doubts about its long-run viability.

Although it coincided with a period of rapid growth in the leading economies, the life of the Bretton Woods regime was very brief. This

---

[1] "In a swap arrangement, each central bank would extend to the other a bilateral line of credit. Typically, the Federal Reserve would borrow to purchase dollars held abroad instead of selling gold. To repay the swaps, the Treasury would issue Roosa bonds, that is, long-term bonds denominated in foreign currencies. By issuing Roosa bonds, the U.S. monetary authorities avoided reducing gold reserves" (Bordo 1993, 59). While recognizing the political pressure exerted by the U.S. on other countries, Eichengreen (1989, 277–8) draws attention to the latter's interest in defending the international public good of a fixed exchange rate system.

is one of the most intensely debated aspects of postwar monetary history.[2] Thus, Barry Eichengreen has observed: "Even today, more than three decades after its demise, the Bretton Woods international monetary system remains an enigma" (1996, 93).

The solution to this enigma lies ultimately in the foundations of the postwar architecture. The present book focuses on the intellectual efforts to construct the new monetary order, analyzing the underlying principles and possible inconsistencies. Understanding the origins of the malfunctioning of the Bretton Woods system is of great importance because its collapse led to the end of commodity money, an epoch-making break in monetary history.

Bretton Woods was the final stage in the transition to fiat money, a last, vain attempt to maintain a link with the commodity standard. History offers other examples of fiat money, such as in Britain's North American colonies and in France during the Revolution. But, except for paper currency in China (Tullock 1957; Davies 1994, 179–83), these were bound up with exceptional circumstances, geographically limited in scope, and brief in duration. By contrast, the current diffusion of a fiat money standard is well established, generalized, and probably irreversible. Milton Friedman has remarked: "The world's current monetary system is, I believe, unprecedented. No major currency has any link to a commodity" (1986, 643). The transformation of the monetary system over the last century is therefore unique, as was, not coincidentally, the set of rules established at Bretton Woods. At a conference organized on the occasion of the twenty-fifth anniversary of the agreements, Robert Mundell (1972) underscored this point. After distinguishing between the concepts of a monetary "system" and a monetary "order," which define, respectively, the mechanism that links the world's currencies in different markets and the body of rules within which this system

[2] The collection of papers edited by Bordo and Eichengreen (1993) aims to answer various questions "about why Bretton Woods was statistically so stable and why it was so short lived" (Bordo 1993, 4).

operates,[3] he identifies only three monetary orders: the Roman-Byzantine empire, the gold standard, and Bretton Woods. The differences between them are substantial. The first, which spanned an immense period, originated with the exercise of imperial power. The second was the result of a historical process, whose development generated and consolidated a set of institutions.[4] The Bretton Woods monetary order differs radically from its predecessors, being the product of a formal agreement, the fruit of discussion of reform schemes, that established a framework of rules for the operation of the system.

The uniqueness of the Bretton Woods agreements, emphasized by Mundell, is in reality related to the transition to fiat money. The gold standard, while leaving a certain degree of discretionary power to policymakers, was based on maintaining the gold parity and on other rules of the game that were the product of a shared theoretical paradigm. Hence, it required no formal codification. When that paradigm came under fire and the commodity link loosened, it became necessary to design new rules and institutions.

The change in the conception of the monetary mechanism toward a managed currency originated in the debate over the impossibility of controlling the money stock under the commodity standard. The problem, which had been posed by John Law as far back as

---

[3] "A system is an aggregation of diverse entities united by regular interaction according to some form of control. When we speak of the international monetary system we are concerned with the mechanisms governing the interaction between trading nations, and in particular between the money and credit instruments of national communities in foreign exchange, capital, and commodity markets. The control is exerted through policies at the national level interacting with one another in that loose form of supervision that we call co-operation. An *order*, as distinct from a system, represents the framework and setting in which the system operates. It is a framework of laws, conventions, regulations, and mores that establish the setting of the system and the understanding of the environment by the participants in it. A monetary order is to a monetary system somewhat like a constitution is to a political or electoral system. We can think of the monetary system as the *modus operandi* of the monetary order" (Mundell 1972, 92; italics in the original).

[4] In a recent article, Ronald McKinnon noted: "[For] the pre-1914 gold standard ... there was no collective 'founding treaty' nor major regime changes. Countries opted unilaterally to follow similar rules of the game that proved remarkably robust" (1993, 3).

1705, was addressed in the nineteenth century but gained additional importance after World War I. The magnitude of that shock made it extremely difficult to reinstate the gold standard and especially to comply with one of its fundamental tenets, the restoration rule, which imposed a return to the original parity after any suspension of convertibility. The United Kingdom's return to the pre-war parity in the mid-1920s in observance of this rule imposed a high welfare cost. Meanwhile, new theoretical work was weakening the classical paradigm that underpinned the gold standard. The severe turbulence in the monetary system and the economy in the interwar period helped to generate new strands of economic analysis. Until the Great Depression, the prevailing view considered the gold standard as optimal, because, in addition to being immune from political interference, it coherently reflected an equilibrium model. The depression discredited this hypothesis and produced a paradigm shift, a watershed in the history of economics.[5] The discussion of the institutional framework broadened. In examining the Bretton Woods negotiations, therefore, one must consider the advances in economic analysis that paralleled the changes in the monetary system in the 1920s and 1930s. This is an aspect that has been somewhat neglected in the literature. In general, monetary theory has always conditioned the evolution of monetary arrangements. However, when the monetary order is no longer ruled by the market for the money commodity but by a plan developed by experts, theory becomes the decisive factor.

1.2. MONETARY SYSTEMS AND MONETARY THEORY

Throughout history, the shape of monetary institutions has been powerfully influenced by the prevailing theory of money. For

[5] This quantum jump in research has been comprehensively analyzed by David Laidler (1999), who argues that the Keynesian revolution had its roots in many original contributions.

thousands of years, monetary systems conformed to the principle of metallism,[6] which, though no longer accepted, dominated monetary thought from Aristotle to the nineteenth century and beyond (Schumpeter 1954, 63). The abstract argument for commodity money may not be easy to distinguish from the policy goal of monetary discipline, but the predominance of metallism for such a long period is nonetheless puzzling.[7]

According to Carl Menger (1871, Chapter 8; 1892), money originated in a spontaneous process driven by market forces. Commodities of greater saleability arise as means of exchange through the unconcerted behavior of each individual "led by [his economic] *interest, without any agreement, without legislative compulsion, and even without regard to the public interest*" (1871, 260; italics in the original). Modern theory upholds Menger's hypothesis, showing formally that some very common good happens to be chosen as a first commodity money because of its market rather than physical characteristics (Jones 1976, 775). In the course of time, all the goods that performed monetary functions – cattle, salt bars, cowry shells, and the like – possessed, to varying degrees, those market properties. The selection was guided by the search for informationally more efficient ways of settling transactions and eventually converged on metals. This advance was conditioned by the state of technology. In fact, progress in metallurgy was essential to start minting coins in Lydia in the sixth century B.C. Likewise, the singular experience of the development of paper money in China in

---

[6] Schumpeter's definition runs as follows: "By Theoretical Metallism we denote the *theory* that it is logically essential for money to consist of, or to be 'covered' by, some commodity so that the logical source of the exchange value or purchasing power of money is the exchange value or purchasing power of that commodity, considered independently of its monetary role. . . . By Practical Metallism we shall denote sponsorship of a principle of monetary policy, namely, the principle that the monetary unit 'should' be kept firmly linked to, and freely interchangeable with, a given quantity of some commodity. Theoretical and Practical Cartalism may best be defined by the corresponding negatives" (1954, 288; italics in the original).

[7] The following five paragraphs synthetize the main arguments put forward in Cesarano (1999a, Section 1).

the ninth century A.D. was favored by the invention of paper, ink, and printing (Tullock 1957, 395).

Menger's theory, showing the emergence of money as the outcome of a natural process (1871, 261–2), exploded the view that money was the product of an agreement or the creation of the state. Yet government soon found its role, replacing merchants in certifying the quantity as well as the quality of the money commodity. Initially, perhaps, the public authority enjoyed the advantage of a higher reputation, but then the function of fixing the standard became instrumental to extracting seigniorage. Aside from this form of disguised taxation, the early appropriation by the government of the issuing function has an important further implication: To operate the system, the money issue monopolist must be guided by knowledge, albeit scanty and rudimentary, of the working of a monetary economy. The theory of money thus becomes a key factor in the development of monetary institutions; and even before economics was recognized as a discipline, it was decisively affected by various propositions, true or otherwise.

The ill-fated experience of the Law System in France in the early 1700s is a case in point. Originally motivated by the scarcity of money in Scotland, John Law's reform proposals were marred by technical inadequacies, despite his grasp of a number of principles of money and banking. The eventual collapse of the Law System, then, struck a fatal blow to the introduction of fiduciary elements into monetary arrangements, strengthening the case for metallism well into the 1800s and right up to World War I. On the other side, much earlier Copernicus (1526) advocated strict coinage rules and opposed debasement of the currency on the basis of a principle that would eventually come to be known as Gresham's Law. As these cursory examples show, the impact of monetary theory, whether right or wrong, on the monetary system can be momentous. Of course, this consideration bears on the "core" of the monetary system – that is, the ground rules governing the standard – not on innovation in the payments system or the development of inside money, which are both propelled by competitive market forces.

In contrast with the unplanned spread of banking and finance, the early role of government as sole issuer of money demanded rules, to be designed on the basis of current knowledge, however backward. This was no easy task, even when monetary theory was fairly advanced, as in the eighteenth century, because different, antagonistic approaches proceeded in parallel yet antithetic fashion.[8] This has been a characteristic trait in the advancement of monetary economics. Central to this controversial subject are two issues, particularly relevant to the operation of the monetary system: the nature of money and the effects of changes in the money supply.

The classics fully grasped the functions of money, but they seldom made the further analytical step to recognize that the performance of those functions does not require an intrinsically useful object. Even the most insightful, who intuited the conventional character of money, stopped short of advocating a paper standard. Ferdinando Galiani (1751, 67–71) put forward the key modern notion of money as a record-keeping device and a mechanism for enforcing budget constraints. David Hume (1752a, 35–6) contrasted the nature of money with that of commodities, recognizing the greater security and transportability of paper money but rejecting it because of its inflationary effects.[9] The lack of monetary

---

[8] In the preface to his *Critical Essays*, John Hicks remarks: "It is useful to recognize that pre-Keynesian monetary economics was not monolithic, in order to understand how it is that in our day monetary economics is not monolithic either. Some of our present differences echo much older differences. There is one in particular, that came to the surface in the Currency School–Banking School controversy of the eighteen-forties (but is older than that), and which persists to this day. We still have a Currency School, seeking in vain – but one sees why – for a monetary system that shall be automatic. It is represented, over its long history, not only by Lord Overstone and his friends, but by Ricardo himself; not only by Mises and Hayek and Friedman, but also by Pigou. The Banking School (or Credit School, as I wish they had called it) has a history of almost equal antiquity. It has greater names upon its roll than that of Tooke: Mill and Bagehot among the Victorians; Hawtrey and Robertson, as well as Keynes, in the twentieth century" (1967, vii–viii).

[9] In a letter sent to André Morellet dated 10 July 1769, Hume, while still arguing for a commodity standard in order to prevent inflation, pointed out the conventional nature of

discipline was indeed a major concern of classical economists. The commodity standard effectively answered this need and, moreover, was coherent with the equilibrium hypothesis of the economy as a self-adjusting system. In the nineteenth century, this approach prevailed and, notwithstanding the Birmingham School proposals for an inflationary policy to sustain employment, provided the theoretical basis for the gold standard. So widespread and firmly held was this view that the gold standard came to be considered as the realization of an ideal system that finally dispatched government meddling with currencies.

Nonetheless, the commodity standard may suffer from an excess of rigidity, not allowing sufficient control of the money stock to stabilize the price level. Hence, the deflationary pressure of the last quarter of the nineteenth century, following the upward trend in prices caused by the gold discoveries of 1849–51, prompted a debate on monetary reform to avoid prolonged purchasing power variations. Several proposals to improve the operation of the commodity standard without altering its basic properties were advanced. Yet the very idea of a money supply control mechanism sowed the seeds of the modification of the gold standard, no longer held as the ideal system. In this respect, the value of gold ceased to be regarded as a natural phenomenon, but was seen as subject to supply and demand like any other price. Accordingly, the gold standard came to be viewed as just one of various possible monetary systems, to be assessed on its own merits (Laidler 2002, 20–1).

money. "It is true, money must always be made of some materials, which have intrinsic value, otherwise it would be multiplied without end, and would sink to nothing. But, when I take a shilling, I consider it not as a useful metal, but as something which another will take from me; and the person who shall convert it into metal is, probably, several millions of removes distant. . . . Our shillings and sixpences, which are almost our only silver coin, are so much worn by use, that they are twenty, thirty, or forty per cent below their original value; yet they pass currency which can arise only from a tacit convention. Our colonies in America, for want of specie, used to coin a paper currency; which were not bank notes, because there was no place appointed to give money in exchange; yet this paper currency passed in all payments, by convention; and might have gone on, had it not been abused by the several assemblies, who issued paper without end, and thereby discredited the currency" (1970, 214–5).

Economists, in short, do not work in an economic vacuum. The prevailing theoretical paradigm, upon which institutions are built and policies are implemented, responds to the stimulus of actual problems. Even at the height of classical apriorism, which asserted the validity of economic laws in the abstract independently of their predictive power, the role of introspection and observation of economic reality in establishing the premises was not denied.[10] The question of the influence of economic history on economic theory reflects, at a certain remove, the contest between the absolutist and relativist approaches to the history of economic thought (Blaug 1997, 1–6). The former considers the evolution of economic analysis as a cumulative process that is independent of political and social conditions. The latter stresses a relationship of dependence and attributes a considerable impact on the development of economic theory to major events and, more generally, to the economic environment. Maffeo Pantaleoni (1898) was a fierce critic of relativism, but admitted that a given set of environmental conditions can, without affecting the characteristics of the analytical construction, bring about a derived "demand for scientific products."[11] Thus, the

---

[10] In a recent paper, Paul Samuelson has drawn attention to the importance of economic history for economic analysis, stigmatizing the aprioristic approach: "To me economic history is any documentation of *empirical experience* – across space and time. Put this way, only a nineteenth century *deductive* economist or a naïve *a prioristic* philosopher could fail to understand that the fruitfulness of any deductive syllogism cannot originate inside itself. Somewhere in the axioms of a relevant paradigm ('model') there must have already been put in relevant (and testable) factual assertions. Garbage in: Garbage out. Tycho Brahe's good astronomical measurements in: Keplerian gold out" (2001, 272; italics in the original).

[11] "What influence has the environment ever had on the doctrines of chemistry? I appreciate that the environment may create a *demand* today, let's say, for explosives, just as earlier it created a *demand* for philters: research aimed at discovering some properties rather than others. But the *result of the research* is independent of the environment. The properties of bodies are what they are and discovering them, or not discovering them, is a question of ingenuity, method and intellectual training, so that even a chance event can prove fertile.... As for the link between economic institutions, or economic affairs, on the one hand, and economic theories, on the other, it is evident that it is of the kind already mentioned when we were examining the influence the environment could have on other sciences. The demand creates the good.... But, the demand of the market does not dictate

observation of empirical regularities, the grasping of novel stylized facts, and the emergence of anomalies stimulate and nourish the theorist's work. Subsequently, theories are tested against the empirical evidence, whose relevance, in contrast with classical methodology, is now taken for granted. The relationship between facts and theory, therefore, gives rise to a circular process of continuous interaction. Observation of economic reality raises problems and poses puzzles, hinting at models to analyze them. The results of empirical testing, either corroborating or falsifying the hypothesis, then feed back into the set of observed phenomena that, according to their magnitude and importance, again stimulate new hypotheses or draw attention to unorthodox ones.

In fact, distinguished economists have often put forward models anticipating the solution of future problems. As early as 1898, in the heyday of the gold standard, Knut Wicksell (1898, 193) suggested the introduction of an international paper standard to stabilize the price level. And Milton Friedman, in his criticism of the Phillips curve (1968a), foresaw the explanation of the stagflation of the 1970s. In both instances, subsequent events proved decisive to mainstream acceptance of the innovative theory, marking a turning point in the state of the art. The occurrence of major shocks does have a substantial effect, either quashing innovative ideas (e.g., the failure of the Law System) or increasing the demand for "scientific doctrines" to the point of prompting a paradigm shift. In this regard, the malfunctioning of the international

the result of the research that is undertaken in response to the demand itself. The social question, just as it gives rise to the works of George, gives rise to the works of Mallock and Leroy-Beaulieu. And, ultimately, the demand created by the environment is not a direct demand for scientific products. It is a demand for measures, i.e. for practical steps, and only to the extent that these require a theoretical basis do scientific doctrines receive an impulse. If the navy grows, indirectly, hydrostatics, pure mechanics and thermodynamics will be of interest to more people. But in no way does the environment color scientific doctrines, nor from such a link is it possible to deduce any justification for treating the truths that are discovered and the stupidities that are invented as twins" (Pantaleoni 1898, 418–20; italics in the original; author's translation).

monetary system in the interwar years provides almost a laboratory experiment. The seemingly intractable problems inherited from World War I[12] compounded the Great Depression and led to an irreparable crisis of the gold standard, undermining the foundations of commodity money. These monetary disturbances helped power the diffusion of once heterodox ideas that paved the way to the introduction of new monetary arrangements.

The prevailing paradigm, resulting from the interaction of major events and economic analysis, is thus essential in determining policy choices and in designing institutions.[13] The success of the gold standard was sustained, above all, by the widespread acceptance of the equilibrium model of classical monetary theory. No government, at that time, would have dared to enact policies in contrast with the gold standard rules in order to improve the economy's performance, precisely because the rules were thought to lead to the optimal solution. So diffuse was the acceptance of the classical model that, among policymakers, adherence to the gold standard continued after World War I until the overwhelming impact of

[12] While pointing out the theoretical contributions to managed money after 1870, David Laidler recognizes the decisive effect of the World War I shock in shifting mainstream opinion in favor of such a system. "Whether the idea of managed money would have triumphed over tradition and practice to destroy the Gold Standard had World War I not happened is hard to say. My own instinct is to doubt it: exponents of the quantity theory were, on the whole, more satisfied with the monetary status quo on the eve of the war than they had been twenty years earlier. Though they did not give up arguing the theoretical superiority of other ways of organising matters, they did recognise that the Gold Standard, or to be more precise the Gold Exchange Standard, seemed to be working, and working rather well at that. At the same time, I find it even less likely that notions of managed money would have attracted so much support so quickly in the 1920s and 1930s, had their intellectual foundations not been so firmly developed in the preceding forty years or so" (1991, 2).

[13] In an article published before Britain's return to gold, Keynes remarked: "The supporters of monetary reform, of which I, after further study and reflection, am a more convinced adherent than before, as the most important and significant measure we can take to increase economic welfare, must expound their arguments more fully, more clearly, and more simply, before they can overwhelm the forces of old custom and general ignorance. This is not a battle which can be won or lost in a day. Those who think that it can be finally settled by a sharp hustle back to gold mistake the situation. That will be only the beginning. The issue will be determined, not by the official decisions of the coming year, but by the combined effects of the actual experience of what happens after that and the relative clearness and completeness of the arguments of the opposing parties" (1925a, 193).

the Great Depression produced a major change in the state of the art. In this respect, the contrast between two key episodes of British monetary history is telling. The ephemeral return to gold in April 1925 was preceded by a heated debate, but, in the event, the widespread consensus on the gold standard model was decisive to Winston Churchill's decision (see Chapter 3, Section 1, and, in particular, note 6). In September 1931, the intellectual climate was diametrically opposite, witness the Macmillan Committee's report issued two months before, and Britain abandoned the gold standard.

While the role of theory in determining the structure and properties of the monetary system has often been underrated, political factors have been emphasized. However, these can significantly condition the evolution of monetary institutions only insofar as they impinge on theory and, particularly, on the analytical framework accounting for the welfare implications of alternative monetary regimes. In this connection, the interests of pressure groups may affect the policymaker's objective function. For example, importance assigned to unemployment was much less in the early decades of the gold standard than in the twentieth century, when universal suffrage and the rise of labor parties and of trade unionism made employment conditions a more sensitive issue. Nevertheless, aside from some possible effects on the economists' "vision," political factors have little or no influence on the theoretical structure of the model of the economy on which – rather than on the objective function – the most bitter controversies have constantly focused.[14] In this regard, a characterizing quality of the gold standard – that is, the insulation of central banks from domestic politics – is accounted for by the predominance of an equilibrium approach that

[14] The opening paragraph of Milton Friedman's presidential address to the American Economic Association makes this point: "There is wide agreement about the major goals of economic policy: high employment, stable prices, and rapid growth. There is less agreement that these goals are mutually compatible or, among those who regard them as incompatible, about the terms at which they can and should be substituted for one another. There is least agreement about the role that various instruments of policy can and should play in achieving the several goals" (1968a, 95).

dispensed the monetary authorities from pursuing any goal other than maintaining the gold parity. In exceptional circumstances with major repercussions on public finances, the rules of the game could be suspended, but only as long as those circumstances persisted. The great resilience showed by the gold standard, a key reason for its success and for the unyielding support it received even after the disruptive shock of the Great War, was grounded in the dominant paradigm of classical economics, which shaped economic policy design and the rules of the monetary system.

The development of monetary arrangements is certainly too complex to lend itself to monocausal explanations, so politics, together with several other factors, may influence the evolutionary path. Yet such influence must stand the ultimate test of theory. To exemplify, a recurrent feature of Keynes's several proposals for monetary reform was retention of a role for gold in order to safeguard the interests of gold producers. This feature was only apparent, however, because it could not conflict with the theoretical framework underlying Keynes's proposals, which, in fact, aimed at dethroning gold.

In conclusion, economic history and economic theory are closely intertwined, although the link is not unidirectional or regular in pattern, not lending itself to uniform, straightforward interpretation.[15] The uninterrupted flow of events, theories, and

---

[15] Interviewed on this matter, Milton Friedman has recently recognized the influence of history on his own work while admitting at the same time the intricacies of showing exactly the ways in which this influence was exerted: "I have no doubt that economic history did influence my work on economic theory, but I have great difficulty in saying precisely how or through what channels. For example, consider my book *A Theory of the Consumption Function*, in which I developed the permanent income hypothesis. That hypothesis was developed to reconcile a conflict between two sets of historical data: time series data accumulated by Simon Kuznets and budget data, first collected systematically by Frédéric LePlay in the middle of the nineteenth century. The Kuznets data indicated that savings had constituted roughly the same fraction of national income over a long period of time despite a major rise in the level of national income. The budget data by contrast showed that within each sample the higher the income of the individual family the higher the fraction of income saved. These historical data set the problem, but the theory I suggested to explain them owed more to pure economic theory than to any characteristics of data or to economic history more generally. As another example,

hypothesis testing is a circular process that ultimately molds the state of the art.[16] As mentioned above, the dynamic interaction of theories and events was especially intricate in the evolution of the monetary system between the wars, when the interplay of major shocks and monetary analysis was so intense that, at any given moment, several contrasting viewpoints could be found among economists and policymakers. The uneven pace at which positions progressed substantially heightened the monetary imbalances of that period. Monetary arrangements were left in disarray, impelling the reconstruction of an international monetary order from the ground up. The present work on the genesis of the Bretton Woods agreements shows that, whatever the relevance of other factors, economic theory played a central role.

1.3. A BRIEF OUTLINE

The interwar years were characterized not only by severe shocks and monetary gyrations but also by important advances in

consider the article on *The Utility Analysis of Choices Involving Uncertainty* by L. J. Savage and myself. It provided a theory to explain the tendency for individuals simultaneously to buy insurance and to gamble, superficially contradictory activities. Economic history surely entered in. For example, we studied carefully historical experience with lotteries – how they had developed, what form they had taken, and the like. Moreover, it was history that gave us the phenomena which we tried to study and explain. However, here again it is hard to see how history affected the particular hypothesis we set forth. That rested much more on a rich theoretical literature dealing with utility, probability, and choice" (2001, 127–8).

[16] Recalling important historical episodes and stylized facts referred to in his main essays, Friedman has underscored the complexity of the link between facts and analysis pointing out the bivalent function fulfilled by empirical evidence. "As economists, we can only reason about a world we know something about, and our major source of knowledge about that world comes from economic history. However, it is seldom possible to trace the precise connection between particular historical episodes and specific theoretical propositions. History defines our problems and tests our answers" (2001, 129). Along the same lines, Pantaleoni remarked: "Naturally it has never occurred to anyone to maintain that the environment does not supply the premises for economic doctrines, that it does not represent a continuous, direct demand for practical rules, or that it does not serve to confirm or confute theories. Truth to tell, however, rarely do the facts actually constitute either the demonstration or the disproof of a theory, because events generally take a form so complicated as to render their testimony inconclusive, like the vociferations of a clamoring throng" (1898, 424; author's translation).

monetary economics. This study concentrates on the international monetary system, inquiring into the theoretical debate that prepared the ground for Bretton Woods. In this respect, the development of monetary theory was momentous, because it laid the foundations for the new monetary architecture. In a sense, after World War I theory came to play a more effective, indeed crucial, role: No longer confined to academic debate and analysis of the variants of the commodity standard, it became instrumental to designing the monetary system. The main focus therefore is on the history of theory rather than on the history of events.[17]

This book is organized in three parts. The first examines the main developments in the international monetary system in the interwar period. In 1914, the gold standard was at its peak and thus provided the natural benchmark for assessing proposals for monetary reform. Examining the main features of the gold standard model (Chapter 2), an alternative interpretation of Hume's essay clarifies the alleged weaknesses of the specie-flow mechanism. In particular, the lack of empirical evidence about significant price differentials and sizeable gold flows between countries, far from falsifying Hume's hypothesis, actually corroborates it. The rules of the game reflecting this model are the basis of the main properties of the gold standard, which account for the successful performance of the system over four decades. After 1918, the transition to the gold exchange standard spoiled the main properties of the system, especially credibility, leading to recurrent crises. This is reflected in the main developments of the monetary system (Chapter 3), because the ephemeral return to gold also introduced elements of flexibility that ran counter to cooperation and actually undermined the coherent structure of the system. The uneven pace

---

[17] The latter aspect has been analyzed in the thorough works of Richard Gardner (1969) on the context of the Bretton Woods debates, Barry Eichengreen (1992a) on the interaction of international monetary arrangements and the world economy between the wars, and Harold James (1996) on the functioning of the Bretton Woods monetary order and its aftermath.

at which economists and policymakers distanced themselves from the gold standard model heightened monetary imbalances, making the operation of the monetary system a powerful source of instability. The Great Depression, then, turned received ideas definitively away from the gold standard.

The second part of the book focuses on the economic analysis of the international monetary system. After World War I (Chapter 4), although policymakers' consensus on the gold standard was largely unshaken, economists criticized the lack of adequate control of the money supply, which made stabilizing the price level unfeasible and amplified economic fluctuations. This new mainstream view was opposed by both radicals and conservatives, giving rise to a lively academic debate. The optimality of the gold standard had now been called into question, opening a crack in doctrine, which, for over 2,500 years had been based on commodity money. In the 1930s (Chapter 5), mainstream economists, still following the classical equilibrium approach, underscored the fall in the price level as the distinctive feature of the Great Depression and offered a monetary explanation. The widely held hypothesis that the malfunctioning of the monetary system had spread the effects of the depression further spurred the quest for monetary reform. However, despite seminal contributions anticipating modern results, original reform proposals were few. And even after the paradigm shift determined by Keynes's *General Theory*, the critical appraisal of the gold exchange standard, particularly the lack of central bank cooperation, failed to produce a commonly accepted scheme. On the eve of World War II, therefore, the need for a full-fledged reconstruction of international monetary arrangements was urgently felt.

The third part of the book starts (Chapter 6) with an examination of the intellectual efforts that produced the Keynes Plan and the White Plan. Both sought to deal with the main problems of the interwar period – the abandonment of fixed exchange rates, hindrances to multilateral trade, asymmetry in the adjustment process – but they took different routes. Keynes's innovative proposal was founded on the principle of bank clearing to overcome the slow and cumbersome adjustment of the gold standard, as well as on the introduction of an international money managed by a supranational authority; resort to capital controls would have permitted countries to adopt independent full-employment policies. Harry White, instead, took a more conservative approach, seeking to improve on the gold exchange standard and eschewing controls. Both plans allowed for financial facilities to overcome temporary balance-of-payments difficulties and admitted parity changes in case of a persistent disequilibrium. Shortly after their publication, economists pointed out several weaknesses in the proposals, anticipating subsequent criticisms of the Bretton Woods agreements. In particular, activist economic policies, in response to the paradigm shift brought about by the Great Depression, conflicted with exchange rate stability; furthermore, the variegated operating characteristics of the schemes blurred the nature of the adjustment mechanism.

The Bretton Woods conference inevitably ended in a compromise, giving rise to a hybrid construction (Chapter 7). Yet the commonplace that the outcome mainly reflected the U.S. proposal disregards the momentous impact of the *General Theory*, and of Keynes's view of international monetary arrangements, on the main features of the Bretton Woods architecture. Not only was the idea of independent economic policy generally accepted, but the emergence of various malfunctions and, eventually, of fiat money were closely related to the predominance of Keynesian economics.[18]

---

[18] Downplaying postwar price and wage rigidity, Obstfeld emphasizes the substantial change in the conception of economic policy with respect to the gold standard. "Even if many countries' wages and prices were only moderately less flexible after 1945 than under the classical gold standard, at least one drastic shift in the policy environment clearly has occurred. Postwar governments, unlike their pre-1914 predecessors, were politically responsible for (or even legally committed to) the maintenance of high employment and economic growth. Recognizing the primacy of domestic employment objectives, the founders of Bretton Woods hoped that IMF credits would allow countries to wait out transitory shocks while avoiding the uncertainty and possible beggar-thy-neighbor effects of frequent exchange-rate changes " (1993, 216).

The bold attempt by the Bretton Woods negotiators to combine full-employment policies with fixed but adjustable exchange rates made the monetary system inherently unstable. The contradiction was aggravated by the early transformation of Bretton Woods into a revised gold exchange standard, virtually dispensing with exchange rate variations. In abandoning the spirit of the treaty, the foundation of the European Payments Union acted as a catalyst for the policymakers' quest to enhance policy credibility and for the United States' concern to discipline other countries' policies in order to prevent parity changes and excessive external debt. These developments accorded with the conservative background of central bankers, witness the steady accumulation of gold reserves and the emphasis given to the Triffin dilemma – that is, the irreconcilability between the convertibility of the dollar and the provision of international liquidity by the center country to meet the growing demand for reserves (Triffin 1960).

The widening contrast between the policymakers' laggard approach and the divergence of the monetary system from the commodity standard on the one hand, and the increasing influence of Keynesian economics on the other, were the prime causes of the demise of Bretton Woods (Chapter 8). Playing the role of the nth country in the Mundellian redundancy problem,[19] the United States could ignore the balance-of-payments objective, but had to take the responsibility for pursuing rigorous monetary and fiscal policies. Until the mid-1960s, the U.S. inflation rate was the lowest among G7 countries and the most stable, so the center country abided by the rule of anchoring the world price level while the others

---

[19] In the appendix to Chapter 13 of his *International Economics*, Mundell analyzed the asymmetry characterizing the postwar monetary order in which gold had been demonetized in private transactions and, virtually, in official transactions as well. Because the balance-of-payments surpluses necessarily match the balance-of-payments deficits, Mundell argued: "Only $n-1$ independent balance-of-payments instruments are needed in an n-country world because equilibrium in the balances of $n-1$ countries implies equilibrium in the balance of the nth country. The *redundancy problem* is the problem of deciding how to utilize the extra degree of freedom" (1968, 195; italics in the original).

created disequilibrium conditions by accumulating gold reserves. Afterward, instead, the expansionary monetary and fiscal policies in the United States triggered the effects of the cumulative imbalances, accelerating the system's collapse. In an intellectual climate dominated by the Keynesian paradigm, price stability was no longer the primary goal and the international monetary system was left adrift.

In this connection, the interwar cultural divide between economists and policymakers persisted, and the recipes for mending the Bretton Woods flaws were not grasped. This lack of understanding cast serious doubt on the viability of the new monetary order, in an accentuation of the initial disequilibria that eventually proved fatal. The "Bretton Woods enigma" posed by Barry Eichengreen can thus be resolved if we gather together the threads of the conflict of theoretical and institutional frameworks as well as economic policies between the United States and the other countries.

The Bretton Woods experience teaches several lessons, chiefly the difficulty of designing a new monetary order at the drawing board. The emergence of fiat money after nearly three millennia of monetary history and the prospective development of nontangible exchange media pose new and radically different challenges to economists and policymakers. In this state of flux, the interplay of theoretical advancement, major shocks, and innovation in payments technology and banking should again be looked at as the driving force of monetary evolution.

2 INTERNATIONAL MONETARY EQUILIBRIUM AND THE PROPERTIES OF THE GOLD STANDARD

I N A DETAILED RECONSTRUCTION OF INTERNATIONAL MONETARY developments between the wars, Barry Eichengreen (1992a) underscores the period's continuity with the gold standard and the decisive role of the monetary system in aggravating the depression and propagating its effects from the United States to the rest of the world. He identifies two factors underlying the success of the gold standard until 1914: the credibility of the official commitment to gold and international cooperation. The loss of credibility after World War I could only have been remedied by even stronger cooperation, whose absence made the crisis inevitable (Eichengreen 1992a, xi).[1] Credibility and cooperation are important elements of the gold standard, but the relation between them appears to be more complex than a simple inverse relation, suggesting a link that is not in the nature of a trade-off. In general, how the gold standard worked has always been controversial. A clarifying analysis of its properties is therefore essential to understanding the evolution of the monetary system in the interwar years, especially the contrast between the success of the gold standard and the failure of the gold exchange standard. The monetary gyrations and economic

---

[1] Ragnar Nurkse had already pointed out the lack of cooperation under the gold exchange standard: "[T]he nucleus of the gold exchange system consisted of more than one country; and this was a special source of weakness. With adequate cooperation between the centre countries, it need not have been serious. Without such cooperation it proved pernicious" (1944, 46).

instability of the 1920s and 1930s showed the need to devise new rules, which eventually led to the Bretton Woods negotiations and the creation of a new international monetary order.

2.1. THE CLASSICAL ADJUSTMENT MECHANISM

Hume's classic essay *Of the Balance of Trade* (1752b) is still the primary reference in the study of the commodity standard,[2] but ever since it appeared it has been at the center of a lively debate with major implications for the history of the monetary system. Under the traditional interpretation, the price-specie-flow mechanism restores equilibrium by means of changes in the price level. A trade surplus triggers an inflow of gold, which causes prices to rise. This encourages imports and penalizes exports, thus reestablishing the balance and eliminating the excess supply of money. According to a recurrent criticism, raised by James Oswald of Dunnikier (1750) even before the publication of Hume's paper, this mechanism violates the law of one price: Ignoring transport costs, arbitrage would ensure that the price of a commodity was the same across countries. Thus, explanations of the adjustment process relied on changes in other variables – namely, income, the interest rate, and relative prices.[3] However, these attempts to rehabilitate Hume's

---

[2] Its importance is emphasized by Eichengreen: "The most influential formalization of the gold-standard mechanism is the *price-specie flow model* of David Hume. Perhaps the most remarkable feature of this model is its durability: developed in the eighteenth century, it remains the dominant approach to thinking about the gold standard today" (1996, 25; italics in the original). However, Hume had a number of important forerunners: Isaac Gervaise, Jacob Vanderlint, and Richard Cantillon.

[3] In the 1930s, Harry White (1933), who studied under Frank Taussig at Harvard and would later be one of the negotiators of the Bretton Woods agreements, published a book analyzing other adjustment mechanisms in the absence of any empirical evidence supporting the hypothesis of the price-specie-flow mechanism. In this regard, Whale remarked: "It is noteworthy that Taussig, although in a way he has been the leading exponent of the classical explanation, has often warned his readers that the evidence gives the theory very doubtful support. Further, I think it may be said that on the whole the attempts at historical verification undertaken by the younger members of the Harvard School have increased rather than diminished the doubts.... The point which has troubled Taussig most is that in many cases the adjustments appeared to have occurred

theory are unsatisfactory and sometimes involve "sophisticated fallacies" (Samuelson 1980, 141). Only more recent contributions, such as the monetary approach, are consistent with the law of one price, basing the model on the "desired" level of real balances. The apparent conflict between Hume's analysis and modern empirical and theoretical work has lent weight to the view that the price-specie-flow mechanism, and specifically its automatic character, is a myth that in no way reflects how the gold standard actually worked. Hence, historical research would appear to have lost the support of the classical model in explaining the adjustment process, which is a key issue in understanding the gold standard.[4]

In reality, the intricate debate that has run on for two-and-a-half centuries is the product of an erroneous interpretation (Cesarano 1998a). In Hume's essay, the law of one price is not violated and in fact is the foundation of his analysis: It is the equilibrium condition underlying the "natural" distribution of the stock of money. This point is already made in his reply to Oswald (Hume 1750): It is precisely because of the law of one price that the ratio of the money stock to output is the same across countries.

more immediately and with less friction than his theory would lead one to expect" (1937, 45–6). The data reported by Robert Triffin (1964, 142) show that between 1870 and 1960 the price index of exports by the eleven leading countries moved in the same direction in 89 percent of cases and in the opposite direction in only 11 percent.

[4] As Eichengreen (1985, 9) asserted in citing Marcello De Cecco: "How the adjustment process worked prior to 1913 is 'the ritual question' posed by students of the gold standard (to adopt the phrase of De Cecco)." In the following quotations, the idea of the gold standard as a myth shared by scholars emerges clearly: "[A] whole book ought to be written to analyse the *Myth* of the Gold Standard" (De Cecco 1984, viii; italics in the original); "We might speak here of the myth of the (automatic) price-specie-flow mechanism whereby a country with a balance of payments deficit would have to pay for it by losing gold which would cause its money supply to fall thereby inducing a fall in prices and an increase in competitiveness leading to balance of payments equilibrium; this process would be simultaneously reinforced by rising prices in the rest of the world due to a gain of gold. It is now quite clear that the pre-WWI gold standard did not work in this simple way" (Redmond 1992, 347); and "[T]his vision of the gold standard, like the unicorn in James Thurber's garden, is a mythical beast" (Eichengreen and Flandreau 1997, 3). The first part of the book edited by Michael Bordo and Anna Schwartz (1984) contains a broad, detailed discussion of the interpretation of Hume's theory and, in particular, of the contrast between the traditional approach (Bordo 1984) and the monetary approach (McCloskey and Zecher 1984).

"Of the Balance Trade" is a critique of mercantilism, demonstrating that it would be impossible for a single country to accumulate gold forever. The money stock is divided among the different countries in such a way that they all have the same ratio of money to income, which, abstracting from the velocity of circulation, is equal to the price level. The stability of equilibrium precludes the continuous outflow of specie. The country's gold stock is ultimately governed by its growth capacity. Under the law of one price, a given increase in output gives rise, *ceteris paribus*, to an accumulation of gold.

[A]ny man who travels over Europe at this day, may see, by the prices of commodities, that money, in spite of the absurd jealousy of princes and states, has brought itself nearly to a level; and that the difference between one kingdom and another is not greater in this respect, than it is often between different provinces of the same kingdom. Men naturally flock to capital cities, sea-ports, and navigable rivers. There we find more men, more industry, more commodities, and consequently more money; but still the latter difference holds proportion with the former, and the level is preserved. (Hume 1752b, 66)

Hume's contribution, although based on a simplified version of the quantity theory that followed the theoretical orientation of the time, has considerable explanatory power and, albeit focusing on money supply rather than demand, achieves results that are consistent with the modern literature. As in the monetary approach, equilibrium in the money market is the center of the model and the balance of payments is viewed as a monetary phenomenon. The interpretative error that has led to the attribution of a different model to Hume is the emphasis placed on a single passage[5] cited out

---

[5] "Suppose four-fifths of all the money in Great Britain to be annihilated in one night, and the nation reduced to the same condition, with regard to specie, as in the reigns of the Harrys and Edwards, what would be the consequence? Must not the price of all labour and commodities sink in proportion, and everything be sold as cheap as they were in those ages? What nation could then dispute with us in any foreign market, or pretend to navigate or to sell manufactures at the same price, which to us would afford sufficient profit? In how little time, therefore, must this bring back the money which we had lost,

of context. A careful rereading within the essay's overall analytical structure dissolves the presumed theoretical contradictions and divergences from the empirical evidence. The central message regards the stability of long-run equilibrium and not, as the standard interpretation would have it, the transition from one equilibrium to another, a dynamic problem that Hume investigated in his other essay on money (1752a) in a closed economy setup. Indeed, in the paragraph immediately following the over-quoted one of footnote 5, he clearly illustrates the meaning of his analysis that does not regard the effects of actual changes in money supply and prices but represents a thought experiment showing the mechanism that prevents conspicuous departures from equilibrium.

Now, it is evident, that the same causes, which would correct these exorbitant inequalities, *were they to happen miraculously, must prevent their happening in the common course of nature,* and must for ever, in all neighbouring nations, preserve money nearly proportionable to the art and industry of each nation. All water, wherever it communicates, remains always at a level. Ask naturalists the reason; they tell you, that, were it to be raised in any one place, the superior gravity of that part not being balanced, must depress it, till it meet a counterpoise; and that the same cause, which redresses the inequality when it happens, must for ever prevent it, without some violent external operation.

(Hume 1752b, 63–4; italics added)

Variations in the money stock, then, are clearly notional in character and are proportional to changes in output, because arbitrage equalizes prices across countries. The absence of large-scale gold

and raise us to the level of all the neighbouring nations? Where, after we have arrived, we immediately lose the advantage of the cheapness of labour and commodities; and the farther flowing in of money is stopped by our fulness and repletion. Again, suppose, that all the money of Great Britain were multiplied fivefold in a night, must not the contrary effect follow? Must not all labour and commodities rise to such an exorbitant height, that no neighbouring nations could afford to buy from us; while their commodities, on the other hand, became comparatively so cheap, that, in spite of all the laws which could be formed, they would be run in upon us, and our money flow out; till we fall to a level with foreigners, and lose that great superiority of riches, which had laid us under such disadvantages?" (Hume 1752b, 62–3).

flows and significant price differentials among countries lends support to this alternative version based on the law of one price. Thus, a correct reading of Hume rehabilitates his contribution, which far from giving rise to a myth actually demonstrates an essential property of the gold standard: It dampens movements away from equilibrium.[6] This proposition is consistent with the speed of the adjustment mechanism pointed out by Frank Taussig (see footnote 3) and stressed also in modern literature (Bayoumi, Eichengreen, and Taylor 1996, 7–9).

The seeming contrast between the traditional interpretation of the price-specie-flow mechanism and the empirical evidence prompted scholars to conclude that the gold standard was a managed rather than automatic mechanism. Over the course of the nineteenth century, central banks undoubtedly played an increasingly active role in influencing monetary aggregates, but this could not emerge from Hume's analysis, which considers fiduciary money as a substitute for metallic money with no effects on his results. The extension of the model to incorporate other variables, and particularly capital movements, is reflected in the "rules of the game."[7] Thus, in the event of an outflow of specie, Bagehot's rule would impose an increase in the discount rate to attract foreign capital

---

[6] Having described the several contagious crises during the gold standard, Eichengreen and Flandreau remarked: "And yet what is striking about the gold standard is that none of the major powers was forced to depart from it for any extended period of time. This statement holds for North America, Western Europe, and Britain's overseas Dominions and Commonwealth, as well as for the Austro-Hungarian and Russian Empires after 1890. Throughout this area, exchange rates were impressively stable. Although there was no shortage of shocks to commodity and financial markets, disturbances to the balance of payments were dispatched without destabilizing exchange rates or otherwise undermining the solidity of the gold standard system" (1997, 10). However, they attribute the capacity for adjustment not to the functioning of the gold standard but rather to the especially favorable conditions prevailing in the various economies, chiefly rapid industrialization.

[7] The coinage of this expression, summarizing the behavior of monetary authorities under the gold standard, is usually attributed to Keynes (1925b, 220), but it may have been current in British financial circles; Walter Layton, editor of *The Economist*, referred to "the rules of the game in regard to gold" (1925, 189) in an article published before *The Economic Consequences of Mr Churchill* of July 1925.

and thus ease the deflationary pressure and smooth the adjustment process.

In the interwar period, the domestic and foreign assets of the central banks moved in opposite directions, preventing any liquidity drain in the event of an outflow of reserves (Nurkse 1944). Arthur Bloomfield (1959) observed the same phenomenon in the pre-1914 period as well. This stylized fact, however, rather than a violation of the rules of the game, demonstrates that there was significant room for maneuver to smooth the effects of the monetary mechanism on domestic money supplies (McKinnon 1993, 9–10) but not enough to govern the system as a whole. The price level was determined in the gold market, and Keynes's assertion that the Bank of England was the "conductor of the international orchestra" (1930, Vol. 2, 307) must be reassessed. The followers of the monetary approach see the United Kingdom as too small a part of the world economy to have decisive influence over prices and, assuming the validity of the law of one price, the Bank of England, paraphrasing Keynes's analogy, was a "triangle player" (McCloskey and Zecher 1976, 359).[8] Finally,

---

[8] More recent research has taken an intermediate stance, considering the United Kingdom at the same level as France and Germany. "There is no question that the Bank of England exercised more influence over discount rates (the rates at which central banks extended credit to institutional customers) than did any other national central bank. There is no question that her discount rate provided a focal point for the harmonization of discount policies internationally. But the Bank of England was no more able to neglect changes in discount policies abroad than were foreign central banks able to neglect changes by the Bank of England. It is untrue, moreover, that the Bank of England monopolized the role of international lender of last resort. More frequently than not, it was the international borrower of last resort, reduced to dependence, as we will see, on the Bank of France and other foreign sources in its battle to defend the sterling parity. The key to the success of the classical gold standard lay rather in two entirely different areas: credibility and cooperation. In the countries at the center of the system – Britain, France, and Germany – the credibility of the official commitment to the gold standard was beyond reproof. Hence market participants relieved central bankers of much of the burden of management. If sterling weakened, funds would flow toward Britain in anticipation of the capital gains that would arise once the Bank of England intervened to strengthen the rate. Because the central bank's commitment to the existing parity was beyond question, capital flows responded quickly and in considerable volume. Sterling strengthened of its own accord, usually without any need for government intervention. Speculation had the same stabilizing influence in France, Germany, and other European countries at the center of the gold standard system" (Eichengreen 1992a, 30). In this regard, the empirical results

when the stock of gold is small in relation to fiduciary money, the lender of last resort could face a conflict between the objective of safeguarding banks and that of maintaining convertibility. Under the gold standard, the intervention of the central bank did not reach such a critical level as to undermine the stability of the system, owing both to the limited development of the lender-of-last-resort function and the great credibility of the fixed exchange rate thanks to the restoration rule.

In short, under the gold standard central banks did not play a merely passive role, but this does not mean that the system lacked an adjustment mechanism. The contrast between the managed aspect of the gold standard and its automatic nature is only apparent. The key point is the stability of equilibrium. The very properties of the system were such as to prevent any monetary imbalances from leading to substantial departures from equilibrium.[9] The intervention of monetary authorities did not supplant the adjustment mechanism but rather facilitated its operation and, above all, reduced the welfare costs of a more volatile money supply. The effectiveness of this intervention was founded precisely on the characteristics of the gold standard that derived from its commodity link. The anchoring of the parity in these circumstances was highly credible and forced economic policies to achieve that objective, thus explaining the long life of the system.

---

of Tullio and Wolters "show strong mutual feedbacks between London, Paris and Berlin with maybe just a slight dominance of London" (1996, 422). Furthermore, McKinnon (1993, 3–4) notes that even if we acknowledge the importance of the London financial center, the price level under the gold standard was in any case determined in the gold market, giving the system a symmetry that the architects of Bretton Woods tried in vain to re-create.

9 In his penetrating analysis of the international transmission of the trade cycle under the gold standard, Hawtrey contended that, together with the slowness and inertia in the monetary mechanism, this was a central feature of the actual operation of the system. "These gold movements made the progress of a credit expansion or a credit contraction irregular and discontinuous, but the irregularities were never so great as to obscure the general trend for any considerable period. The credit movement would always be resumed till equilibrium was restored in the world gold position" (1929a, 73).

Throughout history, the commodity nature of money was considered an essential feature. Even when the metallist principle was finally refuted in theory by focusing on the functions of money rather than on the object used to perform those functions, metallism continued to be advanced as a counterweight to government meddling with money creation. Hence, Schumpeter (1954, 289) points out that rejecting theoretical metallism is not inconsistent with accepting practical metallism. This position is most clearly analyzed by John Stuart Mill (1848, 542–55). An inconvertible paper money can undoubtedly circulate on the sole basis of convention, and its value is regulated by the monetary authority by fixing the quantity in circulation. Nonetheless, the introduction of paper money is strongly opposed because, allowing discretion in monetary management, it would have pernicious effects.

Such a power [of issuing inconvertible currency], in whomsoever vested, is an intolerable evil. All variations in the value of the circulating medium are mischievous: *they disturb existing contracts and expectations*, and the liability to such changes renders every pecuniary engagement of long date entirely precarious. . . . Not to add, that the issuers may have, and in the case of a government paper, always have, a direct interest in lowering the value of the currency, because it is the medium in which their own debts are computed.   (Mill 1848, 544; italics added)

Mill's analysis is both original and modern because, besides underscoring the risk of government interference, it considers the impact of the monetary regime on expectations (Cesarano 1996).[10] From a theoretical point of view, purchasing-power variations meddle with the price system and heighten uncertainty about long-run

[10] Mill's position stands in contrast to that of Thomas Attwood, who favored the introduction of inconvertible paper money in order to pursue full employment (Cesarano 1998b). While Attwood and the Birmingham School left no enduring imprint on the history of economic thought, Henry Thornton (1802) made a major contribution to various aspects of monetary theory: the lender of last resort, the effectiveness of monetary impulses, the rejection of the real bills doctrine, the transfer problem. However, before his "rediscovery" by Friedrich Hayek, who edited the 1939 reprint, Thornton's classic work was virtually unknown.

commitments. This approach is founded on an equilibrium hypothesis that rules out increasing output by monetary expansion. This theoretical paradigm translates into policy norms aimed at checking money creation and into an institutional framework apt to attain this goal. In particular, the high information content of the commodity standard makes it especially well suited to effectively constraining policymakers' behavior. A metallic system based on convertibility is, therefore, preferred to a rule requiring the stabilization of the price of gold because it is simpler and therefore more understandable. Violations of convertibility would then be easily recognized, discouraging monetary authorities from using this device and thus enhancing the credibility of the system.

Mill's position is important in that, in addition to representing the received view of monetary economics in the second half of the nineteenth century, it clearly identifies the foundations of the commodity standard. His analysis is grounded in the hypothesis of equilibrium, not just in the money market and in the "natural" distribution of precious metals, but rather in the economy as a whole. This conception excludes an active role for the monetary authorities[11] because, by disturbing the equilibrium, they would reduce the level of welfare. Although theoretically weak, the metallist postulate complements this equilibrium approach. The assumption that the commodity characteristic is an essential requisite for money carries important implications for the operation of the system. First, policymakers cannot affect the money stock, which is determined by the market. Second, the great credibility of fixed exchange rates, and monetary discipline in general, makes it possible to use small variations in interest rates to restore equilibrium quickly. If the

---

[11] Mill illustrated this point in a frequently cited passage from the *Principles*: "There cannot, in short, be intrinsically a more insignificant thing, in the economy of society, than money; except in the character of a contrivance for sparing time and labour. It is a machine for doing quickly and commodiously, what would be done, though less quickly and commodiously, without it: and like many other kinds of machinery, it only exerts a distinct and independent influence of its own when it gets out of order" (1848, 488).

rules of the game are respected, a commodity standard is effectively a monetary union because no country can control the money stock. It is not surprising that Mill described the existence of a plurality of currencies a "barbarism," blaming it upon the desire of states to have a tangible sign of their sovereignty (1848, 615).

2.2. THE PROPERTIES OF THE GOLD STANDARD

The search for a less costly medium of exchange and the development of credit and financial instruments, fostered by market forces, have continuously reshaped monetary arrangements, bringing in innovative features and raising new questions. In his *Critical Essays*, John Hicks (1967a, Chapter 1) shows how the evolution of an exchange economy, from indirect barter to the banking system, brings forth a set of institutions – a clearing house, a court of justice, a central bank – necessary to the smooth operation of more advanced forms of monetary organization. These innovations, together with a deeper understanding of monetary problems, widened and perfected the operating rules of commodity money, the gold standard representing the peak of this evolutionary process.

Fixing the unit of account and free coinage are the fundamental principles governing the gold specie standard. In the gold bullion standard, a further rule earmarks gold reserves to back banknotes and coinage. On analytical grounds, the distinction between the gold specie standard and the gold bullion standard may be irrelevant, and in fact Jürg Niehans (1978, 141–2) considers them equivalent forms of the pure gold standard. On policy grounds, however, this equivalence has been doubted by conservative economists, like Mises and Hayek, who saw Ricardo's ingot plan as the germ of a process enlarging central bank powers, eventually leading to the abandonment of commodity money. Such transformations were the result of the progressive development of monetary arrangements, bringing about, *pari passu*, an extension of the rules of the game. Hence, according to Ronald McKinnon (1993, 3–4), in the heyday of the international gold standard, the system was also characterized by "implicit" rules: the Bagehot rule, the restoration rule, and the price level rule.[12] The implicit rules, it should be emphasized, are elements of a coherent whole in that each supports the others. For instance, if there is an external drain the central bank raises the interest rate, in application of the Bagehot rule, thus attracting capital from abroad and attenuating monetary restriction. The effectiveness of such a policy is enhanced by the virtual absence of exchange risk due to the restoration rule. The latter, in turn, is strengthened, at a remove, by the price level rule, which prevents governments from resorting to domestic inflation.

These mutual influences are important because they help to clarify the nature of the relationship linking the implicit rules to the properties of the gold standard, which lay behind the successful operation of the system. First, the Bagehot rule, moderating the fluctuations in the money supply, enhances the overall stability of the economy. Acting as the lender of last resort, the central bank can effectively tackle short-run liquidity crises, thus avoiding major imbalances in financial markets and in the real economy as well. Second, the restoration rule is the cornerstone of the standard's credibility. Ensuring that suspensions of convertibility are temporary and admitted only under particular conditions whose exceptionality is easily verified (Eichengreen 1996, 37),[13] the rule

---

[12] The latter term was not coined by McKinnon, who left the third of these implicit rules unnamed. His definition of what is here termed the price level rule runs as follows: "Allow the common price level (nominal anchor) to be endogenously determined by the worldwide demand for, and supply of, gold" (1993, 4).

[13] Almost 250 years earlier, Ferdinando Galiani advanced the same proposition regarding the effects on the prince's credibility of a once-and-for-all increase in the money stock: "Finally, in augmenting the currency, faith in the ruler does not waver except when this is not appropriate. Failure to fulfill one's promise, when it is necessary, does not diminish faith, it increases compassion. We saw this occur in the republic of Genoa not too many years ago. Misfortunes that proceed from natural causes do not make men fearful, but vices and bad faith do, when they cannot be checked by anxious fear or superior authority. The prince will be just and people will have faith in him. He will augment the currency when necessary and none shall complain. He will not pay when he cannot, and his not being able to do so is not his fault. He will not be pitied any more; he will be helped with great fervor" (1751, 178–9).

provides a formidable constraint on economic policy design, bending it to the long-run commitment to a fixed parity. Hence, the restoration rule solves the time inconsistency problem of monetary policy. The consequent background of monetary stability dissipates long-run uncertainty so that economic agents can confidently enter into long-term contracts. Third, the price level rule, whereby the world price level is determined in the gold market, makes the monetary system entirely symmetrical. Changes in purchasing power would produce different effects inside a country; but from an international point of view, the system is characterized by symmetry. Gold being a truly international money, the redundancy problem (Mundell 1968) does not emerge. Indeed, not even Britain undertook the task of stabilizing the world price level despite its predominant role in the system (McKinnon 1993, 10–1).

Therefore, the implicit Bagehot, restoration, and price level rules respectively provide the basis of three main properties of the gold standard – stability, credibility, and symmetry – although the link between them is more complex than a simple one-to-one correspondence. The rules are mutually reinforcing in that each contributes indirectly to the effectiveness of the others, and they are, thus, interdependent. This essential characteristic is congruent with the fact that the properties of the commodity standard originate from a commonly accepted model based on the equilibrium hypothesis. The vision underlying the advancement of economics from the mid-eighteenth century to the 1920s reflected a frictionless, self-adjusting economy inspired by classical mechanics.[14] This conception was widely shared; hence, there was no need for formal recognition of the international monetary arrangements stemming

---

[14] Pointing out the influence of Isaac Newton on classical economics, Waterman remarked: "Hume and Malthus were among the more distinguished of those who attempted to apply the Newtonian mechanical model to that branch of 'moral philosophy' which acquired an independent existence during their own time as Political Economy. The characteristic image of the model was that of gravitation; and its conceptual corollary, the mathematical representation of stable equilibrium. . . . 'Nature,' as conceived by the post-Newtonian mind, abhorred disequilibrium" (1988, 93).

from it in an explicit agreement or pact. The properties of the gold standard are intimately connected with the equilibrium hypothesis. If the actual characteristics of the economy differ from those consistent with that hypothesis, the rules of the game become unbearable, making it impossible for some countries to join the system. However, so strong was the ideal of the gold standard that those countries that refrained from formally adhering to the system often behaved as if they had joined it.

The implicit rules complemented the traditional ones, thus corroborating the essential properties of the commodity standard. The origin of some rules, in fact, was the development of credit and financial markets bringing about new institutions (witness the transformation of banks of issue into central banks). Hence, the debate about the automatic or managed character of the gold standard is a false start. The increasing role played by monetary authorities was a necessary implication of those developments, but it did not contrast with the operation of a commodity standard; instead, it enhanced its properties. While Hume's abstract model assumed a specie standard, reflecting the monetary arrangements of his time, the introduction of fiduciary elements gave rise to commonly accepted rules – that is, convertibility, absence of restrictions on gold and current or capital account transactions, and backing of banknotes and coinage by earmarked gold reserves. These rules, together with the implicit ones, were the basis of a common, but uncodified, pattern of behavior. The rationale of the rules of the game was to constrain the expansion of the money supply after the diffusion of fiduciary money, maintaining the main characteristics of the commodity standard, in which the market sees to the production of the money commodity. Not surprisingly, the gold standard performed better than earlier, less advanced metallic systems because, combining long-run discipline with short-run flexibility, it more easily overcame shocks. The maneuvering room of the monetary authorities was constrained by the rules of the game and was consistent with the viability of the system.

The smooth operation of the gold standard, then, is no myth; its otherwise inexplicable success is accounted for by the correct interpretation of Hume's model and its extension to capital movements. Not that explanations are lacking. Eichengreen and Flandreau (1997, 10–8) group them under three headings: the efficiency view, stressing the automatic nature of the adjustment mechanism; the discipline view, pointing out the restraint on inflationary policies and, more generally, the consistency of the overall economic policy design; and the modern synthesis, emphasizing the credibility and flexibility that made the gold standard a set of credible target zones. The three approaches, however, are not alternative; rather, each focuses on a different feature of the standard, all stemming from the rules of the game. In a metallic standard, the inherent stability of the money stock prevents departures from equilibrium and, in case of disequilibrium, efficaciously dampens its effects.

Ultimately, the essential features of the gold standard derive from the principle of metallism and the equilibrium hypothesis. The gold standard is a homeostatic system. In the event of a shock, equilibrium is reestablished through the specie-flow mechanism, whose operation governs the "natural" distribution of gold in the long term. Furthermore, the quantity of gold is determined in the market, making the system symmetrical. From an economic policy standpoint, the key feature is the limitation of government interference, which is an implication of the analytical foundations we have just described. Interference cannot be entirely ruled out, but any such attempt is immediately recognizable, imposing a high cost in terms of credibility when not justified by exceptional circumstances. Nor is this characteristic limited to monetary policy alone. It also affects other policies and above all acts preventively, inhibiting behavior that is not consistent with maintaining parity.[15]

---

[15] "This residual harmonization of national monetary and credit policies, depended far less on *ex post* corrective action, requiring an extreme flexibility, downward as well as upward, of national price and wage levels, than on the *ex ante* avoidance of substantial

Thus, the main properties of the gold standard – stability, credibility, and symmetry – safeguarded purchasing power in the long run while allowing a certain degree of discretion. Paradoxically, the very rigidity of the system enabled central banks to intervene in a flexible and effective manner thanks to the high credibility conferred by the anchoring of the parity and the monetary regime.[16]

2.3. CREDIBILITY AND THE EVOLUTION
OF THE MONETARY STANDARD

Despite its many useful properties, the gold standard was not entirely free of flaws. The set of rigid rules ensured monetary discipline but put too stiff a straitjacket on the standard, making

disparities in cost competitiveness in the monetary policies which would allow them to develop. As long as stable exchange rates were maintained, national *export* prices remained strongly bound together among all competing countries, by the mere existence of an international market not broken down by any large or frequent changes in trade or exchange restrictions. Under these conditions, national price and wage levels also remained closely linked together internationally, even in the face of divergent rates of monetary and credit expansion, as import and export competition constituted a powerful brake on the emergence of any large disparity between internal and external price and cost levels" (Triffin 1964, 148; italics in the original). Discussing the maintenance of the gold parity by the United States in the decades before World War I in relation to the credibility of a rigorous fiscal policy, Thomas Sargent places the accent on the discipline that the gold standard imposes on fiscal policy: "To adhere to a gold standard, a government has to back its debts with gold or other assets that are themselves as good as gold. In practice as well as in theory, it is unnecessary to hold stocks of gold equal in value to the entire stock of a government's liabilities. Instead, it is sufficient to back debts by sufficient prospects of future government surpluses. By accepting a gold standard rule, a government in effect agrees to operate its fiscal policy by a present-value budget balance rule. Under this rule government deficits can occur, but they are necessarily temporary and are accompanied by prospects for future surpluses sufficient to service whatever debt is generated by the deficit" (1999, 1473).

[16] As Laidler puts it: "The twenty-five years or so that preceded the outbreak of the First World War were the heyday of Bagehot's principles. Monetary policy in those years was very much a matter of discretion in the short-run, constrained by a firm long-term commitment to a gold-standard rule. Even before these principles were firmly in place, however, changes in monetary economics were getting under way that would, in due course, undermine their intellectual authority. If the story of the development of Classical monetary economics after 1797 is one of economic theory catching up with institutional facts, then that of the evolution of Neoclassical monetary economics after 1863 is one of analysis running ahead of those facts" (2002, 19).

other than temporary control of the money supply impossible. The debate in the final decades of the century – the so-called "battle of the standards" (Jevons 1875, Chapter 12) – turned on the problem of purchasing-power stability. This objective was attained over the long term, but a commodity standard may experience considerable short-term variability as well as protracted price rises or declines depending on the discovery of new mines. Beginning in the mid-nineteenth century, production from gold mines in California and Australia caused prices to rise before reversing course in the early 1870s. Afterward, the persistence of deflation for more than two decades stimulated the work of prominent economists, all of whom, however, took the commodity standard as given and did not seek a radical reform of the system.[17] The point is that this literature admitted an embryonic element of discretion for the purpose of stabilizing the money stock, hence prices. Nevertheless, consideration of the idea was limited to academic circles, as policymakers deemed the gold standard to be essential to monetary and, more generally, economic stability. Corroborated by the pre-1914 experience, this was the prevailing view when it came time to reorganize the monetary system in the wake of World War I.

The striking disequilibria of the postwar years brought a substantial loss of credibility. This deprived the system of one of its essential characteristics and helps explain events over the subsequent two decades. In particular, the key question of why cooperation

[17] Jevons (1884) suggested separating the functions of money by using gold as the unit of account for current transactions and a tabular standard, originally developed by Joseph Lowe in 1822, for deferred payments. Marshall proposed "symmetallism" based on a gold and silver basket, whose fluctuations in value would be equal to the mean of the fluctuations of the two metals. Walras supplemented gold with a managed fractional currency (*billon régulateur*), whose issue would help stabilize the money stock. Finally, Wicksell deserves mention because, in contrast with the other schemes, which were all variations on the commodity standard, he argued for cutting the link with gold altogether, a "first step towards the introduction of an ideal standard of value" (1898, 193). Although this is not the appropriate place for an extensive analysis of these projects, the latter should nonetheless be recalled because they substantially broadened the debate over the commodity standard.

had a different effect before and after 1914[18] can be answered by considering the larger role of fiduciary payment media and, especially, the weakening of the rules of the game, which was reflected in risk conditions and radically altered the structure and stability of the standard. The efficacy of capital flows in smoothing adjustment was grounded in those rules and in the gold standard's properties, making the financing of temporary external disequilibria highly profitable. This distinctive feature was the outcome of an "invisible hand" that stemmed from clear-cut incentives. More specifically, small variations in interest rates were enough to trigger short-term capital movements, providing sizeable gains at negligible risk (McKinnon 1993, 8; Eichengreen 1996, 31), even outside a formal cooperative setting.[19] The flow of capital into a country in difficulty was swift precisely because of the great credibility of fixed exchange rates. Hence, credibility cannot be traded off with cooperation, for the two are closely linked.

The strong credibility of the gold standard, which is corroborated by the empirical findings of Alberto Giovannini (1993), is emphasized in the modern literature, particularly with regard to

[18] "Had cooperation (in the shape of reserve pooling) been such an essential ingredient of the functioning of the pre-1914 international monetary system, how could it be that the substantial help (in monetary terms) brought by France to England in 1931 failed? Or conversely, if cooperation per se had not been enough to save the gold standard in 1931 was it so essential before 1914?" (Flandreau 1997, 737).

[19] On the basis of an analysis of relations between the leading banks of issue using documentation from the Rothschild archives, Flandreau rejects the hypothesis that cooperation was a key element of the system before 1914: "In all cases, international help had *not* resulted from the bilateral realisation of common interests. In its most favourable form, it had resulted from the unilateral perception of the possible gains associated with one way co-operation. This might explain why what has been called perhaps too quickly 'co-operation' took place on an ad hoc basis, sometimes succeeding, sometimes failing, but in any case never becoming the keystone of the international monetary system" (Flandreau 1997, 761, italics in the original). In a further article, written with Jacques Le Cacheaux and Frédéric Zumer, Flandreau emphasizes the success of the gold standard despite the failure of various international monetary conferences: "The many international monetary conferences that took place between 1865 and 1892 called for extensive policy coordination, but they failed to achieve very much, if anything. Yet most of Europe ended up on gold, without collectively agreed targets for debt, deficits, inflation, exchange rates or long-run interest rates. To the extent that it succeeded, the European gold standard appears as a case of stability without a pact" (1998, 118).

restricting the discretionary power of monetary authorities, thus solving the problem of the time inconsistency of monetary policy (McKinnon 1993, 11). Bordo and Kydland (1995) interpret the gold standard as a policy rule with an escape clause that permits suspension of the rule in the event of major shocks. Moreover, as noted above, the restoration rule requires the reestablishment of the original parity in order to ensure *ex ante* credibility and avoid any *ex post* redistribution of wealth among debtors and creditors.[20]

By contrast, a fixed exchange rate system linking a number of fiat moneys, such as the European Monetary System, could not achieve the same objectives through cooperation.[21] The stabilizing effect of capital movements, therefore, depends on the properties of the standard, not the other way around, so that to interpret the evolution of the monetary system in terms of the speed and size of capital flows is to concentrate on the effect, not the cause. This is a key point in analyzing monetary developments in general, and not just between the wars. The different impact of capital flows on the stability of equilibrium under the gold standard and under the

---

[20] Other recent analyses of the nature of the constraints imposed by the gold standard identify a variety of mechanisms, including a political constraint (Gallarotti 1995), which underscores the interest of the conservative elite in maintaining price stability, as their wealth was mainly invested in fixed-income securities, and a market constraint (Bordo and Rockoff 1996), which emphasizes the incentive for each country to comply with the rules of the gold standard in order to avoid being penalized by higher yields.

[21] Obstfeld and Rogoff clearly illustrate the limits of cooperation in this context: "Like fixed exchange rates, target zones can, in principle, be made more credible through bilateral or multilateral cooperation. As always, any constraints posed by lack of foreign currency reserves disappear when central banks cooperate to defend mutual exchange-rate targets. However, the same incentive problems that bedevil unilateral exchange-rate pegs (regular or "lite") imply practical limits to the extent of cooperation. International coordination can in principle spread the pain of any needed adjustments to monetary policy, but in practice it is often difficult to get the strong currency partner to compromise its domestic goals significantly. On paper, for example, the EMS commits all member countries to unlimited intervention in defense of the agreed parities. However, Germany's Bundesbank, backed by the German government, has interpreted its obligations to extend only to interventions that, in its view, do not threaten its prime objective of low domestic inflation" (1995, 92).

gold exchange standard[22] depends on the presence or absence of a credible monetary anchor. Today, this contrast emerges distinctly because the transition from commodity money to fiat money has been complete for some time now, and the sheer diversity between these two systems and their respective properties highlights the determinants of the transformation of monetary institutions. The liberalization and growth of capital flows has made the return to fixed exchange rates a "mirage" just because "a fixed exchange rate is very costly for a government to maintain when its promises not to devalue lack credibility. At the same time, developing and maintaining credibility has become increasingly difficult" (Obstfeld and Rogoff 1995, 74).

Underlying the fall in credibility, there is the general diffusion of fiat money, diametrically opposed to commodity money. The change in the money "object" is thus the decisive factor making the return to fixed exchange rates unlikely. This development cannot be accounted for by free capital movements alone, as these were an essential element of the gold standard, the epitome of a fixed-rate regime. Capital mobility per se does not connote a specific exchange rate regime; thus, the forces driving the evolution of monetary arrangements must be sought elsewhere. In reality, the viability of monetary standards is ultimately determined by their essential properties, not by contingent factors or temporary imbalances, witness the performance of the gold standard during which shocks were not lacking (see Eichengreen and Flandreau's remark in footnote 6).

[22] The change in the effectiveness of capital flows has been lucidly described by Nurkse: "After the monetary upheavals of the war and early post-war years, private short-term capital movements tended frequently to be disequilibrating rather than equilibrating: a depreciation of the exchange or a rise in discount rates, for example, instead of attracting short-term balances from abroad, tended sometimes to affect people's anticipations in such a way as to produce the opposite result. In these circumstances the provision of the equilibrating capital movements required for the maintenance of exchange stability devolved more largely on the central banks and necessitated a larger volume of official foreign exchange holdings" (1944, 29).

In the final decades of the nineteenth century, the full-fledged development of the gold standard was facilitated by a number of factors: advances in minting technology, which made the counterfeiting of fractional coinage more difficult; the weakening of political opposition to demonetizing silver; and the new balance of power following the Franco-Prussian War (Cooper 1982, 44–5; Eichengreen 1996, 13–20).[23] These are tangible signs of path dependence that remain, however, within the confines of commodity money. By contrast, the articulated process that led to designing a new monetary order at Bretton Woods, and eventually to the introduction of fiat money, produced an unprecedented break in monetary evolution that cannot be explained in terms of contingent factors. The hypothesis of path dependence thus appears to be difficult to argue. Such a sweeping transformation came by way of a complex process in which theoretical advancement played a key role.

---

[23] The transition from bimetallism to the gold standard was an *in vitro* experiment with the emergence of a new vehicle currency. As Paul Krugman (1984) explains, this phenomenon is characterized by an element of circularity, as choosing a means of exchange in itself fosters its diffusion. Krugman's hypothesis is based on the production and transmission of information that underlies the role played by money.

3 THE INTERNATIONAL MONETARY SYSTEM
BETWEEN THE WORLD WARS

I N THE 1920S, INTERNATIONAL MONETARY DEVELOPMENTS WERE dominated by the interaction between the shocks of war and the aim of restoring the gold standard when the conditions for achieving that goal rapidly and without major welfare costs were lacking. Furthermore, the new cultural climate undermined the theoretical framework that had sustained a credible commodity standard. On the one hand, the advancement of monetary theory was uneven, offering conflicting solutions to the problems inherited from the war. On the other hand, policymakers remained attached to the gold standard, leading to take actions that actually aggravated the crisis.[1] Indeed, the malfunctioning of the monetary system was

---

[1] The central bankers' inadequacy to cope with the difficulties brought about by the First World War is underscored by Hawtrey: "The art of central banking is something profoundly different from any of the practices with which it is possible to become familiar in the ordinary pursuits of banking or commerce. It is a field within which a certain degree of technical knowledge is necessary, even to take advantage of expert advice. Yet it seems to be taken for granted that a central banker should be like a ship captain who knows nothing of navigation, or a general who does not believe in the Staff College. The central banker is even reluctant to admit that there exists an art of central banking. If central banks *can* do these things, what a formidable responsibility rests on those who direct them! Nothing but complete scepticism as to the power of central banks to do anything whatever promises a quiet life for their directorates. If they cannot avoid taking decisions, then conformity with a few easily understood shallow empirical precepts will enable them to face criticism. Yet it is only in recent years that this scepticism has become firmly established. A hundred years ago the directors of the Bank of England were not only interested in economic ideas but were actually taking the lead in evolving the art of central banking. After 1866 the art had become more nearly fixed, and perhaps it was the comparative smoothness with which credit regulation worked that gradually dimmed the memory of the underlying principles. The result has been not merely that the world

a main factor in the onset of the depression and the worldwide transmission of its effects.

In reconstructing the monetary history of those years, it is common to subdivide the period according to the exchange rate regime in place (Redmond 1992, 346): an initial phase of floating rates that ended with Britain's return to the gold standard in April 1925; a short stage of fixed rates ending in September 1931, when sterling abandoned the gold standard; and a final phase of managed floating rates until the outbreak of World War II. A temporal division of monetary developments is even more significant from a different perspective, focusing not on the exchange rate regime, but on the rules and properties of the system. To clarify this point, let us recall that both the gold standard and the "hard" EMS a century later were based on fixed exchange rates, but the effect of capital flows was stabilizing under the former, destabilizing under the latter. This difference reflects the nature of the two systems, one a highly credible commodity standard in which the money stock was determined by the market, the other an agreement between the several fiat monies, with diametrically opposed properties. Thus, for both historical and purely theoretical reasons, the analysis of the standard must focus on its distinguishing characteristics and on the rules that govern its operation in addition to the exchange rate regime in itself.[2] In this connection, the aftermath of the depression and Britain's abandonment of the gold standard in September 1931 produced a momentous break in monetary evolution, powering a continuing transformation that eventually led, after the parenthesis of Bretton Woods, to the definitive diffusion of fiat money.

has been insufficiently prepared to deal with the new problems of central banking which have arisen in the years since the war, but that it has failed even to attain the standard of wisdom and foresight that prevailed in the nineteenth century" (1932, 246–7; italics in the original).

[2] Renewed interest in the design of monetary standards was stimulated by the work of Black (1970), Fama (1980) and Hall (1982), which originated the paper by Greenfield and Yeager (1983) and a new strand in the literature, the "new monetary economics" (Cesarano 1995).

3.1. THE POSTWAR LEGACY AND THE RETURN TO GOLD

After World War I, the return to the gold standard was considered essential to restoring a stable monetary order.[3] At the same time, however, the imbalances generated by the war had left a burdensome legacy. The large and differentiated rise in prices, the reparations question, the decline of about a third in gold production between 1915 and 1922 (Nurkse 1944, 27), and political and social turmoil made it extremely difficult to restore the gold standard without disruptive deflation, which postwar economic conditions could not bear. To counter these trends, at the Genoa Conference in April 1922 it was proposed to supplement gold with convertible currencies and stabilize its relative price through central bank cooperation.[4] Even under the gold standard, countries had held small amounts of foreign currencies (12 percent of the reserves of

---

[3] As John Redmond observed: "[P]olicy makers (and, indeed, virtually everyone else) were anxious to restore [the gold standard] as soon as possible after the war. In fact the commitment to do so was undertaken in Britain before the war actually ended. The Interim Report of the Cunliffe Committee provided an unequivocal definition of postwar British monetary policy in 1918: 'In our opinion it is imperative that after the war the conditions necessary to the maintenance of an effective gold standard should be restored without delay.' In short, a return to gold as soon as possible; moreover, the rest of the world (or at least the parts that mattered) concurred with this view" (1992, 347). According to Edwin Kemmerer, the impact of wartime inflation rallied the general public behind restoring the gold standard: "[T]he war probably left no conviction stronger with the masses of the people of Europe than that *never again* did they want to suffer the evils of such an orgy of inflated paper money. Everywhere there was a popular longing to get back to a 'solid' monetary standard, to something in which the people had confidence; and in the distracted world of that time there was no other commodity in which they had so much confidence as gold" (1944, 109; italics in the original).

[4] The final report of the Financial Commission chaired by Sir Robert Horne, Chancellor of the Exchequer, established: "Resolution 9. These steps [balancing of budgets, adoption of gold as a common standard, fixing of gold parities, cooperation of central banks, etc.] might by themselves suffice to establish a gold standard, but its successful maintenance would be materially promoted . . . by an international convention to be adopted at a suitable time. The purpose of the convention would be to centralize and coordinate the demand for gold, and so avoid those wide fluctuations in the purchasing power of gold which might otherwise result from the simultaneous and competitive efforts of a number of countries to secure metallic reserves. The convention should embody some means of economizing the use of gold by maintaining reserves in the form of foreign balances, such, for example, as the gold exchange standard or an international clearing system" (quoted in Nurkse 1944, 28).

fifteen European central banks in 1913). In the following decade, this percentage rose substantially: for twenty-four central banks, foreign currency balances accounted for 27 percent of reserves in 1925 and 42 percent in 1928 (Nurkse 1944, 29). Besides, the circulation of gold coins, which had virtually disappeared during the war, was discouraged by imposing a minimum purchase limit (in the case of the Bank of England, 400 ounces, equal to £1,730; Eichengreen 1996, 61). These developments go far beyond the change in reserve composition and in fact reflect structural change. Central banks began to play a much more important role. Whereas under the gold standard capital movements were largely generated by the private sector, after the war intervention by the monetary authorities expanded not just in size but also in information content. These were the first signs of the transformation of a commodity-based system, whose rules ensured monetary discipline, into a managed system, with greater discretionary scope. As Keynes argued in the *Tract*: "[T]he war had effected a great change. Gold itself has become a 'managed' currency" (1923, 167).

While policymakers were still convinced of the superiority of the gold standard, its foundations were increasingly called into question by academic economists advocating a managed currency. Until 1914, monetary theory, centered on metallism and the equilibrium hypothesis, oriented economic policies toward maintaining gold parity. After the war, the return to the gold standard in an environment that lacked the features necessary for its operation threw monetary institutions into crisis. In particular, the change in the price level during and after the war differed from country to country, making it impossible in a number of cases to apply the restoration rule. Also, central bankers, reluctant to accept the innovations of the gold exchange standard, often conducted policies inconsistent with the new rules, thus undermining the system.

The return to the prewar parity in the United Kingdom reflected a desire to quash all doubts as to the country's intention to comply with the rules of the game and reestablish credibility. The reconstitution of the gold standard was considered essential to economic stability, as was expressly indicated in the Cunliffe Committee report in 1918: "Nothing can contribute more to a speedy recovery from the effects of the war, and to the rehabilitation of the foreign exchanges, than the re-establishment of the currency upon a sound basis" (Committee on Currency and Foreign Exchanges after the War 1918, 232). Those appearing before the committee were unanimous in arguing that returning to the gold standard would eliminate the monetary uncertainty that was weakening the country's trade relations and its position at the center of international finance (237–8). In this connection, compliance with the restoration rule underpinned the Cunliffe Committee's approach, serving as the reference paradigm at the subsequent Genoa Conference.

In an interim report published in August of the same year [1918], the [Cunliffe] committee presented a classical description of what its authors took to be the working of the pre-1914 gold standard. The report is relevant for this study because its international monetary model was in many respects the one that was accepted by virtually everyone at Genoa and even eleven years later by the Continental European countries that participated in the London conference. It was, of course, a system in which the parities of currencies were assumed to be permanently fixed in terms of gold and in which gold movements associated with payment imbalances brought equilibrating adjustments in domestic interest rates, wages, prices, and spending. The conception was of a unified world in which the component national economies adjusted in order to maintain international monetary stability. Not only was this view accepted without dissent by the committee, but its members conducted their discussions *on the assumption* that sterling would eventually be stabilized at its prewar parity equivalent to $4.86. (Clarke 1973, 11–2; italics in the original)

The influence of Keynes's famous pamphlet, *The Economic Consequences of Mr Churchill* (1925b), helped spread the view that the return to gold had been an error committed by Winston Churchill's economic advisers in order to favor the financial sector at the expense of industry. In reality, Churchill was aware of the debate and the critique by Keynes and others, underscoring the deflationary effects of the adjustment process (Sayers 1960). The overvaluation of the pound – by between 5 and 15 percent according to various estimates (Eichengreen 1996, 59) – was known to the advocates of restoration, but it was felt that the costs during the transition would be outweighed by the long-term benefits. In March 1925, the Federation of British Industries wrote an open letter to Churchill asking for a return to gold without mentioning that the fall in prices had not been large enough so that the prewar parity would ensure equilibrium (Sayers 1960, 88 and note 4). The position of the British industrialists, the first to suffer from the overvaluation of the pound, clearly shows how deeply rooted was the belief in the benefits of restoring the gold standard. In fact, "alternatives to the restoration of the gold standard were not seriously considered" (Redmond 1992, 350). A broad majority shared this view,[5] which was decisive politically. As Churchill's secretary, James Griggs, recounted in his memoirs, the arguments for and against a return to the gold standard were aired during a dinner at the end of which the chancellor placed the issues in a political context.[6] Churchill made his decision only after having carefully

[5] At the end of his article, Walter Layton remarked: "British opinion is in the main represented by the conclusion of Professor Pigou, who has recently declared that 'so far as the United Kingdom is concerned, until the gold standard has been re-established, more elaborate improvements in our monetary system are not practical politics'" (1925, 195). After the return to gold, the British press was unanimously in favor: "*The Times* (29 April) claimed that the great majority of businessmen would rejoice in the return to gold. *The Economist* (2 May) expected it to effect 'a definite broadening of the base of British commerce'; the new policy was subject for congratulation to the Chancellor and was 'the crowning achievement' of Montagu Norman. The *Yorkshire Post* (2 May) and the *Manchester Guardian* (5 May) were equally comfortable. The President of the Federation of British Industries had much more to say about other (now forgotten) aspects of the Budget, but did find a moment in which to welcome the return to gold as a step towards a revival of foreign investment and the conquest of new markets" (Sayers 1960, 87). For a detailed reconstruction of Britain's return to gold, see Moggridge (1972).

[6] Richard Sayers summarized Griggs's account: "Plenty was said about the risks of unemployment, falling wages, prolonged strikes and the contraction of some of the heavy industries. I suspect that Keynes was not at his most effective: he did not in those days carry his later weight, and he was always liable to have an 'off-day.' At any rate, Churchill was not completely convinced by Keynes's gloomy prognostications and turned

assessed the size of the majority in favor of restoration. On a purely technical plane, renewed monetary stability was supposed to set the stage for the recovery of world trade, helping to lower unemployment by boosting exports. Under the classical approach founded on the equilibrium hypothesis, the gold standard would ensure stability and foster full employment by disciplining monetary policy conduct. Thus, there was no conflict between the price level and the employment target: "[T]he gold standard was essentially an employment policy" (Sayers 1960, 89).

In dissent, Keynes pointed out that the insufficient flexibility of domestic costs would aggravate the imbalances in the British economy (as in fact happened). However, the importance of his 1925 essay goes beyond the criticism of the return to gold. As he had done in greater detail in the *Tract* (1923), Keynes also attacked the classical model underlying the gold standard and, underscoring the frictions inherent in the adjustment mechanism, argued for active monetary control – that is, a monetary policy in the modern sense of the term, aimed at "preserving the stability of business, prices, and employment" (1923, 173). The pamphlet's vehement attack on Churchill derived from the same principles. The chancellor's decision was blamed on the "clamorous voices of international finance" (1925b, 212) that dominated at the time, and Keynes rightly foresaw that, given the rigidity of wages, the greatest impact of the resumption of gold payments would be on employment.

By what *modus operandi* does credit restriction attain this result [of reducing money wages]? *In no other way than by the deliberate intensification of unemployment.* The object of credit restriction, in such a case, is to withdraw from employers the financial means to employ labour at the existing level of prices and wages. The policy can only attain its end by intensifying unemployment without limit, until the workers are ready

to McKenna, who had wobbled somewhat in his latest public pronouncements. Churchill in effect asked McKenna: 'This is a political decision; you have been a politician, indeed you have been Chancellor of the Exchequer. If the decision were yours, what would it be?' McKenna, after wobbling to the end, replied, 'There's no escape; you have got to go back; but it will be hell'" (1960, 89).

to accept the necessary reduction of money wages under the pressure of hard facts. This is the so-called "sound" policy, which is demanded as a result of the rash act of pegging sterling at a gold value, which it did not – measured in its purchasing power over British labour – possess as yet. It is a policy, nevertheless, from which any humane or judicious person must shrink. So far as I can judge, the Governor of the Bank of England shrinks from it. But what is he to do, swimming, with his boat burnt, between the devil and the deep sea? At present, it appears, he compromises. He applies the "sound" policy half-heartedly; he avoids calling things by their right names; and he hopes – this is his best chance – that something will turn up. (Keynes 1925b, 218–9; italics in the original)

In the presence of price stickiness, the effects of any departure from equilibrium fall on quantities. In general, Keynes emphasizes friction in the economy, which undermines the classical equilibrium hypothesis.[7] Keynes was in a minority, but his position broke with the received view, casting doubt on the theoretical reference paradigm from which the essential properties of the commodity standard were derived. This paradigm was the foundation of the high credibility of commodity money; moreover, by anchoring the actions of the monetary authority, it created a *de facto* form of co-operation between countries.

Because credibility had weakened and maintaining the gold parity was no longer the only objective of central banks, the system was missing the necessary element for its success.[8] Hence, the gold

---

[7] This emerges clearly in the following passage, in which we can discern the presentiment of a major crisis: "The gold standard, with its dependence on pure chance, its faith in 'automatic adjustments,' and its general regardlessness of social detail, is an essential emblem and idol of those who sit in the top tier of the machine. I think that they are immensely rash in their regardlessness, in their vague optimism and comfortable belief that nothing really serious ever happens. Nine times out of ten, nothing really serious does happen – merely a little distress to individuals or to groups. But we run a risk of the tenth time (and are stupid into the bargain), if we continue to apply the principles of an economics, which was worked out on the hypotheses of laissez-faire and free competition, to a society which is rapidly abandoning these hypotheses" (Keynes 1925b, 224).

[8] Comparing the prewar gold standard with the interwar period, Hallwood, MacDonald, and Marsh remarked: "What is important and worth emphasizing, however, is the (joint and individual) significance of the explanatory variables for the interwar equations. This contrasts quite sharply with the picture for the Classical period and indicates that

exchange standard, seemingly only a simple transformation of the gold standard, had radically different characteristics. In this regard, it is useful to recall the distinction drawn by Friedman (1961) between "real" and "pseudo" gold standards: Under the former, gold is used as money; in the latter, the government sets the price of gold. Similar in appearance, the essential properties of the two systems nevertheless differ by the presence, in the latter, of an active policymaker. Moving to a gold exchange standard, there-fore, implied the abandonment of a monetary mechanism that was governed by a consistent set of rules, relatively immune to exter-nal interference, and thus highly credible. The consequent loss of credibility could hardly be offset by closer cooperation since any such trade-off can be excluded. In addition, the sheer magnitude of the shocks that buffeted European economies after World War I together with the change in approaching the monetary mechanism induced policymakers to consider domestic objectives as well, often embracing different policy stances.

It is difficult to imagine how close cooperation could take the place of the rules of the gold standard if the convention of central bankers planned for the Genoa Conference to implement the new monetary arrangements was never held.[9] The scepticism of Benjamin Strong,

governments may have been pursuing goals in addition to the maintenance of gold par-ity. Thus the evolution of the fundamental variables was felt by the markets to have an impact on the credibility of the governments' links to gold" (1996, 154). It should be recalled that, as with other innovations in the monetary field, the development of the gold exchange standard was rooted in an actual problem. After having set the parity of the rouble in 1894, Russia made up for its lack of reserves by taking out loans and invest-ing most of the funds in liquid assets denominated in marks, which were convertible into gold. Both India and the Austro-Hungarian Empire also followed Russia's example, which had two advantages: Countries earned interest on their reserves, and there were fewer disturbances in the international gold market (Hawtrey 1947, 60–1).

9 The testimony of the governor of the Bank of England before the Macmillan Committee is eloquent in this respect: "It always appeared impossible, during those years when we were waiting, to summon such a conference for the excellent reason that the people would not come. They would not come, not because they were unwilling to co-operate, but because they were unwilling to face the publicity and the questionings in their own countries, which would arise if they attended any such conference, and all the attempts that I made to that end failed" (quoted in Hawtrey 1947, 102).

the influential chief of the New York Fed, on the effectiveness of the gold exchange standard was shared by other central bankers. After restoring the gold standard at an undervalued parity, France immediately accumulated a considerable gold stock, reserves doubling between 1926 and 1929 and quadrupling by 1931. After the traumatic experience of hyperinflation, Germany, too, maintained tight monetary discipline. Hjalmar Schacht, president of the Reichsbank, was a firm advocate of the gold standard.[10]

At the origin of the crisis of the monetary system was the inconsistency between the rules of the gold exchange standard, which called for active monetary control, and the behavior of those central banks that still stuck to the prewar gold standard. The responsibility of the central banks is stressed by Hawtrey in his analysis of the causes of the depression:

For, even if there were non-monetary causes at work in 1929 and 1930, which were tending to produce a violent compression of the consumers' income and collapse of demand, it remains true that the action of the great Central Banks at that time was independently tending to produce precisely that result. For the curtailment of the flow of money, the Central Banks, as the sole sources of money, must bear the responsibility. That responsibility is hardly less if they are shown to have used their power to reinforce disturbing causes which they might have counteracted, than if they themselves originated a disturbance in conditions otherwise calm. The collapse of demand is another name for the appreciation of gold. It means the offer of less gold in exchange for commodities. And we may regard the responsibility of the Central Banks as arising from their control over the market for gold. If some of them absorb a disproportionate amount of gold, the others find themselves short of it, and between them they force its wealth-value up. The responsibility of Central Banks for determining the

---

[10] The dominance of those opposed to the gold exchange standard was illustrated by David Williams: "Once the chief results of the gold exchange standard had been achieved – stabilisation of exchange rates and the strengthening of monetary reserves – there was increasing pressure by some important countries to revert to a gold bullion standard. The gold exchange standard was never accepted as anything but a temporary palliative by France; Germany and the smaller countries of West and Central Europe had a strong desire to hold as much gold as was possible. The gold exchange standard in the 'twenties was regarded not only as an expedient, but as a temporary expedient" (1963, 95).

wealth-value of gold had been recognized at the Genoa Conference, but by 1929 the Conference had been forgotten and the responsibility disclaimed. The Central Banks had reverted to the ideas of the nineteenth-century gold standard, which limited their responsibility to restraining the expansion of credit whenever it outran the available gold reserves. Here was an objective which made no demands on the reasoning faculty; it could be treated as an article of faith. Under the conditions of the nineteenth century faith worked well enough, because the wealth-value of gold was fairly stable. Only in the severe depressions of 1876–9 and 1884–6 were there searchings of heart. In face of the wild vagaries of the wealth-value of gold in the years following the war, faith was no longer enough.

(1947, 140–1)[11]

The rigorous policies of France, Germany, and the United States were adopted for domestic purposes and conflicted sharply with Great Britain's need to return to equilibrium from the overvalued level of the pound. Such conflict between internal and external objectives could not arise under the gold standard, as the overall thrust of economic policy was directed toward maintaining parity. The gold exchange standard weakened the credibility of fixed exchange rates and the underlying policies, with major implications for the adjustment mechanism. The de facto cooperation under the gold standard ceased to exist and capital movements no longer played a stabilizing role.[12]

[11] In *The Art of Central Banking*, Hawtrey emphasized the consequences of the death of Benjamin Strong, underscoring the central banks' rejection of the gold exchange standard: "It was a disaster for the world that Governor Strong died in the autumn of 1928, and the experiment came to an end. And meanwhile the Genoa Resolutions have been thrown aside. . . . But whatever Governments or Parliaments or experts may say, the opinion and the practice of central banks have become rigidly adverse to the Genoa plan. Far from regulating credit 'with a view to preventing undue fluctuations in the purchasing power of gold,' they have systematically excluded any such purpose from consideration, and have approximated to the purely mechanical system of gold reserve proportions, which was accepted by the theory if not by the practice of the nineteenth century" (1932, 209). On the role that the central banks should play in stabilizing the purchasing power of gold, see also Young (1929).

[12] Friedman summed up his assessment of the characteristics of the monetary system in the 1920s as follows: "It was a period when the acceptance of the idea of independent central banks was at its zenith, even the U.S. having finally come most of the way. It was the era of the great Central Bank Governors: Moreau in France, Schacht in Germany,

The fluctuation of exchange rates and the succession of crises after World War I, especially in France and Germany, radically transformed the macroeconomic framework and, consequently, investor sentiment. In addition, economic policy in the leading countries diverged. Paradoxically, those that applied the restoration rule, such as the United Kingdom, lost credibility owing to the difficulties of implementing deflationary policies, while those that did not return to their prewar parities, such as France and Italy, were able to adopt rigorous, credible policies, helped by the fact that the disequilibrium accumulated over the course of the war was partly offset by depreciation. The reduced credibility of the system was reflected in an increasing preference for gold reserves. In this initial stage of the transition from commodity money, the monetary system was buffeted by a variety of forces that irreversibly altered the reference scenario.

3.2. THE GREAT DEPRESSION AND THE END
OF THE GOLD STANDARD

The peculiarity of the monetary mechanism in the gold exchange standard, exchange rate disequilibria, and the pursuit of domestic policy objectives often in conflict with those of other countries set the stage for a disruptive crisis. The key factor was the deflationary impulse consequent on the fall of the money multiplier exacerbated by bank failures.

The contraction is in fact a tragic testimonial to the importance of monetary forces. True, as events unfolded, the decline in the stock of money and the near-collapse of the banking system can be regarded as a consequence of nonmonetary forces in the United States, and monetary and

Strong in the U.S., and above all, Norman in Britain, and of continuous interchange and cooperation among them. It was also, as Mr. Rueff has so tellingly stressed, the era of the gold-exchange standard, which, as I fully agree with him, made the system much more vulnerable to monetary mistakes than it had been" (1968b, 273). Note that in this passage the meaning of central bank "independence" is quite different from its modern sense. In fact, it relates to the pursuing of discretionary monetary policy.

nonmonetary forces in the rest of the world. Everything depends on how much is taken as given. For it is true also, as we shall see, that different and feasible actions by the monetary authorities could have prevented the decline in the stock of money – indeed, could have produced almost any desired increase in the money stock. The same actions would also have eased the banking difficulties appreciably. Prevention or moderation of the decline in the stock of money, let alone the substitution of monetary expansion, would have reduced the contraction's severity and almost as certainly its duration. The contraction might still have been relatively severe. But it is hardly conceivable that money income could have declined by over one-half and prices by over one-third in the course of four years if there had been no decline in the stock of money.

(Friedman and Schwartz 1963, 300–1)

This hypothesis of Friedman and Schwartz (1963)[13] was developed further by Eichengreen (1992a), who highlighted the spread of the deflationary process through the workings of the gold exchange standard. Eichengreen's analysis of the decline in nominal income does not necessarily conflict with that of Friedman and Schwartz,

[13] Frank Steindl (1991) and David Laidler (1993) show that Lauchlin Currie's contribution anticipated that of Friedman and Schwartz. In the 1930s, other leading economists, such as Cassel, Fisher, and Hawtrey, had identified the fall in the money stock as an essential factor in the events of the period. Irving Fisher, underscoring the decline in bank deposits, remarked: "Between 1926 and 1929, the total circulating medium increased slightly – from about 26 to about 27 billions, 23 billions being check-book money and 4 billions, pocket-book money. On the other hand, between 1929 and 1933, check-book money shrank to 15 billions which, with 5 billions of actual money in pockets and tills, made, in all, 20 billions of circulating medium, instead of 27, as in 1929. The increase from 26 to 27 billions was inflation; and the decrease from 27 to 20 billions was deflation. The boom and depression since 1926 are largely epitomized by these three figures (in billions of dollars) – 26, 27, 20 – for the three years 1926, 1929, 1933. These changes in the quantity of money were somewhat aggravated by like changes in velocity. In 1932 and 1933, for instance, not only was the circulating medium small, but its circulation was slow – even to the extent of widespread hoarding" (1935, 5). Furthermore, John Williams pointed out the multiplicative effect of gold flows: "The fixed exchange process is more roundabout; international transfer of money may have effects upon the internal economy incommensurate with, and not directly related to, the initial change in the balance of payments, particularly if, as in a fractional reserve against deposits system, the monetary expansion-contraction is a multiple of the gold movement" (1937, 24). Recently, Lastrapes and Selgin (1997) have emphasized the effect of the check tax, in force between June 1932 and December 1934, on the rise in the currency ratio and, therefore, on deflationary pressure. Bordo and Eichengreen (1998, 404–5) have summarized the various positions of contemporary scholars on the causes of the 1929 crisis.

but rather qualifies and extends it by considering the effects of economic policy failures on other countries.[14] Eichengreen overturns the generally accepted interpretation of the impact of infringing the rules of the game, according to which so-called competitive devaluations aggravated the crisis. In reality, the countries that took the lead in abandoning their ties to gold came out of the depression sooner and with lower welfare costs. Far from enhancing stability, the gold exchange standard helped intensify and spread the contraction in economic activity. Because in the short run the stock of gold is given, large fluctuations in the multiplier have a strong impact on the money supply (Bernanke 1993, 257–8).

An additional problem was the asymmetry between the policies of countries that lost reserves and those that accumulated them. Whereas the former necessarily suffered a reduction in the money stock, because they would have otherwise been unable to defend the parity, the latter were able to sterilize the increase, thus intensifying the deflationary impact. France and the United States accumulated gold to the point that in 1932 their holdings represented 70 percent of the world stock. In this regard, Herbert Grubel (1969, 133–4) suggests two main reasons for countries' preference for gold instead of foreign exchange assets: first, the prestige deriving from their currencies serving as reserves for other nations, which required convertibility and thus holding conspicuous gold reserves; second,

---

[14] "Traditional debates (such as the Friedman/Schwartz–versus–Temin debate in the U.S. context) have faced off essentially monetary explanations versus explanations based on 'real-side' maladjustments (e.g., overbuilding, excess capacity, underconsumption). While some evidence could be found for many of these stories (and there is no question that the Depression is an enormously complex event with multiple causes), many or most of them suffer from being specific to one or a few countries. Eichengreen's impressive achievement is to have found the *common* shock that can explain the nearly simultaneous onset of the Depression around the world. As it happens, this common shock was transmitted through national money supplies, so at least in a proximate sense Eichengreen's work validates the monetarist thesis" (Bernanke 1993, 263–4; italics in the original). Eichengreen (1996, 75 note 38) does disagree with Friedman and Schwartz on one point. According to the latter, the Federal Reserve could have prevented the crisis given the large stock of gold it held, whereas Eichengreen rejects this analysis. The question is still open. In a recent essay, Bordo, Choudhri, and Schwartz (2002) restrict the validity of Eichengreen's hypothesis to small open economies.

the expectation of a return on gold, in the form of capital gains stemming from repeated devaluations, higher than the yield on foreign exchange. Devaluation also heightened the uncertainty of the value of foreign currency assets, which reduced their usefulness as reserves. It thus became very difficult to reconcile protection of the banking system with the maintenance of the gold parity. From another perspective, the possible conflict between these two objectives highlights an essential aspect of the evolution of monetary institutions during the period. The gold exchange standard, which was intended to limit the deflationary impact of the return to gold, undermined credibility, thus triggering behavior that produced the opposite effect and actually worsened the deflationary process.

Before World War I, by contrast, even critical situations did not erode credibility. Exceptional events would be coped with by suspending convertibility; verification of such exceptionality, which was needed to ensure that policymakers were not violating the rules of the game, was immediate. During the 1920s, the need for greater flexibility in economic policy to face the postwar difficulties loosened this verification mechanism, giving rise to diffuse instability. At the same time, central banks continued to refer to the gold standard model, failing to take account of the restrictive effects of the gold exchange standard on the money stock. Underlying the crisis in the monetary system between the two wars was a failure to perceive the implications of moving from an "automatic" to a managed system, which required continuous and above all coherent action to maintain stability. In fact, because the consensus on the functioning of the monetary system had dissolved, countries often had different views and interpretations. In the United Kingdom, the severity of the crisis was blamed on lack of liquidity, while France ruled out monetary expansion because it would have aggravated the situation.[15] Underlying these contrasting views are

---

[15] This uncertainty on the correct economic policy strategy is clearly described by Stephen Clarke with regard to the United States in the decade following the Genoa Conference: "Most important, the international side of United States economic activity was dwarfed

distinct paradigms. The first, accepted by Keynes and the critics of the return to gold, assigns economic policy a crucial role in driving the economy toward a higher welfare path; the second is based on an equilibrium model that precludes any such policy role. The conflict and, in general, the lack of a universally accepted model was reflected in the inadequate behavior of central banks that ultimately led to a disastrous deflation.

Countries had to choose between policy objectives – that is, either maintaining parity or safeguarding the banking system. Austria opted for the latter and introduced exchange controls to cope with the crisis at Credit Anstalt, the country's largest bank, in May 1931.[16] Difficulties spread to Germany and Hungary and, in July 1931, Germany abandoned the gold standard and imposed exchange controls. In Britain, the looser ties between banks and industry initially warded off any problems, but the deterioration in the trade balance, which was at first offset by a surplus in invisibles, eventually became unsustainable and triggered large outflows of reserves. Beginning in 1930, the collapse in world trade and the effects of protectionist measures imposed by many countries had aggravated the crisis. The one-point increase in the discount rate on 23 July 1931 and a further one-point hike the following week were not enough to stem the capital outflow in the face of plummeting expectations for the exchange rate. The crisis culminated on 21 September 1931 with the formal suspension of sterling convertibility, marking the symbolic end of the gold standard.

by the domestic side. The key to the experience of the decade seemed therefore to lie in domestic economic management. Here, however, the verdict on orthodox principles was contradictory. Laissez-faire and the reduction of government debt had been associated both with the good times of the twenties and also with the crash. Thereafter, heroic efforts to balance the budget and so maintain confidence in the government's credit had been accompanied by a worsening of the depression. In their perplexity, some concluded that the remedy lay in an even stricter implementation of orthodox principles, while yet others held that alternative policies – then regarded as radical and inflationary – were required" (1973, 20–1).

[16] This paragraph and the following one are based on Eichengreen's reconstruction of interwar monetary developments (1996, 77–88).

In the aftermath of these developments, we find three groups of countries: One group continued to cling to the gold standard – the United States, the Latin American countries whose currencies were pegged to the dollar, and part of Europe, mainly France, Belgium, Switzerland, Czechoslovakia, and Romania; a second, in Central and Eastern Europe, employed exchange controls to defend the exchange rate; the third, consisting of countries linked to the United Kingdom, maintained a fixed exchange rate with the pound. The countries that kept their link with gold lost competitiveness and suffered the impact of their restrictive policies. Until 1932, President Herbert Hoover, while taking some expansionary fiscal measures to get through the depression, kept the gold standard as a key point of his program and maintained a conservative policy stance (Temin and Wigmore 1990). The election of Franklin Roosevelt altered the course of American politics, producing a shift in the policy regime. The dollar shed its ties to gold, with convertibility suspended in April 1933, and the price of gold was allowed to rise. The objective was to foster an increase in the price level, but there was no clear, comprehensive economic policy design.[17] In January 1934, the gold

[17] Eichengreen underscores the shortcomings of Roosevelt's advisers: "Neither Roosevelt nor his advisers had a coherent vision of international economic policy. Fred Block calls them 'notoriously inept' in their grasp of economics. FDR's views were heavily influenced by the ideas of two Cornell University agricultural economists, George Warren and Frank Pearson. Warren and Pearson had uncovered a correlation between the prices of agricultural commodities (which they took as a proxy for the health of the economy) and the price of gold. To encourage the recovery of agricultural prices they urged Roosevelt to raise the dollar price of gold, indirectly bringing about the devaluation of the dollar" (1996, 87 note 61). Clarke also describes Roosevelt's peculiar, improvisational approach to the London Conference and economic policy in general: "Franklin Roosevelt's mishandling of United States participation in the London economic conference is generally recognized and understood. The elements in the debacle range from the President's monetary idiosyncrasies to his intense concern to maintain the momentum of domestic economy recovery. During the first hundred days of the New Deal, the President encouraged a great diversity of programs and proposals, some of them inconsistent with each other. Among other things, he agreed to participate in a world economic conference that would promote cooperative recovery measures but simultaneously complicated cooperation by taking the United States off the gold standard. He favored a tariff truce but sanctioned restrictions against imports under the National Recovery and Agricultural Adjustment Acts. After the gloomy immobility of the Hoover administration, the new regime was experimenting, keeping its options open, and choosing its course according to the

parity, which had been $20.67, was fixed at $35 an ounce. The exit of the United States weakened the other gold standard countries, and they, too, eventually abandoned the standard. In 1936, France, the Netherlands, and Switzerland suspended convertibility.

The transformation of monetary institutions in that period and the difficulty of defining their characteristics, related to the transition process from commodity money to fiat money, are illustrated by Friedman and Schwartz:

It is easier to describe the gold policy of the United States since 1934 than it is to describe the resulting monetary standard of the United States. It is not a gold standard in the sense that the volume of gold or the maintenance of the nominal value of gold at a fixed price can be said to determine directly or even at several removes the volume of money. It is conventional to term it – as President Roosevelt did – a managed standard, but that simply evades the difficult problems of definition. It is clearly a fiduciary rather than a commodity standard, but it is not possible to specify briefly who manages its quantity and on what principles. The Federal Reserve System, the Treasury, and still other agencies have affected its quantity by their actions in accordance with a wide variety of objectives. In principle, the Federal Reserve System has the power to make the quantity of money anything it wishes, within broad limits, but it has seldom stated its objectives in those terms. It has sometimes, as when it supported bond prices, explicitly relinquished its control. And it clearly is not unaffected in its actions by gold flows. So long as the exchange rate between the dollar and other currencies is kept fixed, the behavior of relative stocks of money in various countries must be close to what would be produced by

immediate effects of diverse policies on the economy. And it was on the domestic economy, perforce, that the President focused most of his attention. Preparation of the position that the administration expected to present at the conference was left in the hands of a very few subcabinet officials who had had little or no previous diplomatic experience. In this preparation, guidance from the President was minimal. When Roosevelt gave his formal written instructions to the delegation prior to its departure for London, James Warburg, who had drafted them, experienced an 'uncomfortable feeling' that the President had, for some reason, lost interest in the conference. Roosevelt's insouciance may also account for the poor quality of his appointments to the United States delegation, whose members were unable to work in harness, were diplomatically inexperienced, and were sometimes totally uninterested in the work of the conference. The success of a cooperative recovery effort would have been problematic in any event; with such a delegation it was altogether unlikely" (1973, 36–7).

gold standards yielding the same exchange rates, even though the mechanism may be quite different. Perhaps a "discretionary fiduciary standard" is the best simple term to characterize the monetary standard which has evolved. If it is vague and ambiguous, so is the standard it denotes.

(1963, 473–4)

The return to floating exchange rates differed from that in the immediate postwar years, an experience that was viewed negatively owing to the marked instability of the period, which was blamed on speculation. Accordingly, in the second half of the 1930s the dominant approach was managed floating, in which monetary authorities intervened to limit fluctuations in exchange rates. The first countries to abandon the gold standard quickly emerged from the crisis. Floating exchange rates made it possible to pursue expansionary policies, improve competitiveness, and thus increase exports. Such action to boost the economy was taken independently by each country, focusing primarily on its own objectives. The attempt to revive international cooperation at the London Conference in the summer of 1933 failed. Three years later, the Tripartite Agreement would do no better (Eichengreen 1992a, 379–82). There was no coordination of economic policies, for which the very premises were lacking. Rather, it was the pressure of events, especially the severity of the depression and the grave malfunctioning of the monetary system, that exerted a decisive influence. When the rigidity of rules no longer left room for maneuver to attain welfare targets, the commodity standard was abandoned, leaving policymakers with no clear idea of an alternative system. As Stephen Clarke remarked:

The failure of the London conference left the international monetary system in disarray. The harmony in official monetary thinking that had prevailed at Genoa had been destroyed. The old orthodoxy was still championed by the gold bloc but was given little more than lip service in Britain and the United States. The traditional international monetary conception was dying without having been replaced by another more acceptable model.

(1973, 40)

3.3. THE PROPERTIES OF THE MONETARY SYSTEM AND
THE ROLE OF MONETARY THEORY

One of the key problems for scholars is the contrast between the success of the gold standard up to 1914 and its subsequent collapse. The diversity of the explanations advanced testifies to the analytical difficulty. And most of the explanations suggested are unsatisfactory, because, as Eichengreen and Flandreau (1997, 20–2) note, they are based on elements that were present both before and after the war: (1) the inclusion in central banks' reserves of foreign exchange assets as well as gold; (2) the dominance of the United Kingdom in exports of capital goods and as a financial center (yet the weight of France, Germany, and the United States was anything but negligible); and (3) Britain's role as "conductor of the international orchestra," or hegemonic power (Kindleberger 1973).

Gathering up the threads of the arguments presented in this and the previous chapter, a hypothesis can be suggested about the evolution of the gold standard in the period straddling World War I. Until 1914, the rules of the game, and especially the implicit rules and the relative properties, provided for a consistent institutional framework, so that the distribution of the money stock among the various countries and the adjustment process were governed by an "automatic" mechanism hinging on a highly credible gold parity. After the war, this characteristic evaporated. Although this has recently been acknowledged, we still lack a convincing analysis of the determinants of credibility. A number of elaborate hypotheses have been suggested[18] but their composite nature saps their explicative power. In reality, the many factors can be reduced to a single hypothesis: the dominance of the paradigm of classical economics, which was the basis of the gold standard rules and their generalized acceptance. In the four decades before the Great War,

[18] "In the late nineteenth century, the credibility of governments' commitment to the maintenance of gold convertibility rested on foundations grounded in economics, diplomacy, politics, and ideology" (Eichengreen and Flandreau 1997, 18).

equilibrium was subject to tensions and shocks that, while less intense than those of the 1920s and 1930s, were far from unusual. Yet the disciplinary force of the gold standard was so great that any pressure, however strong, in the direction of expansionary policies was doomed to yield to the rules of the game.

What pressure existed for the pursuit of other policy goals was exceptional and, ultimately, limited. At the gold standard's European and North American core, its political, ideological, and economic underpinnings sufficed to sustain the system. When push came to shove and the authorities in these countries had to choose between interest-rate increases to keep the gold standard from collapsing and interest-rate reductions to stimulate production, they never hesitated to opt for the former.

(Eichengreen and Flandreau 1997, 19)

In other regions of the world, like Latin America, economic and political conditions were too weak to comply with the gold standard rules. However, as Eichengreen and Flandreau argue, "[T]he very contrast with Europe highlights what was unique and distinctive about the gold standard system. At its core – in the industrial nations of Northern Europe and their overseas dependencies – the commitment to gold convertibility remained paramount" (1997, 19). In fact, notwithstanding adverse shocks and the quest for expansionary policies to counter them, belief in the gold standard principles was so deeply rooted as to make any substantial deviation unthinkable. Although monetary authorities resorted to discretionary action in the short term, they avoided meddling with the rules of the game because this would presumably lead to instability, interfere with the allocative mechanism, and create inefficiencies in the productive process, ultimately compromising growth.

After the war, the consensus on the classical model began to weaken. Although policymakers remained convinced of the validity of the model, economists reiterated their quest for a more perfect monetary system with a view to stability of prices and of the economy in general, questioning the optimality of the gold standard and hence the contention that there were no alternatives capable of attaining a higher level of welfare. For the first time in two and a half millennia, the commodity standard began to lose its uniqueness in the scenario of monetary arrangements.

The innovations suggested at the Genoa Conference were apparently innocuous, mainly the greater resort to convertible currencies and the stabilization of the relative price of gold, but their implications, not fully understood at the time, were momentous. Stuck to the gold standard model, central bankers simply would not consider gold and convertible currencies as on an equal footing, and the very idea of discretionary action to stabilize the price level was alien to them. The proposed reform asked central bankers to leave the sea of tranquillity of the gold standard and set sail for uncharted waters. Their resistance to change is no surprise.

The gold exchange standard explicitly changed only one of the rules governing the gold standard: the price level rule. However, the difficult postwar situation made the restoration rule inapplicable for several major countries and prompted measures, such as restricting gold convertibility, that tainted the rules and undermined the properties of the system. Given the interconnection between the rules, some properties not directly affected by the innovations were also impaired. With regard to Bagehot's rule, for instance, interest rate increases could no longer attract capital inflows given the weakened credibility of the fixed parity, thus invalidating the stability property. Hence, the bold attempt to improve on the design of the gold standard, in reality, harmed the system irreparably, opening the Pandora's box of crises between the world wars.

The major change in paradigm is evident in the contrast between the approach and results of the Cunliffe Committee of 1918 and the Macmillan Committee of 1931, which influenced the conferences of Genoa (1922) and London (1933), respectively. The Cunliffe Committee emphasized the benefits of the gold standard and the need for its restoration, while the Macmillan Committee accepted the idea of a managed currency aimed not only at maintaining parity but also at stabilizing the price level, output, and employment (Committee on Finance and Industry 1931, 5, 118–9).[19] These developments overturned the vision of the monetary mechanism and the economic system in general, which reveals Keynes's influence on the Macmillan Committee, of which he was a member. In the early 1930s, a consensus had not yet formed on any single paradigm, and various views coexisted.[20] Keynes's position was decidedly innovative, in contrast to the orthodoxy that held sway among central bankers. The fuzziness of the state of the art shows that opposing forces were at work, which gave rise to hybrid monetary arrangements.

Explaining the crisis in the gold standard in terms of the dominant role of theory in designing the rules and thus the economic policy framework does not conflict with the other approaches but rather encompasses them, reducing them to a single hypothesis.

[19] Clarke underscored this point in summarizing the conclusions of the Genoa and London conferences: "Although both the Genoa and London conferences must be classed as failures, the records of the negotiations and the memoirs of participants provide a fascinating account of the interaction between economic developments and international monetary thought. At Genoa the traditional gold-standard view, as formulated by British thinkers, was accepted almost without question. Eleven years later this view was championed primarily by the French and other Continental Europeans but was rejected in practice by the United States, Britain, and the countries that were to comprise the sterling area. With this shift in monetary views came two other crucial changes. At Genoa the aim was a unified monetary system based on parities fixed in terms of gold – a system in which domestic economies would have to adjust in order to maintain international equilibrium. By 1933 only the inflation-scarred Continental Europeans were clinging to the traditional order of priorities, while Britain and the United States gave domestic recovery precedence over external stability. The further outcome of London was to accelerate international monetary disintegration, with the sterling area, the European gold bloc, and the United States each dealing as best it could with its special regional problems" (1972, 2).

[20] The uncertainty over the evolution of the monetary system was emphasized by Marco Fanno on the last page of his *Lezioni*: "The abandonment of the gold exchange standard by many countries virtually returned the world monetary situation to the state in which it was before 1925 without offering even a glimpse of an immediate way out. In the meantime, in the midst of such severe monetary disorder, a wide variety of strange proposals was advanced. Some argued for the global rehabilitation of silver and the restoration of bimetallism, while others suggested abandoning metal-based systems altogether in favor of managed currencies. It is too early and difficult to discern the fate of such proposals, but even though the current concentration of gold in France and the United States hinders the monetary readjustment of the other gold standard countries, it seems unlikely that the world is ready to leave gold once and for all" (1932, 312; author's translation).

In fact, the properties of commodity money, above all credibility, depend on widespread acceptance of the underlying theoretical model. Furthermore, the flexibility of prices and factor use, the efficiency of the adjustment mechanism, and the ability to respond to various types of shock are all characteristics that reflect the adherence of policymakers and individuals to a laissez-faire vision and to an equilibrium model.[21] To use a recurrent analogy, the commodity standard acts like an anchor: When a shock occurs, the economic system as a whole undergoes a number of adjustments necessary to stick to the parity, just as waves and undersea currents shift the position of a sailboat around its anchor. Uncertainty about maintaining the fixed parity deprives the system of its anchor or center of gravity, thus leaving the monetary mechanism adrift.

Political factors may also have influenced the evolution of the monetary system, but their effectiveness originated in the prevailing monetary theory. In this regard, Britain's resumption of gold payments in April 1925 is eloquent. As Keynes argued, not returning to the gold standard would have avoided a substantial welfare cost, but Churchill was persuaded to opt for restoration (see footnote 6) by the overwhelming dominance of the classical paradigm, which considered that cost a necessary part of reestablishing a stable monetary system and, consequently, renewed growth.

---

[21] "[I]n spite of all counterarguments, the 'automatic' gold standard remained almost everywhere the ideal to strive for and pray for, in season and out of season. Again: why? At present we are taught to look upon such a policy as wholly erroneous – as a sort of fetishism that is impervious to rational argument. We are also taught to discount all rational and all purely economic arguments that may actually be adduced in favor of it. But quite irrespective of these, there is one point about the gold standard that would redeem it from the charge of foolishness, even in the absence of any purely economic advantage – a point from which also many other attitudes of that time present themselves in a different light. An 'automatic' gold currency is part and parcel of a laissez-faire and free-trade economy. It links every nation's money rates and price levels with the money rates and price levels of all the other nations that are 'on gold.' It is extremely sensitive to government expenditure and even to attitudes or policies that do not involve expenditure directly, for example, to foreign policy, to certain policies of taxation, and, in general, to precisely all those policies that violate the principles of economic liberalism. *This* is the reason why gold is so unpopular now and also why it was so popular in a bourgeois era" (Schumpeter 1954, 405–6; italics in the original).

In addition to the crisis in the gold standard, this hypothesis also clarifies another problem: the reluctance to abandon the gold standard even after it was observed that the countries outside the system had avoided the ruinous effects of the Great Depression. Some interpretations again look to political factors, arguing that the return to gold headed off a distributive conflict, making it possible to reconstitute an orderly economic policy framework after the considerable uncertainty generated by the shock of the early postwar years. However, the distributive conflict simply reflects the sheer size of disequilibria during that period, stemming from a multiplicity of factors all leading to a deterioration of the economies involved and ultimately to inflation. The gold standard, then, was viewed as the institutional setup that would reestablish monetary and economic stability. Underlying this view, firmly held by policymakers, was the equilibrium model, which was believed to have been the basis of the successful performance of the monetary system in the four decades before World War I. The continuing intellectual appeal of this model, therefore, explains the reluctance of central bankers to deprive themselves of an efficacious, long-tested institutional framework. As Eichengreen noted:

Nothing guaranteed that governments suspending gold convertibility would take reflationary action. Abandoning the gold standard permitted the adoption of reflationary initiatives but did not compel it. Recovery required discarding not just the gold standard statutes but also the gold standard ethos. Six months to a year of experience with inconvertibility typically was required before governments abandoned that ethos and began to experiment cautiously with expansionary initiatives. Policymakers in some countries went to incredible lengths to defend the gold standard, precluding all option of reflationary policies. Shifting political coalitions go some way toward explaining these cross-country variations in economic policy responses to the Great Depression. But to simply tote up the number of creditors and debtors, or to attempt to weigh the political influence of producers of traded and nontraded goods, is to miss what was special about the political economy of economic policymaking in the 1930s. The single best predictor of which countries in the 1930s allowed their currencies to depreciate and pursued reflationary initiatives, instead of clinging to the gold standard or adopting equally stifling exchange controls, was the experience with inflation a decade before. Countries that had endured persistent inflation in the 1920s were loath to permit currency depreciation and to expand their money supplies. They continued to associate depreciation and monetary expansion with inflation, even in the midst of the most catastrophic deflation of the twentieth century. They showed remarkable persistence in rejecting arguments for devaluation and reflation in the face of incontrovertible evidence of their beneficial effects in other countries. (1992a, 393–4)

The crucial point remains the policymakers' widely held belief, based on the classical paradigm, that the gold standard would restore monetary and economic stability. In this approach, periods of deflation – even long ones, such as that over the last quarter of the nineteenth century – were seen as natural features of the system, and any impact on employment and output was considered a temporary inconvenience compared with the lasting benefits of a stable monetary setting. This model was deeply ingrained in the policymakers' cultural baggage and influenced their behavior even after 1929. The abandonment of the gold standard was imposed by the pressure of events, not freely chosen. The changes suggested at the Genoa Conference to revive the system were in fact a fatal blow. They solved some immediate problems, but at the same time they permanently undermined the rules of the game and the related properties, particularly the cornerstone of the gold standard: credibility. The erosion of the economic model underlying the commodity standard was ultimately the cause of its irreversible crisis. The central role played by economic analysis in shaping institutions clearly emerges. It would become crucial in designing the Bretton Woods monetary order.

4 THE MONETARY SYSTEM IN ECONOMIC
ANALYSIS: THE CRITIQUE OF THE
GOLD STANDARD

TO THE MONETARY HISTORIAN, THE 1920S IS THE DECADE OF THE return to gold. Mindful of the long period of relative stability enjoyed before the war, policymakers wanted above all to restore the gold standard, because orderly monetary conditions were considered to be the prerequisite for renewed growth. Yet, the great difficulties in the way of quickly reinstating the old rules posed new questions and cast serious doubt on the smooth working of commodity money. The economists' advocacy of monetary reform thus gained momentum, with a critical reflection on the optimal design of the institutional framework that had only limited impact on central bankers but nevertheless set in motion the transition toward fiat money. Innovation, however, was necessarily founded on an alternative theoretical model, able to challenge the received view underpinning the gold standard. The spread of a new paradigm sparked a lively debate and clashed with policymakers' reluctance to forsake a monetary order that had proved to be so successful. Hence, proposals of monetary reform seldom considered severing the link with gold altogether. The watershed in the debate was the disruptive shock of the depression, which shattered the intellectual status quo. Before it, the gold standard had continued to predominate and the economists' innovative suggestions had exerted little influence. Afterward, the critique of commodity-based monetary standards gathered momentum and the need to construct a novel system began to emerge.

4.1. THE MAINSTREAM AND THE EMERGENCE OF THE GOLD EXCHANGE STANDARD

In the aftermath of World War I, economists focused on floating exchange rates and the related analytical apparatus, purchasing power parity theory. Cassel's hypothesis was widely discussed with examination both of its theoretical consistency and of its empirical relevance,[1] but the floating exchange rate regime was seen as a transitory situation soon to be succeeded by the return to gold. Nonetheless, the gold standard came under scrutiny because the long-range swings in purchasing power in the nineteenth century exerted a perceptible influence on the economy, particularly during the deflation of the last quarter of the century (Robertson 1922, 116–7). In addition to this problem, which related to the very nature of the commodity standard, the reestablishment of prewar parities would have imposed a substantial adjustment cost in terms of output and employment. These two criticisms had far-reaching implications, because they respectively undermined the price level rule and the restoration rule. Besides, given the link between the implicit rules, Bagehot's rule was also impaired by the consequent loss of credibility. In the effort to overcome postwar hardships, therefore, the suggested modifications of the gold standard eventually tainted the very properties of the system, the basis of its success.

Some of the arguments in support of monetary reform, especially the desirability of a stable price level, had already been advanced before the war. Irving Fisher (1911, Chapter 13) drew a clear picture of the state of the art at the acme of the gold standard, considering all the possible models for organizing monetary institutions in relation to the objective of stabilizing purchasing power. Starting from the proposition that only unexpected changes in prices produced

[1] The topic originated a vast literature, Bickerdike's 1920 article being a main contribution. Other works included: Angell (1922), Bickerdike (1922), Pigou (1922), and Fanno (1923), a collection of papers previously published in the *Giornale degli Economisti*.

effects on the real economy, Fisher called for better forecasts of price movements to mitigate economic fluctuations. That is, wider knowledge of the quantity theory, which he considered to be "an exact law of proportion, as exact and as fundamental in economic science as the exact law of proportion between pressure and density of gases in physics" (1911, 320), would improve the ability to calculate expectations and, by reducing entrepreneurs' exposure to inflationary "surprises," reduce the amplitude of cyclical swings. This decidedly modern argument postulated an inverse relationship between the intensity of the cycle and the information available to economic agents. Rejecting several variants of the metallic standard and inconvertible paper money[2] as well, Fisher proposed a system that combined the characteristics of the gold exchange standard with those of the tabular standard, under which deferred payments are linked to a price index. These ideas led to the plan for a "compensated dollar" (Fisher 1913a), with the gold content of the monetary unit changing with the price level so as to keep purchasing power constant. This solution was meant to be acceptable to economists of opposite schools: "conservatives" who admitted no change to the gold standard and "radicals" whose reform proposals were ineffective (Fisher 1920, 335). In reality, as Fisher himself recognized in connection with the tabular standard (1911, 335), the project was tantamount to generalized indexation and not a true mechanism for price stability. The analogy with measures of length and weight is thus not very convincing because, actually,

---

[2] Government interference in the issue of paper money was the greatest drawback to this solution, which, anticipating Friedman's simple rule, Fisher indicated as a "seemingly simple way" to stabilize the level of prices. "It is true that the level of prices might be kept almost absolutely stable merely by honest government regulation of the money supply with that specific purpose in view. One seemingly simple way by which this might be attempted would be by the issue of inconvertible paper money in quantities so proportioned to increase of business that the total amount of currency in circulation, multiplied by its rapidity, would have the same relation to the total business at one time as at any other time. If the confidence of citizens were preserved, and this relation were kept, the problem would need no further solution. But sad experience teaches that irredeemable paper money, while theoretically capable of steadying prices, is apt in practice to be so manipulated as to produce instability" (Fisher 1911, 329).

standardizing the dollar[3] implied its being continually adjusted as prices changed.

Fisher's contribution, therefore, did not consist so much in the actual plan for a compensated dollar as in its analytical foundations. Besides analyzing the redistributive effects of price instability, he underscored the role played by the uncertainty of inflationary expectations in generating economic fluctuations (1920, Chapter 3). In retrospect, his approach is not at odds with that of today's new classical macroeconomics but leads to a different result, showing the effectiveness of monetary impulses because it assumes a smaller information set for agents (Cesarano 1983a). The suggestion of disseminating knowledge of the quantity theory, considered to be the "true" model of the economy, can be seen as a way of increasing the information available to individuals in order to improve the accuracy of forecasts and reduce the variability of income. There is thus a link between information and social welfare. By eliminating the uncertainty of an unstable monetary unit, the compensated dollar would result in more precise calculation of the variables on which the economic agents' behavior depends, thus enhancing the stability of the economy.

[T]he fluctuating dollar hopelessly conceals the facts. It blinds the eyes of the mass of men whose right it is to know the facts and whose duty it ultimately is, under our democratic form of government, to choose one or more remedies for such evils as exist. The fluctuating dollar keeps us

[3] The main objective was to remedy the lack of a standardized monetary unit. "The truth is, that the purchasing power of money has always been unstable. The fundamental reason is that a unit of money, as at present determined, is not, as it should be, a unit of purchasing power, but a unit of weight. It is the only unstable or inconstant unit we have left in civilization – a survival of barbarism" (Fisher 1920, xxvi). In an appendix to the second edition of his classic work on the quantity theory, published in 1922, he remarked: "We have standardized even our new units of electricity, the ohm, the kilowatt, the ampere, and the volt. But the dollar is still left to the chances of gold mining.... With the development of index numbers, however, and the device of adjusting the seigniorage according to those index numbers, we now have at hand all the materials for scientifically standardizing the dollar and for realizing the long-coveted ideal of a 'multiple standard' of value. In this way it is within the power of society, when it chooses, to create a standard monetary yardstick, a stable dollar" (Fisher 1911, 502).

all in ignorance; whereas a stabilized dollar would lay bare the facts. It is no exaggeration to say that stabilizing the dollar would directly and indirectly accomplish more social justice and go farther in the solution of our industrial, commercial, and financial problems than almost any other reform proposed in the world to-day; and this it would do without the exertion of any repressive police force, but as simply and silently as setting our watches. Uncertainty is a mark of an undeveloped civilization, and its demolition (through applied science, insurance, safeguards, and standardization) is one of the chief characteristics of a highly developed civilization. Our uncertain dollar is simply a relic of the Stone Age. It is an anomaly to-day.   (Fisher 1920, 111–2) [4]

The compensated dollar proposal attracted wide attention in a period still dominated by the gold standard and in any case constitutes evidence of the change in the intellectual climate.[5] After 1918, the debate centered on price stability and its eventual

[4] Fisher's proposal still draws some interest today. According to Robert Hall (1997), substantial adjustment of the monetary unit would have been necessary to attain the objective of price stability, because the purchasing power of gold had varied considerably over time. Discretionary monetary policy would achieve better results than the compensated dollar because, by using the information available, it could prevent fluctuations in the price level. Hall's observations, already put forward by Pigou (1927, 294), are a corollary to the proposition that Fisher's project amounted to generalized indexation, with account taken *ex post* of the change in prices, and not a monetary reform in the strict sense, concerned with the characteristics and quantitative control of the means of exchange.

[5] In May 1911, Fisher began urging President Taft to organize an international conference on price stabilization. The Senate approved the project in April 1912 and authorized an expense of $20,000, but Congress failed to examine the proposal in time. Fisher (1913b) also indicated President Taft's successor, Woodrow Wilson, as a supporter of the conference, together with four hundred other personalities, including the leading economists of the day. The construction of a monetary system capable of guaranteeing price stability engaged Fisher throughout his life, not only as a public figure, but also as an academic, and by 1937 he had devoted no fewer than 331 writings to this topic (Gayer 1937, 441–2). In the aftermath of World War I, he thought this goal to be within reach. "Only one real obstacle stands in our way – conservatism. But to-day, as a result of the war, there is a new willingness to entertain new ideas. That is, the war has loosened the fetters of tradition. It was the French Revolution which led to the metric system. It would not be surprising if, as is being suggested, this war should give Great Britain a decimal system of money, revise the monetary units of the nations so that they shall be even multiples of the franc, give us an international money and stable pars of exchange and, as the greatest reform of all, as well as the simplest, give us a monetary system in which the units are actually units of value in exchange, as they ought, and were intended, to be" (Fisher 1920, xxviii).

incoherence with the rules of the gold standard, leading to consideration of an alternative system, "managed" instead of a "natural" money. Economists nonetheless held widely divergent views on the changes needed and hence the amount of discretion to be granted to monetary authorities. Simplifying, three approaches can be distinguished. The most prevalent embraced a concept of managed money that aimed at stabilizing the price level but maintained a link with gold;[6] the radical approach, mainly represented by Keynes, proposed a further departure from the commodity standard, broadening the objectives of monetary policy; a conservative one, chiefly supported by exponents of the Austrian school like Mises and Hayek, staunchly advocated the gold standard.

The dominant approach reflected the idea that the monetary order should serve the objective of stable purchasing power. Starting from the analysis of the effects of a variable price level on the efficiency of the price system and on income distribution (Hawtrey 1919, 428–9; Fisher 1920, 54–9), the argument against variability was extended to the impact on output and employment and, more generally, on business fluctuations. An ideal unit of account

---

[6] In the opening paragraph of a lecture delivered at the London School of Economics, Gustav Cassel clearly described the mainstream position: "The desirability of . . . [the] restoration [of the gold standard] is generally taken for granted, and is no controversial matter. Perhaps even too little so. The gold standard has without doubt its drawbacks. Even in the conditions obtaining before the war, gold had by no means a constant value, and the binding up of our standard with gold subjected it to all the variations in value which the yellow metal experienced. Economists paid much attention to these variations and to the inconveniences which the corresponding fluctuations in the value of money or in the general level of prices caused to the economic life of modern society. But few of them would then have gone so far as to propose the abolition of the gold standard and the establishment of a scientific paper standard built on the principle of stabilization of the purchasing power of money" (1923, 171). That this was the prevailing view was recognized by one of its fiercest critics, Friedrich von Hayek: "We have all been brought up upon the idea that an elastic currency is something highly to be desired, and it is considered a great achievement of modern monetary organisation, particularly of the recent American Federal Reserve system, to have secured it. It does not seem open to doubt that the amount of money necessary to carry on the trade of a country fluctuates regularly with the seasons, and that central banks should respond to these changes in the 'demand for money', that not only *can* they do this without doing harm, but that they *must* do so if they are not to cause serious disturbances" (1931, 108–9; italics in the original).

maintains its value through time so that, in every market, obligations arising from contracts represent "an invariable command over wealth" (Hawtrey 1919, 429). According to Hawtrey, the gold standard, fixing the price of one commodity whose accumulated stock is extremely large relative to the supply flow, is a crude but effective solution in the very long run.[7] On the other hand, Keynes (1923, Chapter 1) argued, substantial changes in purchasing power like those after 1914 produce disruptive distributive effects with momentous repercussions on growth. Inflation, driven by governments' financial needs and by the political influence of the debtor class, saps confidence and discourages both investment and saving; deflation benefits the *rentier* at the expense of the productive classes and increases unemployment. Furthermore, changes in prices also affect output via expectations: Entrepreneurs, anticipating the rising or falling prices, expand or contract productive activity. The relationship between price dynamics and economic fluctuations suggested a monetary hypothesis of the business cycle – "the trade cycle is a *purely* monetary phenomenon" (Hawtrey 1922, 298; italics in the original) – entailing the implementation of credit policies to prevent price level variations. But this is no easy task. Besides the problems posed by interpreting variations in the price index, both lags and imperfect knowledge of the transmission mechanism – that is, the arguments supporting Friedman's simple rule – make policy targets difficult to attain. As Hawtrey remarked:

[W]hat is almost more fundamental, a change in the monetary supply may manifest itself at first not in a change of prices at all, but in a change in the volume of purchases; it may have made material progress before the index number is affected. Stabilisation cannot be secured by any hard-and-fast rules. The central banks must exercise discretion; they must be

---

7 Thus, the gold standard was often likened to a large lake (Fisher 1920, 95) with small flows, in and out, that make adjustment in either the level of the water or in the intensity of the flows very gradual and lengthy (Niehans 1978, 147 note 5). In this respect, Keynes (1923, 11–2), emphasizing the stability of the price level in the century preceding World War I, noted that the price index was the same at the beginning and at the end of the period.

ready to detect and forestall any monetary disturbance even before it has affected prices. The policy can only be perfected by long experience.

(1922, 300)

These difficulties notwithstanding, the widely shared objective of price level stability called for an appropriate institutional framework. According to Hawtrey, the gold exchange standard was "the favourite of currency theorists" (1919, 437), allowing increases in the demand for money to be satisfied with fiduciary money. However, besides warning against excessive monetary creation, Hawtrey warned against the deflation caused by accumulation of gold reserves while returning to the gold standard. Indeed, a highly debated issue, impinging on the viability of the postwar monetary system, was the adequacy of the gold stock. Some deemed it redundant given the increase in mining since the turn of the century (Snyder 1923, 277) and the accumulation by the United States (Bellerby 1924, 185) or, more simply, because "a perfectly conducted gold standard does not require any gold at all, or practically none" (Keynes 1924a, 171).[8] Others, looking at the events following the onset of the gold standard and antithetically interpreting the gold accumulation by the United States, warned of a possible scramble for gold, as envisaged by the resolutions of the Genoa Conference (Hawtrey 1922, 293). And finally, the supporters of the gold exchange standard, while weighing both possibilities,

---

[8] A few years later, Keynes recognized his failure to predict gold accumulation by central banks, attributing it just to the "rashness and want of foresight of our monetary authorities." He emphasized the incoherence of central banks' scramble for gold with the recommendation of the Genoa Conference that reserves be allowed to be held in foreign exchange. ". . . I was forgetting that gold is a fetish. I did not foresee that ritual observances would, therefore, be continued after they had lost their meaning. . . . [I]f the legal reserves of the central banks of the world are fixed at a high figure, and if they prefer gold in their own vaults to liquid resources in foreign centres, then there may not be enough gold in the world to allow all the central banks to feel comfortable at the same time. In this event they will compete to get what gold there is – which means that each will force his neighbour to tighten credit in self-protection, and that a protracted deflation will restrict the world's economic activity, until, at long last, the working classes of every country have been driven down against their impassioned resistance to a lower money wage" (1929, 776).

considered the question much less important since what mattered was the stability of the price level, which could be attained by the controlled issue of convertible paper money (Hawtrey 1919, 437–8; 1922, 293–4; Cassel 1922, 281). In the main, the range of opinions mirrored theoretical differences: Radicals, envisaging the demise of the role of gold, neglected the question of gold stock inadequacy, while conservatives, supporting the gold standard, were more sensitive to the problem.

Analyzing this topic, Feliks Mlynarski (1936a) emphasized a general question. In a secular perspective, the demand for gold, fostered by output and population growth, tends to increase more than the supply, raising its relative price. The fixed gold parity thus comes under pressure and devaluation eventually follows.[9] Mlynarski's proposition is a corollary to the principle of incompatibility between price stability and commodity standard. In the *Tract*, Keynes had already underscored the deflationary bias of commodity money in the course of centuries, interpreting the monetary manipulations of the Middle Ages as an attempt to remedy the problem (1923, 162–3).

With the benefit of hindsight, it was the resilience of the gold standard model that eventually led to the accumulation of enormous reserves, that proved the undoing of the gold exchange standard. Central bankers, in fact, had no confidence in the postwar innovations and, faithful to the gold standard, followed a policy not always consistent with balanced operation of the monetary system.

---

9 "The historical tendency of the purchasing power of monetary metals is the tendency to increase regardless of annual fluctuations or secular trends. . . . Meanwhile prices paid per kilo of metal either by mints in coins or by central banks in notes have to remain stable, because every monetary system consists in the first line in the stability of this price. Here we discover a problem of cardinal importance to the economic history of the world. It is obvious that in the long run the real exchange value must win and prices must change. The increase in the exchange value must be followed, sooner or later, by an increase in price. To-day's pound sterling is a fraction of the pound as unit of weight. Similarly to-day's franc is a fraction of the livre and to-day's mark a fraction of the original mark of silver as unit of weight. The same can be said about the Roman as of copper. The history of money reveals a tendency towards continual and gradual devaluation, i.e. towards raising the price paid in coins or notes per kilo of the respective metal" (Mlynarski 1936a, 322).

In Hawtrey's analysis (1919, 438–9), international cooperation was to stabilize the relative price of gold under an agreement setting limits on the quantity of paper money in each country, thus compensating for the weakening of automatic mechanisms. Though not unaware of possible inconsistencies between price stabilization and other aspects of the plan, Hawtrey considered it a significant improvement on the past monetary order. A workable solution could be reached through

... an arrangement between England and America, with a view to maintaining their aggregate uncovered paper issues as nearly as possible at a fixed amount, to providing for remittances between them on a gold exchange basis, and to controlling credit with a view to keeping the gold value of commodities, as measured by an index number, approximately constant. The third of these conditions is the most novel, but, if it could be carried into effect, would be the most useful. It might not be consistent with the first, but where they differ it would, at any rate in theory, be the more correct guide to follow, and the paper currency law could be adjusted from time to time as might be necessary. The purpose of such a system would be not merely to restore the gold standard, but to make it a more trustworthy standard than it has been in the past. The demand for gold as currency would, in fact, be so regulated as to make the value of a gold unit itself in commodities as nearly as possible constant.

(Hawtrey 1919, 441–2)

That deep scepticism surrounded this reform project is confirmed by the failure to convene the planned meeting of central bankers.[10] The message of the Genoa Conference was ignored by critics or considered "with misgiving and suspicion as an academic proposal of doubtful practicability" (Hawtrey 1922, 295); the balanced working of the system was hindered by central bankers' clinging to the gold standard model. Accordingly, the gold exchange standard worked

---

[10] According to Hawtrey, the meeting of central bankers would have quite a different significance from the earlier ones. "Another international conference! What, will the line stretch out to the crack of doom? But here there is a difference. The calling in of the central banks is a recognition of the principle that currency policy is ultimately credit policy, for the direction of credit policy is the special function of a central bank" (1922, 291).

fairly well in the 1920s, as long as monetary policy, especially in the United States and the United Kingdom, complied with the system's rules. When it diverged, crisis was inevitable.[11]

Policymakers' reluctance to abandon the gold standard was also due to fear of jeopardizing its properties, especially impermeability to government interference. As Pigou noted (1927, 297–9), the problem did not arise in exceptional circumstances, such as war, when any set of rules, no matter how rigid, was necessarily violated. Rather, it concerned "normal" situations in which a paper currency is likely to be abused. In such cases, limiting note issue might be helpful, especially for its value as a signal, because infringing the limit would require ad hoc legislation. The gold standard's property of shielding policymakers from political influence was recognized by most economists. As Robertson put it:

We must remember the enormous impetus to which any banking system is subject, both from within and without, towards increasing continually the volume of its loans, and the formidable difficulty of so regulating the supply of money as really to meet the legitimate needs of trade. We must remember, too, the pressure exerted upon Governments in the name of the consumer to provide this and that – coal or railway-transport or house-room – by some means or other below its economic cost. It is not surprising if both bankers and Governments in their more responsible moments desire to have some charm more potent than a mere metaphysical index-number both to elevate before the people and to contemplate in the privacy of their own cells. There are the same arguments against disturbing the

[11] First the Federal Reserve Board and then the Bank of England after the return to gold had experimented with a policy aimed at stabilizing the price level (Pigou 1927, 278, note 2). A detailed study of these matters can be found in Hawtrey's classic 1932 essay. In another work, he saw France as having played a key role in triggering monetary instability. "A price stabilization policy, such as that framed at Genoa, is in itself a safeguard against inflation. Nor has the experience of the gold exchange standard gained since then supplied any support for the fear of inflation. In the period from 1923 to 1928 when the gold exchange standard was in fairly effective operation, the price level was falling rather than rising. The event which gave the signal for general deflation in 1929 was the change of policy on the part of the Bank of France, which ceased to buy foreign exchange, disposed of 6 milliards of the foreign assets it already held in that form, and began to absorb gold at the rate of 10 milliards in a year. It was the *reversal* of the previous adherence to the gold exchange standard in one important case that disturbed a pre-existing equilibrium" (1947, 230–1; italics in the original).

simple faith of the banker and the City journalist (the politician perhaps
has none) as against disturbing that of the pious savage. If a gold standard
had never existed, it might be necessary to invent something of the kind
for their benefit. (1922, 121–2)[12]

The overriding purpose of price stability stimulated analysis of
both the strategical and tactical aspects of monetary policy. Despite
a nonsuperficial understanding of the handling of the discount rate
and of other tools – open market operations, reserve requirements,
moral suasion, and rationing (Gregory 1925) – economists were
hardly confident that they had sufficient knowledge of the transmission mechanism and of the techniques necessary to attain that
goal. In particular, attention was drawn to changes in velocity that
might have the same sign as changes in money supply, thus reinforcing the latter, and to lags in policy effects. Monetary impulses
first impinged on expenditures and income before affecting prices,
making monetary control a complex task (Hawtrey 1922, 296–300;
1929, 74). The stylized fact relating price variability to output variability suggested a policy norm much like Friedman's simple rule
(Bellerby 1924, 181). By contrast, the gold standard would ham-
per price stabilization, heightening cyclical fluctuations (Keynes
1924a, 169–71), and transmitting them to all the countries adhering to what was in fact a "centralized system" (Hawtrey 1929a, 70).
The quest for a managed money to attenuate such volatility instead

---

[12] Recalling the singular experience of the island of Yap with stone money (Friedman
1992, 3), Robertson noted: "Just so gold is a fetish, if you will, but it does the trick"
(1922, 123). In the fourth edition of *Currency and Credit*, Hawtrey gave an effective
description of the contrast between the theoretical shortcomings of metallism and the
defense of this principle by policymakers to avoid inflationary pressures. "This severe
and uncompromising doctrine [metallism] owed its success rather to its practical utility
than to its theoretical perfection. It grew up out of the political contests which raged from
time to time about currency questions. Attacked and defended by a thousand politicians
and pamphleteers, it long held the field as the one theory which provided an intelligible,
self-consistent, workable system. The economists did not pay such unreserved homage
to it as the practical men. They saw that the precious metals themselves cannot provide
an invariable standard of value, and they speculated on ideal currency systems based on
index numbers of prices and similar devices. But on the whole for most people sound
currency meant a metallic currency. In it they saw the only bulwark against inflationism,
that attractive but insidious financial vice" (1950, 416–7).

implied an active role for the monetary authorities. Thus, according to Hawtrey, the country most fit to take up this role was the United States because "a central banking system has been established there" (1929a, 76). These reform proposals carried momentous consequences; they marked the departure from the commodity standard, originating the birth of modern monetary policy.

The optimality of a stable price level was also examined within the framework of sophisticated analyses of the business cycle. It was argued that, given long-term contracts, uncertainty regarding purchasing power hindered the smooth working of the capital and labor markets, eventually amplifying cyclical fluctuations (Marshall 1923, 16–9). Price stability, widely accepted as a policy aim (Cassel 1932a, 510; Pigou 1927, 251–7), was a "natural view" (Robertson 1922, 111; 1928, 59) insofar as it eliminated the factors interfering with contracts and expectations that gave rise to disequilibria in the economy. This result was open to one recurrent objection: the exclusion of recipients of fixed income from the welfare gains deriving from an increase in productivity and obtained through an increase in purchasing power. Accordingly, it was held that in cases of great productivity growth prices should be left to diminish, allowing workers to benefit without the need for explicit and difficult wage demands. At all events, excluding exceptional circumstances, the objective of stable prices remained preferable.[13]

The importance of this conclusion lies in its contrast with the rules of commodity money. In the past, the unquestioned need to limit government interference had always prevented not only the introduction of inconvertible paper money but also any accentuation of the fiduciary elements of the commodity standard. After World War I, this preclusion was not so clear-cut. The sheer

[13] The issue was thoroughly analyzed in Robertson's contribution to the Study Group on the International Functions of Gold (1931) and in the discussion of his paper by several economists. For a thorough, perceptive analysis of business cycle theory in the interwar period, see Laidler (1999).

magnitude of the shock had suggested that the rules of the game might actually undermine the viability of the system. In particular, the return to the prewar parity might have been feasible if it had been done quickly, in the exceptionally serious situation obtaining in the immediate aftermath of the war; once the emergency no longer existed, resumption became problematical (Robertson 1922, 121). The criticism of the restoration rule, the cornerstone of the credibility of the gold standard, tied in consistently with the objective of purchasing power stability, breaking the price level rule, to complete the attack against the gold standard.

Far from complying with a principle of distributive justice, restoration would have safeguarded prewar loans but would have more than offset the losses on those granted during the war. Because the latter were much larger than the former, the redistributive effect of the rule would have been the opposite of that desired. This argument was advanced not only by radical economists like Keynes (1923, 148), but also by central bankers like Sir Charles Addis (1924a, 168). The main focus, however, was on the macroeconomic implications. Besides increasing the burden of the public debt, the deflation needed to restore the prewar parity would have had adverse repercussions on output and employment. Enforcing the restoration rule in countries whose currency had depreciated sharply was "almost inconceivable" (Snyder 1923, 276),[14] and the debate thus focused on more manageable cases, chiefly the United Kingdom. The essential point of the restoration was credibility. As Hawtrey remarked in a paper to the Royal Economic Society:

Well, some people would argue that there is no very great harm in devaluing the pound. There is no special virtue in the pre-war gold value of 113

---

[14] Allyn Young's opinion was even more trenchant: "So far as the immediate future is concerned, such a return is not only undesirable but impossible. The rapid rise of prices was attended with economic injustice, unevenly distributed. But drastic deflation would bring with it a new series of burdens and injustices, only in small part compensating for the old ones. It would be a new instance of two wrongs failing to make a right" (1923, 5–6).

grains of fine gold. It might be reduced to 100 grains or thereabouts, and in a way it is true there is no great virtue in pre-war parity. But there is one fundamental advantage in getting back to pre-war parity if we can: that is, that if we have got back there with a certain amount of struggle, have regarded it as an end for several years, and finally achieve it, everybody believes we shall stay there. If we devalued, though we started with 100 grains, it might be convenient to change it to 85 grains later, and there would not be that confidence in the gold value of the currency which is so valuable in great financial affairs. (1924, 165)

The crucial importance of the restoration rule to credibility was also recognized, in the other camp, by Keynes: "It is of the essence of the argument that the *exact* pre-war parity should be recovered" (1923, 150; italics in the original). Supporters of restoration were quite aware of its distribution and output costs (Kemmerer 1920, Chapter 3), but considered this a price worth paying: "By facing a period of tribulation we can get back to a sound currency, and shall reap our reward in having a clear future before us;" devaluation, instead, is "open to the imputation that public faith is not kept" (Hawtrey 1919, 434). Where the price level was not too far from the equilibrium exchange rate, the return to the prewar parity would restore monetary stability and foster exports and growth. However, restoration would be excluded if it imposed high welfare costs. The prevailing view at the beginning of the 1920s did not maintain the rigid application of the gold standard rules, allowing some discretion in reconstructing the monetary system.[15]

[15] In the following passages, Cassel criticized the return to the prewar parity and provided a good description of the difference between the traditional and innovative points of view. "I believe, on these grounds, that upon a discussion as to the most suitable level for the value of the new monetary unit the wisest course will be to disregard the point of view of justice and to keep to the purely economic points of view. As is all economics, it is then a question of directing our gaze to the future. We must indeed ask ourselves this question: How can we at the earliest possible moment restore such conditions to the economic life of the world as will prevent the world from going under? As far as this question affects the value of money, there can be no other answer than this: We must, as soon as possible, and with the least possible friction, restore stability not only in the internal values of the various currencies, but also in their international exchange rates. The level at which the value of money is then fixed is, relatively speaking, a matter of secondary importance" (1922, 255–6).

The criticisms and possible rejection of the restoration rule turned the concept of the monetary mechanism upside down and created the conditions for a modern approach. *Prima facie*, the return to a given parity entailed a once-and-for-all adjustment of the monetary equilibrium with the aim of reaffirming the fixed nature of the monetary anchor. In reality, the rule would also have indirectly influenced the conduct of monetary policy as a continuous process, insofar as it forestalled the problem of time inconsistency. Furthermore, it would also have supported Bagehot's rule, maintaining the credible gold standard parity as the cornerstone of the country's economic policies. The emphasis on deflation cast doubt on the validity of the traditional model and paved the way to a broader, more active role for central banks. Accordingly, the repercussions of the war went well beyond the debate on the return to gold and began to erode the fundamental principles underlying commodity money.

4.2. RADICALS AND CONSERVATIVES

The numerous problems inherited from World War I gave rise to a highly variegated range of opinions about the reconstruction of the monetary system. A good sample is the "Discussion on Monetary Reform" at the 1924 meeting of the Royal Economic Society, where the conservative, mainstream, and radical views were epitomized by Cannan, Hawtrey, and Keynes, respectively. The contribution by Addis, a Bank of England director, illustrated the policymaker's standpoint, akin to the conservative position in the academic world.

The most controversial issues arose from the radical critique of the mainstream attempt to revive the prewar monetary order through the gold exchange standard and advocacy of a more innovative system, further detached from commodity money. The chief exponent of this heterodox opinion was Keynes, whose *Tract on Monetary Reform*, although overshadowed by the *General Theory* and even by the much criticized *Treatise on Money*,[16] deserves close examination for its treatment of fundamental analytical issues in the attack on the gold standard. The emphasis was on inflation expectations: An expected change in the price level was deemed sufficient to trigger a mechanism with a cumulative effect on income and employment (Keynes 1923, 36–8). Monetary control was thus essential to prevent wide fluctuations in purchasing power.

It is one of the objects of this book to urge that the best way to cure this mortal disease of individualism is to provide that there shall never exist any confident expectation either that prices generally are going to fall or that they are going to rise; and also that there shall be no serious risk that a movement, if it does occur, will be a big one. If, unexpectedly and accidentally, a moderate movement were to occur, wealth, though it might be redistributed, would not be diminished thereby. To procure this result by removing all possible influences towards an initial movement, whether such influences are to be found in the skies only or everywhere, would seem to be a hopeless enterprise. The remedy would lie, rather, in so controlling the standard of value that, whenever something occurred which, left to itself, would create an expectation of a change in the general level of prices, the controlling authority should take steps to counteract this expectation by setting in motion some factor of a contrary tendency. Even if such a policy were not wholly successful, either in counteracting expectations or in avoiding actual movements, it would be an improvement on the policy of sitting quietly by, whilst a standard of value, governed by chance causes and deliberately removed from central control, produces expectations which paralyse or intoxicate the government of production.

(Keynes 1923, 38–9)

The approach adopted by Keynes bent the rules of the gold standard to the pursuit of economic policy goals. This is the idea

---

[16] Milton Friedman is an exception in this respect. "In listing 'the' classic of each of these great economists, historians will cite the *General Theory* as Keynes's pathbreaking contribution. Yet, in my opinion, Keynes would belong in this line even if the *General Theory* had never been published. Indeed, I am one of a small minority of professional economists who regard his *Tract on Monetary Reform*, not the *General Theory*, as his best book in economics. Even after sixty-five years, it is not only well worth reading but continues to have a major influence on economic policy" (1997, 2).

that underlay all of his contributions to the reconstruction of the monetary system right to Bretton Woods (Cesarano 2003a). The actual institutional arrangements varied, of course, with the underlying theoretical model. In the *Tract*, the model was the classical one based on the Cambridge version of the quantity theory developed by Marshall and Pigou, whose validity Keynes stressed: "[T]he price level is not mysterious, but is governed by a few definite, analysable influences" (Keynes 1923, 84). The quantity theory and its extension to an international context, the theory of purchasing power parity, provided the analytical foundation (1923, Chapter 3) on which Keynes based his proposals for monetary reform (1923, Chapters 4 and 5).

According to Keynes, the central bank could control the price level, *inter alia* by offsetting the fluctuations in the Cambridge k by means of variations in the currency stock, whereas under the gold standard this was determined by the demand for and supply of gold (1923, 85). Nonetheless, policymakers had to resolve two separate problems – the once-and-for-all adjustment for restoration and the monetary policy objective – by choosing respectively between deflation and devaluation on the one hand and price stability and exchange rate stability on the other. Keynes's preferred solutions were devaluation and price stability. His criticism of deflation, a necessary consequence of restoration, was based on several arguments: The redistribution of wealth would benefit *rentiers* at the expense of entrepreneurs, the expectation of an increase in real interest rates would discourage investment, and economic activity would slow down. Furthermore, in the countries where the disequilibria caused by the war were most pronounced deflation was unthinkable; restoring the prewar parity would have imposed too heavy a burden.[17] In fact, the restoration rule would have been

---

[17] Italy was one of these countries. "In Italy, where sound economic views have much influence and which may be nearly ripe for currency reform, Signor Mussolini has threatened to raise the lira to its former value. Fortunately for the Italian taxpayer and

effective only if applied rigidly because a partial revaluation would have undermined credibility. Hence, restoration was practicable, as Ricardo had already argued, when the discrepancy from the pre-war parity was not more than 5 or 10 percent. As regards the choice in favor of price stability, Keynes pointed to the growing experience in pursuing this objective and stressed the limits of the gold standard. Where prices in the various countries diverged widely, as in the aftermath of World War I, the classical adjustment mechanism worked slowly and was unable to correct the disequilibria.[18] Consequently, price stability, although difficult to achieve, was the optimal solution.

Keynes's conclusions implied rejection of the gold standard because they violated both the price level rule and the restoration rule. He contended that the advantages of the gold standard (long-run stability of the value of money and exclusion of government interference) no longer held because gold itself had become a managed currency. Central banks regulated the flows of the metal, so that the classical adjustment mechanism no longer operated. In particular, the interest rate was seen as the means of stabilizing prices and income and not of triggering capital movements as under Bagehot's rule (Keynes 1923, 163, 171–2). A managed currency, unlike a natural currency, made it possible to limit the fluctuations in the money stock, in both the short and the long run, in order to stabilize the price level, economic activity, and employment. Keynes

---

Italian business, the lira does not listen even to a dictator and cannot be given castor oil. But such talk can postpone positive reform; though it may be doubted if so good a politician would have propounded such a policy, even in bravado and exuberance, if he had understood that, expressed in other but equivalent words, it was as follows: 'My policy is to halve wages, double the burden of the National Debt, and to reduce by 50 percent the prices which Sicily can get for her exports of oranges and lemons'" (Keynes 1923, 145–6).

[18] Keynes followed the traditional interpretation of Hume's model and made no reference to the law of one price. On the other hand, he stressed the role of the interest rate in triggering capital movements that helped to overcome temporary difficulties while tending to conceal the real problems in the case of structural disequilibrium (1923, 159–60).

stressed these objectives and argued that transcending commodity money would achieve a higher welfare path (1923, 172–3, 176, 196–7).

These analytical results were translated into concrete proposals for reform. The monetary control mechanism, aimed primarily at stabilizing purchasing power, did not preclude an exchange rate objective as well. Furthermore, it did not have to be based on a fixed rule, "a precise, arithmetical formula" (1923, 186), as did Fisher's compensated dollar, but could take the overall picture into account by considering a wide range of variables (1923, 186–9). Keynes accordingly proposed separating the stock of fiduciary money from the gold reserves: The quantity of money would be independent of the uncertainties of the gold market and could serve to stabilize the price level, output, and employment.

It is desirable, therefore, that the whole of the reserves should be under the control of the authority responsible for this, which, under the above proposals, is the Bank of England. The volume of the paper money, on the other hand, would be consequential, as it is at present, on the state of trade and employment, bank-rate policy and Treasury Bill policy. The governors of the system would be bank-rate and Treasury Bill policy, the objects of government would be stability of trade, prices, and employment, and the volume of paper money would be a consequence of the first (just – I repeat – as it is at present) and an instrument of the second, the precise arithmetical level of which could not and need not be predicted. Nor would the amount of gold, which it would be prudent to hold as a reserve against international emergencies and temporary indebtedness, bear any logical or calculable relation to the volume of paper money; – for the two have no close or necessary connection with one another. Therefore I make the proposal – which may seem, but should not be, shocking – of separating entirely the gold reserve from the note issue.   (1923, 195–6)

This succinct yet pregnant passage delineates a full-fledged conception of monetary policy. Instead of tinkering with the gold standard, Keynes rejects it altogether and calls for a monetary mechanism controlled by policymakers.[19] The emergence of a managed currency, then, was considered inevitable.[20]

The *Tract* stands out for the originality that would mark Keynes's reform plans over the next two decades. Its innovative content was nonetheless limited by the difficulty of reconciling the interests of the dominant power with assignment of currency management to a supranational authority. The problem was not only political in that it had important consequences for the working of the monetary system.

In the early 1920s, Keynes's position was an extreme one. Many economists agreed on reforming the gold standard, but without

[19] Wicksell had already envisaged this approach with the overriding objective of stabilizing prices, at a time when the protracted deflation since the early 1870s was giving way to an inflationary trend: "[I]t would be possible to avoid such a rise of prices only by the *suspension of the free coinage of gold*. This would mark the first step towards the introduction of an ideal standard of value. Monetary discussions of recent years have made us more and more familiar with such an international paper standard. While it is usually regarded as a means of meeting a growing scarcity of gold, it might just as well, I think, and must, come into being as a consequence of an over-abundance of gold. In any case, such a prospect need not, on closer investigation, provide cause for consternation. On the contrary, once it had come into being it would perhaps be the present system which would sound like a fairy tale, with its rather senseless and purposeless sending hither and thither of crates of gold, with its digging up of stores of treasure and burying them again in the recesses of the earth. The introduction of such a scheme offers no difficulty, at any rate on the theoretical side. Neither a central bureau nor international notes would be necessary. Each country would have its own system of notes (and small change). These would have to be redeemable at par by every central bank, but would be allowed to circulate only inside the one country. It would then be the simple duty of each credit institution to regulate its rate of interest, both relatively to, and in unison with, other countries, so as both to maintain in equilibrium the international balance of payments and to stabilise the general level of world prices. In short, the regulation of prices would constitute the prime purpose of bank rate, which would no longer be subject to the caprices of the production and consumption of gold or of the demand for the circulation of coins. It would be perfectly free to move, governed only by the deliberate aims of the banks" (1898, 193–4; italics in the original).

[20] "For the past two years the United States has *pretended* to maintain a gold standard. *In fact* it has established a dollar standard; and, instead of ensuring that the value of the dollar shall conform to that of gold, it makes provision, at great expense, that the value of gold shall conform to that of the dollar. . . . We have reached a stage in the evolution of money when a 'managed' currency is inevitable, but we have not yet reached the point when the management can be entrusted to a single authority. The best we can do, therefore, is to have *two* managed currencies, sterling and dollars, with as close a collaboration as possible between the aims and methods of the managements" (Keynes 1923, 198, 204; italics in the original).

entirely excluding a role for gold. An exception was the Dutch economist C. A. Verrijn Stuart who – arguing for price level stabilization because otherwise "the medium of exchange [would] interfere with the natural movements of prices and income" – proposed the introduction of a nonmetallic system that allowed "a complete adaptation of the provision of money to the existing demand" (1923, 144–5). By contrast, the gold standard could not attain price stability, and the gold exchange standard would be an even worse solution because, decreasing the demand for gold, it would entail inflationary effects (Verrijn Stuart 1923, 149).

Although Keynes appreciated Hawtrey's contributions to managed currency, he criticized the resolutions of the Genoa Conference and dubbed international cooperation a "pious hope" (Keynes 1923, 174), given the dominant position of the Federal Reserve Board; and he argued that the gold exchange standard might prove worse than the gold standard, of which it conserved the weaknesses but not the strengths:

[S]ince I regard the stability of prices, credit, and employment as of paramount importance, and since I feel no confidence that an old-fashioned gold standard will even give us the modicum of stability that it used to give, I reject the policy of restoring the gold standard on pre-war lines. At the same time I doubt the wisdom of attempting a "managed" gold standard jointly with the United States, on the lines recommended by Mr. Hawtrey, because it retains too many of the disadvantages of the old system without its advantages, and because it would make us too dependent on the policy and on the wishes of the Federal Reserve Board.   (1923, 176)[21]

[21] Robertson noted that "gold is passing more and more into the position of a Merovingian monarch, with Governors Norman, Strong and Schacht as joint Mayors of the Palace" (1928, 51). The special radicalism of Keynes's approach was graphically described by Ralph Hawtrey in the article "Money" that he wrote for the fourteenth edition of the *Encyclopaedia Britannica*: "The Genoa plan is based on the continued general use of the gold standard. Proposals have been put forward (particularly by Mr. J. M. Keynes) for applying the policy of stabilization of purchasing power to a paper currency entirely dissociated from gold. The practicability of such a plan is a matter of controversy, and the general return to the gold standard throughout the greater part of the world has made the question an academic one. Apart from schemes of the type favoured by Mr. Keynes,

The differences from Hawtrey emerge clearly in the "Discussion on Monetary Reform" at the meeting of the Royal Economic Society, where Keynes (1924a, 172–5) raises two objections: the problem of apportioning the cost of maintaining the price of gold and that of cooperation between central banks. Viewing the latter with sheer skepticism and disenchantment, Keynes pragmatically suggested delaying restoration and experimenting with stabilizing the price level. If this was the aim, then the return to gold, albeit under modified rules, would be only apparent.[22]

In reality, the appreciable effort at Genoa to reconstruct the post-war monetary system was marred by inconsistencies, chiefly related to maintaining fixed exchange rates while pursuing price stability by means of central bank cooperation, that would find their way through the various reform proposals of the interwar period to Bretton Woods. Most economists focused on stabilizing the price level (Cassel 1922, 271–4) but unlike Keynes did not argue for severing the link with gold. Moreover, the behavior of policymakers, firmly grounded on the gold standard model, thwarted the intention of the Genoa Conference.

At the opposite extreme to Keynes, conservative economists had not abandoned the paradigm of commodity money at all.[23] Cannan,

paper money dissociated from gold is a monetary disease. The abuse of paper money became so prevalent during and after the World War, that it has been given an almost disproportionately important place in latter-day monetary theory" (1929b, 698).

[22] "Mr. Hawtrey wants to placate a good deal of feeling that exists in the world by pretending that he keeps gold standard, whereas in fact he establishes a commodity standard. He proposes to erect a façade of gold and then to regulate its value on the same principles as would be adopted by those who aim at the stabilisation of general prices" (Keynes 1924a, 172).

[23] Although central bankers' views are not considered here, brief mention can be made of Sir Charles Addis (1924b, 268–9), who countered Keynes's suggestion to delay the return to gold because it would heighten uncertainty and damage British trade, putting forward a credibility argument: "The whole thing is largely psychological. If we say that we are going to resume the free export of gold and say it in such a way that people will believe it, you can take it as good as done" (1924b, 269). In his contribution to the Royal Economic Society panel on monetary reform, Addis restated this point, stressing the worldwide consensus to restore the gold standard – "the unanimity is complete" (1924a, 166) – and loosely contending that timely central bank policy was feasible also under the gold standard by means of monitoring prices and unemployment data. His conservative stance clearly emerges from a letter thanking Keynes for having sent him a copy of the

though recognizing that price level stability "is naturally far more attractive to the monetary theorist as an ideal to be worked for the future" (1924, 160), favored the reestablishment of the gold standard because of its operative simplicity and its invulnerability to currency manipulation. Furthermore, a conservative strain of thought, represented by such exponents of the Austrian school as Mises and Hayek, opposed any and all forms of discretion. Although price stability was desirable, the limited knowledge of the monetary transmission mechanism made it impossible to achieve.

The ideal of a money with an exchange value that is not subject to varia-tions due to changes in the ratio between the supply of money and the need for it – that is, a money with an invariable *innere objektive Tauschwert* – demands the intervention of a regulating authority in the determination of the value of money; and its continued intervention. But here immedi-ately most serious doubts arise from the circumstance, already referred to, that we have no useful knowledge of the quantitative significance of given measures intended to influence the value of money. More serious still is the circumstance that we are by no means in a position to determine with precision whether variations have occurred in the exchange value of money from any cause whatever, and if so to what extent, quite apart from the question of whether such changes have been effected by influ-ences working from the monetary side. Attempts to stabilize the exchange value of money in this sense must therefore be frustrated at the outset by the fact that both their goal and the road to it are obscured by a dark-ness that human knowledge will never be able to penetrate.... Once the principle is so much as admitted that the state may and should influence the value of money, even if it were only to guarantee the stability of its value, the danger of mistakes and excesses immediately arises again.

(Mises 1912, 269)

Quite apart from the difficulties of implementation, then, a dis-cretionary policy would be open to abuse by the government. The strength of the commodity standard was that it prevented such

Tract: "I find myself in agreement with nearly all of it, I think, except the conclusion. A managed currency may come some day, but I do not believe we are ripe for it yet. It would be ill to work except in an atmosphere of confidence and belief which at present is non-existent" (1923, 163).

behavior; its weakness was the uncontrollability of the money stock, which was clearly considered a lesser evil (Mises 1912, 270). This standpoint reflected absolute faith in an equilibrium system. Accordingly, the postwar crisis of the gold standard was attributed not to defective operation but to a failure to observe its rules as a result of the transformation into a gold exchange standard. In his later treatise, Mises (1949, 780–1) traced this transformation back to Smith and Ricardo, who had favored a currency made up exclusively of fiduciary instruments in order to save resources. Ricardo's "ingot plan" substituted paper money for gold, while introducing some room for maneuver for the bank of issue. Convertibility was to ensure parity, but there was to be scope on occasion for discouraging the conversion of notes. According to Mises (1949, 780): "In dealing with the problems of the gold exchange standard all economists – including the author of this book – failed to realize the fact that it places in the hands of governments the power to manipulate their nations' currency easily."

If the principle of discretion were accepted, fiat money would be a better solution, saving resources in the form of gold reserves. Hence, starting from the diametrically opposite position, Mises (1912, 432) arrived at the same conclusions as Keynes and anticipated the proposition put forward by Friedman (1961, 250–1) to the effect that both extreme models, the gold standard and fiat money, were to be preferred to the hybrid gold exchange standard. Fiduciary instruments nonetheless created the conditions for an inflationary bias; the ultimate defense of the monetary order lay in a social system based on the private ownership of the means of production (Mises 1912, 449).

These arguments were reiterated in a study on economic fluctuations (Mises 1928), that stressed the independence of commodity money vis-à-vis the government. In this respect, the gold standard was seen as a conquest and the United Kingdom's return to gold as an attempt to defend it. Even though the gold standard did not ensure price stability, a discretionary policy was to be rejected, both so as to avoid giving policymakers the power to determine the value of money and because of the technical difficulties of achieving price stability (Mises 1928, 46, 63, 103).

Following the same current of thought, Hayek analyzed the theoretical foundations of a monetary rule. In his works on the business cycle (1929, Chapter 3), he emphasized not stable money but neutral money. The introduction of money can result in the violation of Say's law, a concept already pointed out by Mill (1844, Chapter 2), and hence in disequilibrium. On the other hand, the principle of neutrality could not be immediately translated into a rule of monetary conduct because the conditions of price flexibility and predictability were not satisfied. A suboptimal solution might have been the stabilization of factor prices (Hayek 1933, 161).

In *Prices and Production*, then, Hayek criticized the advocates of active monetary policy to avoid deflation (1931, 1–3), because money must not disturb the allocative mechanism connected with general economic equilibrium (1931, 30–1). This view excluded the objective of price stability; accordingly, a fall in the price level as a consequence of increased productivity was not just costless but also had the advantage of avoiding distortions in the allocation of the factors of production. Unlike Cassel and Pigou, Hayek proposed keeping the quantity of money constant, although he admitted the possibility of variations to compensate for changes in velocity (1931, 121–4). Nonetheless, there remained the difficulty of identifying the natural interest rate that would equilibrate the capital market and of preventing changes in the structure of production due to the expansion of credit. In short, in view of the insufficient knowledge of the monetary transmission mechanism, it was necessary to avoid discretionary action by policymakers as far as possible by relying on a system, such as the gold standard, with a good degree of automatism:

And I would claim for these investigations at least two things. The first is that, as I have said in my first lecture, monetary theory is still so very far

from a state of perfection that even some of the most fundamental problems in this field are yet unsolved, that some of the accepted doctrines
are of very doubtful validity. This applies in particular to the widespread
illusion that we have simply to stabilise the value of money in order to
eliminate all monetary influences on production and that, therefore, if the
value of money is assumed to be stable, in theoretical analysis, we may
treat money as non-existent. . . . The second conclusion to be drawn from
the results of our considerations follows from the first: So long as we do
not see more clearly about the most fundamental problems of monetary
theory and so long as no agreement is reached on the essential theoretical
questions, we are also not yet in a position drastically to reconstruct our
monetary system, in particular to replace the semi-automatic gold standard by a more or less arbitrarily managed currency. Indeed, I am afraid
that, in the present state of knowledge, the risks connected with such an
attempt are much greater than the harm which is possibly done by the
gold standard.   (Hayek, 1931, 126–7)

In an essay devoted to monetary institutions, Hayek (1932)[24]
launched a frontal attack on the results of the Genoa Conference
and Keynes's innovative ideas. The crisis of the gold standard was
not due to its defects but to the fact that its adjustment mechanism

[24] This article first appeared in *Deutsche Volkswirt* immediately after sterling's abandonment of the gold standard. It was republished much later (December 1966) in French in
Revue d'Économie Politique, with an appendix containing a letter Hayek wrote to *The
Times* on 25 November 1931, but never published, in which he anticipated the issues
discussed in the article and criticized the policy of the United Kingdom. By contrast,
Keynes's comment on the abandonment of the gold standard in *The Sunday Express*
on 27 September 1931 was not only positive but looked forward to a radical change in
monetary institutions, as can be seen from the opening and closing sentences. "There
are few Englishmen who do not rejoice at the breaking of our gold fetters. We feel that
we have at last a free hand to do what is sensible. The romantic phase is over, and we
can begin to discuss realistically what policy is for the best. . . . I believe that the great
events of the last week may open a new chapter in the world's monetary history. I have a
hope that they may break down barriers which have seemed impassable. We need now to
take intimate and candid conference together as to the better ordering of our affairs for
the future. The President of the United States turned in his sleep last June. Great issues
deserve his attention. Yet the magic spell of immobility which has been cast over the
White House seems still unbroken. Are the solutions offered us always to be too late?
Shall we in Great Britain invite three-quarters of the world, including the whole of our
Empire, to join with us in evolving a new currency system which shall be stable in terms
of commodities? Or would the gold standard countries be interested to learn the terms,
which must needs be strict, on which we should be prepared to re-enter the system of a
drastically reformed gold standard?" (Keynes 1931a, 245, 249).

was prevented from working by sterilizing inflows of gold and off-setting outflows with an increase in the fiduciary note issue. Underlying these developments was the rise of managed money, the new approach associated with Cassel, Fisher, Hawtrey, and above all Keynes. Its origin can be traced back to the transition from the gold specie standard to the gold bullion standard, Ricardo's well-known "ingot plan," because in the first case an external deficit necessarily resulted in a reduction in the stock of money, whereas in the second the gold had to be withdrawn from the central bank, which could annul the effects of the withdrawal by expanding credit (Hayek 1932, 128–31). The fundamental difference was between a system that, beyond the short run, was independent of the monetary authorities and one in which the latter were ultimately responsible for the quantity of money. Hayek's thesis that money played no role in the 1929 crisis – in contrast with other contemporary interpretations (Hawtrey 1932, 227–8; 1938, 272–3; Currie, Ellsworth, and White 1932; Currie 1934; Laidler and Sandilands 2002) and with the view prevailing today (Friedman 1960; Friedman and Schwartz 1963; Eichengreen 1992a) – was based on reference to the gold *specie* standard, whose automatic nature would have forestalled disequilibria in the market for money.

Although there are some differences between their approaches to methodology and concepts of equilibrium,[25] Mises and Hayek anticipated Friedman's views on monetary policy grounded in the lack of knowledge of the transmission mechanism. Their proposed solutions – gold standard and simple rule – differed because of the spread of fiat money in the intervening period and their different attitudes concerning friction and rigidities in the adjustment mechanism, but the underlying approach was the same. Friedman

---

[25] An instructive comparison of the Austrian and neoclassical schools can be found in a recent article by Sherwin Rosen (1997). In his early writings on the business cycle and money, however, Hayek appeared to refer, like Robert Lucas, to an equilibrium paradigm rather than to an evolutionary model. For an examination of the contributions of the Austrians to monetary theory, see Yeager (1988).

(1960, 81) based his rejection of the gold standard on its cost in terms of resources, making fiduciary instruments preferable, and on the fact that the money stock was not controllable in the long run, which, when prices and wages were rigid, made adjustment very costly. Hayek (1933a, 161) recognized these costs but considered them to be necessary and in any case less than the benefits deriving from a system that was free from government interference and able to ensure the stability of the economy. Their shared scepticism with regard to the gold exchange standard and then the Bretton Woods system reflected a common conception of monetary policy rejecting discretion.

4.3. THE IRREVERSIBLE CRISIS OF THE COMMODITY STANDARD

In contrast with the widely shared tenets of the gold standard, in the 1920s economists' views of the monetary system were diversified. The debate was heated. The immediate consequence was to open a fissure in the commodity standard architecture with momentous implications. The shocks of World War I combined with theoretical advancement to foster the conviction that a managed money could outperform a natural money governed by an "automatic" mechanism. Though still embryonic, these developments greatly influenced the received view, weakening the postwar monetary reconstruction and producing imbalances that culminated in the downfall of the gold standard in September 1931. This epochal change is efficaciously described by Hayek, stressing the rise of a new theoretical paradigm and Keynes's role in it:

This abandonment of the gold standard undoubtedly implies a final break with the unique tradition of more than two hundred years, on the basis of which Britain has repeatedly returned to the gold standard at the cost of great sacrifices, even after periods of temporary shock to its currency unit. This time the sacrifices which had been made since 1921 were in vain, because the responsible authorities were unwilling or unable to exact what probably would have been the smaller sacrifices necessary to ensure the long-term position of the pound. The greatest responsibility for this, however, must be borne by those who initially opposed the return to the gold standard. For although their position was justifiable at that time, they did not abandon it even when the gold standard had been restored at its former parity, and fought with the utmost vigour against all the measures necessary if that standard were to be finally consolidated. It is beyond all doubt that they found an increasingly more receptive hearing within the management of the Bank. If one wanted to describe the abandonment of the gold standard in Britain as 'the economic consequences of Mr Keynes', and there are many reasons to do so, I believe that even today J. M. Keynes would still regard such a statement not as criticism but as praise. (1932, 132–3)[26]

Although Keynes's radical views represented a minority position, the objective of price stability to smooth out cyclical fluctuations was almost a commonplace. However, the economists' effort to translate this theoretical framework into an institutional design introduced elements of flexibility that substantially altered the rules of the game, impairing the properties of the gold standard and depriving the system of the coherence indispensable to viability. In particular, the consistency of price stability with a fixed parity was to be assured by central bank cooperation, but the very assumptions for its realization were lacking. In fact, the arguments in favor of price stability not only violated the price level rule (because the common price level was no longer determined by the world demand for and supply of gold) but also invalidated the restoration rule (rejecting the deflation necessary for its implementation) and, hence, Bagehot's rule, because the resulting loss of credibility tainted the effectiveness of interest rate maneuvers. The latter were no longer used to trigger capital movements but to control

---

[26] Hayek developed these ideas in a series of lessons he held at the Graduate Institute of International Studies in Geneva, in which, among other things, he reaffirmed his opposition to giving policymakers control over the quantity of money because this would introduce an additional factor of instability (1937, 93). Concluding his article, Hayek (1932, 134) correctly forecast that there would not be a rapid return to gold, while he hoped, though in this he was to be disappointed, that the ideas developed within the Macmillan Committee and in Keynes's *Treatise* would soon be discarded.

the money supply with a view to stabilizing prices and output and employment as well. Hence, Hawtrey's suggestion to compensate for diminished credibility with closer international cooperation was no solution. The relationship between these two factors is not an inverse one and thus could not allow a trade-off that would ensure the viability of the gold exchange standard.

The new approach to the monetary mechanism and the related modifications of the institutional setup, therefore, set the overall conception of the monetary standard on its head, moving from a rigid system anchored by the gold parity, to which economic policies and the economy as a whole had to adjust, to a more flexible structure, where the attainment of policy goals was entrusted to the policymaker. This was not a change in degree but in kind. The mainstream view was reflected in the Genoa Conference resolutions, but radicals and conservatives alike were skeptical of their implementation and deemed the gold exchange standard as a hybrid, worse than either the gold standard or fiat money. This variety of opinions, perhaps only to be expected in a moment of transition, played a crucial role in heightening the disruptive monetary imbalances of the interwar period. While monetary arrangements lost their prewar characteristics, central bankers stuck to the gold standard model. Keynes made this point in a letter to Addis, criticizing the quick restoration of the prewar parity, with these prophetic words:

The more I spend my thoughts on these matters, the more alarmed do I become at seeing you and the others in authority attacking the problems of the changed post-war world with – I know you will excuse my saying so – unmodified pre-war views and ideas. To close the mind to the idea of revolutionary improvements in our control of money and credit is to sow the seeds of the downfall of individualistic capitalism. Do not be the Louis XVI of the monetary revolution. For surely it is certain that enormous changes will come in the next twenty years, and they will be bad changes, unwisely and even disastrously carried out, if those of us who are at least agreed in our ultimate objects and are aiming at the stability of society cannot agree in putting forward safe and sound reforms. (1924b, 271–2)

The clash of opinions produced major disturbances that sparked off the epoch-making transformation leading to the end of commodity money. The process was necessarily long, stretching over half a century, and went through various stages. Ultimately, it produced a radical break with twenty-five hundred years of monetary history.[27] The interaction of innovative theoretical work and disruptive shocks irreparably undermined the received view. Eventually, the fatal blow of the depression called the classical equilibrium hypothesis into question, thus driving the state of the art toward a quite novel paradigm.

---

[27] Angela Redish traces the transition from commodity money to fiat money back to the Middle Ages, drawing attention to the fact that coins were not traded by weight and to the diffusion of central banking principles in the nineteenth century. However, she clearly recognizes the effectiveness of the commodity standard properties up to 1914. "By the end of the nineteenth century Bagehot's argument that the currency needed to be managed and that central banks should act as a lender of the last resort had considerable acceptance, especially in the United Kingdom. While the system had become less automatic, the requirement of convertibility provided a credible anchor for the system and in turn limited the scope for governments to try to manipulate the currency to earn seigniorage" (1993, 785). In the same vein, Frank Graham remarked: "Since the introduction of convertible substitutes for hard money there has always been some management of debt currency, but management, in the sense in which the word is here used, *viz.* control over the long-run value of money, did not anywhere appear until after the first World War" (1943b, 11 note 9).

5 THE GREAT DEPRESSION: OVERTURNING
THE STATE OF THE ART

I N THE AFTERMATH OF 1929, THE INTERNATIONAL MONETARY system suffered a fatal blow and the theoretical debate took a new course. Whereas in the 1920s policymakers had sought to make the changes that would allow the restoration and improvement of the gold standard, in the 1930s the way that system worked came to be seen as a cause of the crisis, intensifying the calls for reform. The movement away from the commodity standard quickened, and policymakers were assigned an active role in stabilizing not just the price level but also income and employment. With the definition of instruments and targets, a full-fledged concept of monetary policy as the central banker's solution of an optimization problem came to be widely shared among economic theorists. Monetary arrangements had to be revamped to match that concept,[1] a task whose accomplishment met with substantial difficulties.

The interaction between theoretical advances and exogenous shocks, the driving force of the evolution of the international monetary system, was quite intense in the crisis-ridden interwar years, especially after the onset of the depression, which stimulated intensive research activity and was inevitably policymakers' overriding

---

[1] John Law (1705) was an early proponent of this approach. His original plan, intended to remedy the scarcity of money in Scotland by issuing paper money backed by land, made him "the genuine ancestor of the idea of managed currency, not only in the obvious sense of that term but in the deeper and wider sense in which it spells management of currency and credit as a means of managing the economic process" (Schumpeter 1954, 322). Law's system was nonetheless based on theoretical metallism (Cesarano 1990).

concern. The further move away from commodity money, widening the discretion and the functions exercised by monetary authorities, highlighted the role of theory in molding innovative rules of the game. Knowledge of the direction in which economic analysis advanced is thus essential for an understanding of the reform proposals that would emerge in the early 1940s. The proposals had necessarily to be consistent with the prevailing theoretical paradigm. In this connection, the impact of the depression on economics was overwhelming; it cast doubt on the very foundations of classical economic theory. The analysis of the monetary system reflected these developments: Until the mid-1930s, it was still grounded in the equilibrium hypothesis, which the growing influence of Keynes had begun to undermine.

5.1. THE EQUILIBRIUM HYPOTHESIS AND THE INTERNATIONAL MONETARY SYSTEM

The disruptive shock of 1929 powerfully enhanced the attractiveness of the idea of managed money. In the classical equilibrium approach, a sharp contraction of economic activity was related not to the inherent instability of the economy but to the significant fall in the price level, which called for closer control of the money supply. The theoretical conception of the monetary mechanism, therefore, was turned upside down and the system was refounded on principles quite different from those underlying the received view. The postwar gold exchange standard, indeed, came to be considered as a major factor of disequilibrium. Recent research, too (Choudhri and Kochin 1980; Huffman and Lothian 1984; Hamilton 1987; Eichengreen 1988, 1992a; Temin 1989), has underscored the role played by the international monetary system in exacerbating and propagating the depression, supplementing the hypothesis turning on the sharp decrease in the money stock in the United States (Friedman and Schwartz 1963). Actually, a similar approach was already adopted in the 1930s. The cause of the crisis, in this view, was the monetary contraction, related to the failure of the monetary system. Thus, to account for the downfall of European economies, Stafford remarked: "No one reason can satisfactorily explain the depression, . . . but there can be little doubt that the monetary mechanism has spread and intensified economic maladjustment" (1931, 92–3). And, referring to the early 1930s, Brown noted: "[T]he conviction became widespread that the gold standard was *inherently* deflationary, and that adherence to it involved real costs that were not compensated for by the advantages of a stable system of exchange rates" (1941, 43; italics in the original).[2] The domestic and international aspects of the problem, however, were not clearly distinguished because, in a metallic standard, they were closely linked.

A notable exception was Irving Fisher (1934). He built a theory of the propagation of the Great Depression, identifying the monetary standard as the vehicle of the international transmission of booms and depressions: The monetary standard transmits changes in the price level, which in turn affect business conditions. Fisher corroborated this hypothesis with a sophisticated empirical analysis, showing that after 1929 all the gold standard countries experienced a nearly identical fall in the price level as well as a highly similar impact on output and employment. Furthermore, the closely interconnected countries of the sterling area also moved together and, after sterling went off gold, were able to reverse the price trend and alleviate the depression. By contrast, a third, "miscellaneous" group of countries evolved in significantly diversified fashion. In a

---

[2] Asking what made countries like Great Britain and the United States, which had sought most vigorously to reestablish the gold standard, reject it altogether, Charles Rist answered: "Nothing but the great economic crisis that broke in 1929. That 'crash' caused the fall of the English pound and halted industries and increased unemployment in the United States, thus inclining the two countries which hitherto had been most devotedly attached to the gold standard to question the soundness of that system and take kindly to the notion of a paper currency not convertible into gold, and 'managed' in such a way as to put an end to business depression, raise prices, lighten the crushing burden of debt and thenceforth guarantee a more regular, a more satisfactory, course of business" (1934, 245).

preferred analogy of his (see Chapter 4, note 7), Fisher likened the international transmission mechanism to a system of lakes whose level falls and rises together unless communication is obstructed. Hence, a country outside a given monetary standard is like an isolated lake whose canals to all the others have been cut (1934, 9).[3]

Fisher's theory did not attract the attention it deserved because of insufficient publicity (his 1934 paper was privately circulated and, though published in the following year by the International Statistical Institute, was not listed in the American Economic Association *Index of Economic Journals*; Dimand 2003, 54–5). Yet his full-fledged explanation of the diffusion of the depression anticipated by half a century modern contributions. In any case, the need to control monetary conditions instead of relying on the operation of the gold standard had, by then, been widely accepted. Indeed, the Great Depression wrought a major change in the fundamental principles underlying the monetary mechanism. As Feliks Mlynarski remarked:

The Ricardian theory merely admitted that under the free-trade system the free movements of gold would check excessive fluctuations of price levels, reducing all economic forces to one common world basis. The new doctrine tackles the problem in a more positive way. If attempts to stabilize the purchasing power of gold should be successful, there would be no longer any violent fluctuations, and booms as well as slumps would cease. From this point of view, and especially after the last disastrous economic crisis, this stabilizing problem is the same as that of eliminating excessive fluctuations of price levels, and as such it is the central problem of contemporary theory and practice. The automatic functioning of the gold standard and a system of free trade were the leading ideas of the

---

[3] In his classic essay on the balance of trade, Hume makes the same analogy: "All water, wherever it communicates, remains always at a level. . . . But as any body of water may be raised above the level of the surrounding element, if the former has no communication with the latter; so in money, if the communication be cut off, by any material or physical impediment, (for all laws alone are ineffectual) there may, in such a case, be a very great inequality of money. Thus the immense distance of China, together with the monopolies of our India companies, obstructing the communication, preserve in Europe the gold and silver, especially the latter, in much greater plenty than they are found in that kingdom" (1752b, 63–4).

nineteenth century. The stabilization of the purchasing power of gold, i.e., a relative rigidity of price levels will, in all probability, be the leading idea of the twentieth century. (1937, 273)

Price level stabilization was thus viewed as the means of preventing sharp fluctuations in output and employment. This analytical construction remained within the confines of the classical paradigm hinging on the equilibrium hypothesis. In this respect, Keynes, in a 1934 radio piece eloquently titled "Poverty in Plenty: Is the Economic System Self-Adjusting?" (1934), divided economists into two groups according to whether they replied yes or no to this question. Including Lionel Robbins in the first camp, Keynes lucidly described in just a few sentences the essential principles of the classical position and the importance it attributed to the malfunctions of the monetary system:

Professor Robbins . . . stresses the effect of business mistakes under the influence of the uncertainty and the false expectations due to the faults of post-war monetary systems. These authorities do not, of course, believe that the system is automatically or immediately self-adjusting. But they do believe that it has an inherent tendency towards self-adjustment, if it is not interfered with and if the action of change and chance is not too rapid. (1934, 487)

Keynes, instead, rejected the equilibrium hypothesis outright. The *General Theory*, then, marked the start of decades of alternation in research programs. Looking ahead for a moment, after the predominance of Keynesian economics, it was Milton Friedman who led the counterrevolution in monetary theory and reestablished the link with the classical tradition, especially in the light of the initial results of his work on the monetary history of the United States. As early as 1954, in a lecture in Stockholm titled "Why the American Economy Is Depression-Proof," he identified the abandonment of the gold standard as one of the crucial innovations that, together with changes in the fiscal structure and in the banking system, would prevent bank failures and increase the controllability of the money stock, thereby averting the repetition of a major crisis. From his historical studies, Friedman arrived at the same result as the economists of the 1930s: "[M]onetary contraction or collapse is an essential conditioning factor for the occurrence of a major depression" (1954, 82–3). Friedman qualified this proposition by specifying that he was referring to the most acute types of crisis, not to ordinary business cycles. This conclusion reaffirms the continuity between his approach and the classical approach. In the Rhodes Memorial Lectures, in fact, Gustav Cassel (1932b) had distinguished the cyclical fluctuations prior to 1914 from the Great Depression. The essential feature of the latter was the drastic fall in the price level, which is a monetary phenomenon and therefore admits of only a monetary explanation. Even if shocks of other kinds occurred, monetary equilibrium could always be restored by central bank action. Hypotheses that referred to disequilibria in the market for goods or widespread overproduction were groundless (1932b, 41–51).[4]

Cassel's view was representative of the theoretical framework followed by most of the leading economists of the day. The starting point was the need to limit the amplitude of cyclical fluctuations. A large expansion would be a prelude to an equally large contraction in economic activity, so it was necessary to avoid phases of excessive expansion. This objective was espoused not only by academics (Angell 1933, 64; 1937, 52–3; Hansen 1937b, 89; Hawtrey 1937, 144; Williams 1937, 26) but also by some policymakers, such as Marriner Eccles, Chairman of the Federal Reserve Board (1937, 3–4). Reducing the variability of income was seen as a necessary

---

[4] While acknowledging the presence of contrary opinions, Cassel argued that the sheer severity of the depression pointed decisively to its monetary origin: "The fundamental importance of a stable monetary system for the well-being of mankind has never been so obviously demonstrated as in these hard times. But even now the explanation of the causal connection and of the essentially monetary character of the whole crisis has met with strong opposition. All possible kinds of explanations for the fall in prices have been advanced, but wide and influential circles have obstinately refused to see that the explanation lies in a defective monetary policy" (1932a, 507–8).

condition if the growth path was to be prevented from entering an area in which the stability of equilibrium was not guaranteed.[5] The policy prescription was to stabilize the quantity of money – or better, "the *effective* money supply (MV)" (Hansen 1933, 253; italics in the original). Admittedly, this rule could not cope with smaller cyclical fluctuations, which in any case could not be eliminated and were a negligible problem (Angell 1937, 83). Of course, explanations of the depression were not exclusively monetary. A widespread hypothesis linked output movements to changes in investment stemming from the varying pace of technical progress. But even in analyses based on real factors, monetary policy action was deemed a necessary condition for stabilization, possibly supplemented by other measures. As Alvin Hansen put it: "It is gradually coming to be recognized . . . that it is a responsibility of the central banks to prevent, as far as possible, a general collapse of purchasing power. Yet it is doubtful, as we have seen, if they can perform this function alone, without the aid of the government" (1933, 254–5).

The dominant approach, as described by Hawtrey, centered on the dynamics of the money supply, the control of which prevented major crises. Starting from the money–income relationship, Hawtrey stressed the importance of the stability of the monetary aggregates in preventing wide fluctuations in the economy, which by its nature was stable. Thus, "the underlying cause of the

[5] Eccles made this point clearly: "Those who believe in nature taking its course argue that there are forces that tend to restore the flow of income when it is disturbed. . . . The answer to this argument is that it is true as far as it goes, but it does not go far enough. It assumes a condition of stable national income, and this is precisely the condition that is absent during a general downswing. . . . Similarly, in depressions, when incomes are falling, a reduction in prices may fail to stimulate demand. This is particularly likely to happen if a further continued fall in prices is generally expected. Thus a departure from stability, although it may set in motion corrective forces, also unfortunately produces intensifying and aggravating ones. Our recent experience is grim witness to the fact that these latter forces may far outweigh the corrective forces for an impossibly long period. Before the self-generating forces of deflation in the last depression were exhausted or were offset by positive government action, the national income had been cut in half, and a sixth of our population was being supported out of public funds. Now that we are on the upswing, the self-generating forces of revival might carry us into another boom unless we are prepared to take corrective action in time" (1937, 7–8).

trouble has been *monetary instability*. The industrial depression and unemployment, the insolvencies, bank failures, budget deficits and defaults, are all the natural outcome of a falling price level" (1932, 228; italics in the original). He also attributed the catastrophic outcome of the crisis to inability to understand its causes: a mistaken monetary policy aggravated by the unsatisfactory working of the monetary system. In fact, the massive accumulation of gold in France and the United States was the *primum movens* of a process fuelled by the failure of the adjustment mechanism. The other countries were obliged to adopt restrictive measures to defend their gold reserves, thereby accentuating deflation and hastening the collapse of the system.[6] This interpretation was consistent with an equilibrium approach that saw massive and persistent unemployment as due to monetary causes and therefore requiring a monetary cure. In this connection, prompt action by central banks was crucial. According to Hawtrey (1932, 279–82), when equilibrium is disturbed, the transition to a new equilibrium position is complicated by the lags in the transmission of monetary impulses and by lack of knowledge of the transmission mechanism, the arguments that would be used on behalf of Friedman's simple rule. Monetary policy, therefore, must aim to smooth not the price level, which is the fundamental variable in a static context, but

---

[6] Cassel also made this point: "The fact that the gold-receiving countries failed to use their increasing gold reserves for extending the effective supply of means of payment must be regarded as abnormal and, therefore, as an independent cause of the fall in prices at the side of the maldistribution of gold itself. Had the gold been used in a normal way prices in France and the United States would have risen above the price-level of the outside world. This would have led to an export of gold which would have saved the outside world from a further fall in prices and helped it to maintain the Gold Standard. Thus it may truly be said, that the breakdown of the Gold Standard was the result of a flagrant mismanagement of this monetary mechanism. *The payment of war debts in conjunction with the unwillingness to receive payment in the normal form of goods led to unreasonable demands on the world's monetary gold stocks; and the claimants failed to use in a proper way the gold that they had accumulated*" (1932b, 71–2; italics in the original). See also Cassel (1932a, 507–8) and (1932b, 64–5). That there was both a scarcity and a maldistribution of gold was denied by Edwin Kemmerer (1932), an unyielding supporter of the gold standard, who expected an inversion of the world price trend due to the system's automatic forces.

consumers' income and outlays, driving the economy in the successive stages of the transition without causing further imbalances. Hence, "the art of central banking is *dynamic*" (1932, 279; italics in the original).

Before these contributions, James Rogers (1931, Chapter 6) had closely examined the "golden spiral" accounting for the huge accumulation of gold reserves in the United States. The large inflow of gold brought about by World War I and enhanced by protective tariff policies did not raise the price level in the United States, because it went to the Federal Reserve Banks in payment of member bank borrowings; nor did prices fall in the gold-losing countries, because of trade unions' opposition to wage cuts. The easy monetary conditions prompted the New York financial market boom and attracted further foreign funds, balanced, however, by U.S. investments abroad. The system had lost the automatism of the prewar gold standard, so Rogers called for removing the obstacles to the adjustment mechanism – price rigidities, tariffs, defective banking policies – in order to stop the golden spiral. In this connection, he was not optimistic that the depression could be overcome rapidly and presciently doubted that sterling could remain on the gold standard (1931, 143–6) given the downward rigidity of prices and the resistance to wage reductions, which increased unemployment and ultimately the public deficit. He emphasized the need, in order to break the stalemate of world depression, to raise the price level in the United States and consequently urged the Federal Reserve Banks to refrain from playing "the part of gigantic sponges continually soaking up the ever inflowing golden flood" (1931, 207) and resume the activist, effective policies of the early postwar years.[7]

---

[7] In a subsequent article, Rogers stigmatized the interruption of the expansionary monetary policy begun in February 1932. In an inquiry into the "sources and uses" of "basic credit" (1932, 246) pioneering the modern analysis of the monetary base, he showed how the large open-market purchases were mostly offset by the repayment of member bank borrowings.

The idea of managed money thus gained ground, with a momentous implication: the urgent need for monetary reform to control the stock of money. At the institutional level, the system had to be configured differently from a commodity standard. Pointing out that the monetary system was no longer "automatic," Fisher remarked: "The question now is not at all whether we shall have an automatic (unmanaged) or a discretionary (managed) currency. The question is whether we prefer an irresponsible management or a responsible management with a definite objective of stabilization" (1935, 214). The equilibrium model was not abandoned, and the severity of the crisis was attributed to the unsatisfactory working of the postwar gold standard, related to the weakening of its rules. However, if conservative economists and central bankers attributed this malfunctioning to the substantial but temporary war shock, the mainstream emphasized the irreversible, disruptive changes in the operating conditions of the system, which had thus become definitively unworkable.

The conservative view – held by such economists as Gregory (1931), Jones (1933), and Rist (1934) – was not backed by original arguments and progressively lost ground. An exception was Hayek (1937), who, recognizing the dominance of the tenet of managed money, set out to analyze its theoretical foundations critically.[8] Aiming to show that the benefits of managed money are illusory, he contrasted a truly international monetary system, in which money flows are the result of individual behavior as between the regions of a single country, with other arrangements characterized by a highly developed banking sector and the presence of central banks. His *Monetary Nationalism and International Stability* compares the three setups in a way that the author himself called "rather pedantic" (1937, 5). Essentially, Hayek considered the abandonment of

[8] Hayek focused on theory because he assigned to the prevailing paradigm a decisive influence on the shape of monetary arrangements. "I am profoundly convinced that it is academic discussion . . . which in the long run forms public opinion and which in consequence decides what will be practical politics some time hence" (1937, xii).

the international system as the source of monetary malfunctioning. Although it might seem paradoxical, many of his criticisms of the postwar gold standard – chiefly the (de)multiplier effects of changes in gold reserves on the money stock[9] – were shared by the mainstream. However, while the latter proposed to abandon the gold standard altogether, Hayek called for a system that could mimic it by reducing the multiplier effects of changes in gold reserves in order to stabilize the stock of money (1937, 88–9). But implementing this policy in countries that belong to an international monetary system would be an additional source of instability. Because a supranational monetary authority is utopian, an order based on rules like the gold standard remains the best option (1937, 93–4). Thus, Hayek's reflections yielded no innovative recipes, showing not only his unbending conservative stance but also the difficulty of rethinking monetary arrangements.[10]

By contrast, mainstream economists considered most of the transformations brought about by the war to be irreversible.[11] First,

9 This basic feature of the interwar monetary mechanism, underscored by several of Hayek's contemporaries, is central to the modern literature. With reference to this characteristic, Hayek remarked: "All this is of course only the familiar phenomenon which Mr. R. G. Hawtrey has so well described as the 'inherent instability of credit'" (1937, 80).

10 In this regard, Henry Simons noted: "There is little agreement, and not much relevant discussion, as to how the monetary rules of the game might effectively be altered to prevent or greatly to mitigate the affliction of extreme industrial fluctuations.... The worship of gold, among obviously sophisticated people, seems explicable only in terms of our lack of success in formulating specifications for a satisfactory, independent national currency – and certainly not in terms of the need of stable exchange rates for orderly international commerce. Indeed, it indicates how little progress liberals have made in showing, by way of answer to revolutionists, what kind of money rules might be adopted to make capitalism a more workable system. On the other hand, the desire to hold to something, in the face of perplexity, invites understanding sympathy – for certainly we have made little progress in defining attractive alternative systems" (1936, 162–3, 168–9). Furthermore, Kemmerer (1933), while appreciating the advantages of the gold exchange standard, pointed out its various defects – excessive pyramiding of gold reserves, asymmetry in the adjustment mechanism, and diminished control of reserves deposited abroad – and cast doubts on its future, confining its operation to smaller states and colonies.

11 "In the post-War period a new gold standard was erected, but under conditions widely divergent from [those] prevailing in the pre-War period. These conditions were in part abnormal, being incidental to the War upheaval. In large part, however, they were the

capital flows were now destabilizing. The greater scale of interest arbitrage transactions together with international stock market speculation put increasing pressure on interest rates, giving rise to "abnormal gold movements" (Einzig 1930, 57–8).[12] The gold standard adjustment mechanism was therefore hampered, heightening fluctuations in economic activity (Mlynarski 1937, 271; Williams 1937, 28–9). Second, prices and wages were now much more rigid, hindering the chief channels of adjustment (Gregory 1931, 83–4; Williams 1935, 158; Hansen 1937a, 132–4; F. Graham 1940a, 24–5). Besides, the notion of rigidity took on a more general meaning in that it referred to the diminished adjustment capacity of markets due to protection, fiscal policies, and labor legislation. In fact, the smooth working of the gold standard postulates great flexibility throughout the economy, which must adapt to the anchor of the fixed gold parity. As Mlynarski remarked:

Under the classical gold standard and liberal economy based on free competition, all elements of production were elastic, capable of more or less automatic adjustment, with one exception, namely, the price of gold. The price of gold constituted a kind of central axle with all other elements of production and exchange revolving around it. The situation has changed nowadays. There are fewer and fewer free prices, less and less elasticity in general. Trade-unions fix the prices of labor. Associations of producers fix the prices of goods and regulate the volume of production. Public economy has expanded, hampering private initiative. Moreover, the gold standard has lost its classical principles. The rigid, unchanging price of gold is replaced by a manipulated price. The system of one central axle, constituted under economic liberalism by the price of gold, becomes an anachronism.   (1937, 306)[13]

---

result of deep-seated structural changes in economic institutions, changes which are not likely to pass when the disturbances thrown up by the War have spent their force" (Hansen 1937a, 131).

[12] M. June Flanders (1989, 208) credits Marco Fanno (1935; 1939) with the distinction between normal and abnormal capital movements, the latter being those originating in causes other than differences in the rate of interest and interfering with the classical price-specie flow mechanism.

[13] Besides price and wage rigidity, Hansen drew attention to the possible international policy divergence in several fields: "We have and we shall continue to have institutional

The list of peculiar features cited to account for the malfunctioning of the monetary system could be lengthened almost indefinitely. Paul Einzig (1930, 62–3) pointed to the political factor that led some countries to accumulate substantial gold reserves either for prestige or to exert pressure on other nations. Gregory (1931) considered the sterilization of gold. Mlynarski (1936a, 327–30) summarized the several defects of the gold exchange standard as gold hoarding by central banks, the one-sided character of private gold arbitrage transactions, the notable increase of short-term capital in the gold centers, and the massive stock of gold accumulated by the United States. Actually, most of these developments followed from a single cause, namely the alteration of the basic properties that had underpinned the success of the gold standard until World War I.

5.2. IN SEARCH OF A NEW MONETARY ORDER

In the disaster of the depression, analysis of the monetary system was not limited to its technical *modus operandi*, as in the aftermath of the war, but went to its very foundations. As Hawtrey noted, "[G]old at first preserved something of its sacrosanct character. Only the portentous deflation of the nineteen-thirties broke the spell, . . . bring[ing] the entire traditional monetary system into disrepute" (1950, 423, 426). Although diagnoses were not lacking, there was hardly an unambiguous indication of therapy. In any case, the all but universal call for new monetary arrangements ended the consensus endorsement of the gold standard. What had long been considered an ideal model now came to be seen as the cause of the depression and the prime obstacle to the restoration of stable

arrangements making for wage rigidity; no democratic country can root out trade unions or turn its back on social legislation. We have and we shall continue to have our central banking systems. We have and we shall continue to have powerful centrifugal forces tending to break up the international system. Nationalistic management of money, tariffs, public expenditures, taxation, public debt, and wage rates make an international system unworkable so long as these policies diverge into as many directions as there are nations" (1937a, 134–5).

monetary relations.[14] Together with the urgent problem of massive unemployment, the reconstruction of the international monetary system was a serious intellectual challenge.

Extreme, clear-cut solutions were increasingly rejected. The simple return to the gold standard was deemed unfeasible, except by a handful of die-hard conservatives, owing to the structural changes brought about by the depression. At the same time, in light of the experience of the 1920s, totally flexible exchange rates were considered potentially disequilibrating and, in any case, too radical an innovation.[15] In fact, there was little support for complete flexibility

---

[14] Rogers stressed the particular nature of the depression, its role in the changed approach to the monetary system, and the importance of Roosevelt's policy. "To describe the recent currency experiences of the United States is to recount one of the strangest and most dramatic episodes in monetary history. While occasional depreciation of the world's chief units of value has apparently been the rule rather than the exception in past ages, the motivating influence in every earlier recorded experience seems to have been the financial needs of the sovereign (and more recently of the government) rather than the economic well-being of the country. Until 1933, history had failed to record a single instance of a great country's resorting to currency depreciation for the avowed and sole purpose of reviving internal prosperity. The honor of initiating so drastic and so far-reaching a remedy for domestic ills fell to the United States under the leadership of Franklin D. Roosevelt" (1937, 99).

[15] Despite his bent for unorthodox theorizing, Keynes was an inflexible opponent of freely floating exchange rates. Thus, Moggridge remarks: "By the time Keynes came to draft his proposals for the post–World War II monetary system, he had at one time or another recommended almost every exchange rate regime known to modern analysts except completely freely floating exchange rates" (1986, 66–7). In this connection, Flanders asks whether Keynes's viewpoint stemmed from "his (aesthetic?) distaste for floating rates" (1989, 184). An answer was provided by Keynes himself, on 13 October 1936, in a letter to a German student who had questioned him on the point: "Perhaps my views could be summarised as follows: (1) In general I remain in favour of independent national systems with fluctuating exchange rates. (2) Unless, however, a long period is considered, there need be no reason why the exchange rate should in practice be constantly fluctuating. (3) Since there are certain advantages in stability and knowing as much as possible beforehand what is likely to happen, I am entirely in favour of practical measures towards de facto stability so long as there are no fundamental grounds for a different policy. (4) I would even go so far, in order to get practical agreement, as to give some additional assurance as to the magnitude of the fluctuation which would normally be allowed. I should dislike an absolute pledge. The magnitude of the fluctuation which would be suitable would depend upon the circumstances of the country, but, provided there was no actual pledge, I should think that in most ordinary circumstances a margin of 10 percent should prove sufficient. (5) I would emphasise that the practicability of stability would depend upon (i) measures to control capital movements and (ii) the existence of a tendency for broad wage movements to be similar in the different countries concerned. (CW vol. 11, p. 501)" (quoted in Moggridge 1986, 66).

with only a few exceptions. A notable one was Frank Graham (1940b, 25–6) in his quest to introduce fiat money. Another instance was that of Erik Lindahl (1937, 311–2), who, in order to implement an autonomous monetary policy with the objective of price stability, envisaged a system of "free currencies," in which exchange rates would fluctuate between different currency areas, such as the sterling bloc. In general, underlying the argument for exchange rate flexibility was the need to avoid the disruptive effects, in a deflationary environment, of wage rigidity and the increasing burden of debts, both public and private. This was strongly argued, for example, by Evan Durbin (1935, Chapter 7): Stabilizing money incomes by appropriate monetary and fiscal policies would substantially limit the variability of exchange rates, which would prove far less traumatic than the sudden departures from fixed parities.

The literature mainly focused on middle-of-the-road solutions, taking measures to relaunch the gold exchange standard – extinguish the war reparations, liberalize international trade and capital movements, and reduce central banks' demand for gold reserves (Cassel 1932b, 89–92) – and cooperating to stabilize the relative price of gold. However, the transformation of the international monetary system had undermined the conditions for cooperation, making monetary reconstruction a difficult task indeed. The suggestion of a managed currency remained generic; and given the resilience of the gold standard as a model for policymakers, it sometimes revealed a basic inconsistency between domestic economic objectives and maintenance of the gold parity. This was the crucial problem underscored in Keynes's *Tract*, as Friedman recognized (1984, 157). Today, it is still at the center of the debate on the so-called "irreconcilable trilogy" or "holy trinity" or "eternal triangle": fixed exchange rates, freedom of capital movements, and discretionary economic policy.

The reluctance to abandon gold or a fixed exchange rate regime while calling for activist domestic policies often made reform

proposals very weak, incomplete, or downright wrong. Nevertheless, economists offered useful intuitions. One was the point raised
by Cassel (1936, 240–1) and again by Frank Graham (1940a, 19) on
a provisional gold parity that was perceived to be such by economic
agents. Considering the high probability of a downward revision
of the parity, a particular opportunity for speculation would arise,
a one-way bet, which would be one of Friedman's main arguments
against the Bretton Woods system (Friedman 1953a). Graham sin-
gled this feature out as the "Achilles' heel" in monetary standards
and suggested widening the range of exchange rate changes around
"a predetermined but unannounced norm" (1940a, 21) so that the
monetary authority could, by heightening uncertainty, defeat speculators. Mlynarski proposed technical measures – reducing the legal
reserve requirements, widening the gold points to check short-term
capital movements as suggested by Keynes, and issuing gold certifi-
cates cleared between central banks to create "a gold clearing standard" (1936b, 337; see also Mlynarski 1931, Chapter 6) – which,
together with new forms of credit to shore up debtor countries,
would realize the much-sought-after cooperation. Beside its technical aspects, Mlynarski's analysis is noteworthy because it antic-
ipates some key elements of the Keynes Plan – that is, clearing
and short-term credit to overcome temporary payments imbalances. The intellectual effort to improve the monetary system
while recognizing the difficulties is eminently illustrated by Jacob
Viner:

If I may express an individual view, we know too little as yet of the possibilities of stabilization to take immediately any major steps in that direction.
The hostility of central bankers and the menace of political control are
genuine and important factors in the situation. The gold standard is a
wretched standard, but it may conceivably be the best available to us. Its
past record, bad as it is, is not necessarily conclusive in this respect, as
the only alternatives which have actually been tried have, on the whole,
had an incomparably worse record. But we won't know the possibilities of

alternative currency systems until we try them, and both the prevailing atmosphere and prevailing conditions are favorable to cautious experimentation. (1932, 37–8)

Unlike the advocates of change, Ralph Hawtrey still considered the gold exchange standard an "ideal plan" (1932, 250) that did not suffer from structural defects but from violation of the rules and in particular the failure to cooperate in stabilizing the relative price of gold. In the 1920s, the principles laid down at the Genoa Conference had been observed, but subsequently central banks failed to stabilize the quantity of money and hence income (1932, 243). Instead of looking at changes in the gold reserves, not a timely signal because they emerge after the effect on aggregate demand, other variables had to be considered, such as the price level and output, and credit regulated to attenuate cyclical fluctuations (1932, 257, 262, 301). Reaffirming his belief in the gold exchange standard, Hawtrey (1938, 273) stressed the need to avoid not so much a "managed standard" as "mismanagement" – excessive instability of the money stock. The weak point is the implicit assumption of the invariability of the properties of the monetary system after World War I; the reference to the gold standard as the origin of the cooperation mechanism (1938, 254) appears quite inappropriate given the radical transformation of monetary arrangements, with the weakening of the implicit rules of the gold standard.

The design of a widely shared, innovative monetary system apt to avert major swings in economic activity made little progress.[16]

[16] The lack of consensus was underscored by Viner: "In the late 1930's probably no country was wholly satisfied with the existing monetary situation. But there was no agreement as to the directions in which improvement was to be sought. Some wished for a return to the rigid pre-1914 gold standard, without fundamental change therein. Others dreamed of a new kind of gold standard – an internationally managed one designed to produce both stability of the exchanges and stability of world price levels, so as to cure the great defect of the traditional gold standard, that it made the world subject to sustained deflationary or inflationary price trends resulting from fortuitous developments in the discovery of gold fields and in the technology of gold mining. Still others, and especially the totalitarian countries, sought a permanent and complete divorce of their monetary systems from gold and a further extension and intensification of exchange controls

Nevertheless, some efforts in this direction were made. Irving Fisher (1935, Chapter 7) suggested the then widely debated proposal of a 100 percent reserve ratio (Phillips 1995), a measure that would have prevented the fall in deposits after 1929. In his opinion, disequilibria in the real economy played only a minor role in the major crises, which were due instead to excessive debt to banks accompanied by deflation. By correcting a "faulty system," the reform would have prevented the propagation of the cumulative debt deflation process (Fisher 1933; 1935, 121–4), in which debt repayment, via the fall of deposits, caused a monetary squeeze and increased the real value of the debt. Deflation could be stopped by creating money so as to increase the demand for goods and production inputs and drive prices up. In addition to the death of Governor Benjamin Strong as a factor in the Federal Reserve's policy (1935, 129), Fisher restated the hypothesis set forth in his 1934 paper, assigning a crucial role in spreading the crisis to the international monetary system:

If the "debt-deflation theory" is correct, the infectiousness of depressions internationally is chiefly due to a common gold (or other) monetary standard and there should be found little tendency for a depression to pass from a deflating to an inflating, or stabilizing, country. A study has been made to test the last named hypothesis and it has been found to be substantially correct. For instance, it was found that, in the depression of 1929–35, when one gold standard country had a depression with a rising value of gold, all gold standard countries were practically sure to catch the contagion, because prices fell alike in all. But silver standard countries and countries with a managed paper currency escaped, as their price levels were rising or stable.... In the above analysis it is clear that one essential link is a reduction in check-book money. In still more detail it was shown in Chapter IV how such a reduction is caused by the contest for cash between banks and the public.   (1935, 133–4)[17]

administered on a national basis and with narrowly nationalistic and indeed, in some cases, openly aggressive objectives" (1943, 194). On the same point, see Angell (1937, 53–4).

[17] For an analysis of Fisher's ideas, see the article by William Allen (1993).

An alternative proposal was the commodity reserve currency scheme put forward by Benjamin Graham (1937; 1944) and by Frank D. Graham (1940b). The unit of account was to be a basket comprising set quantities of a number of goods, not just one as in the gold standard, in order to stabilize the price level and prevent crises of overproduction. According to its advocates, the commodity reserve currency, the analysis of which is beyond the scope of this work, had all the strengths of the gold standard without its weaknesses. In reality, in addition to the costs in terms of resources typical of all commodity monies, there is the complexity of its working. The different versions of the plan were distinguished by the degree of emphasis on various essential aspects, such as the accumulation of goods for strategic purposes, an issue also addressed by Keynes (1938), or the stabilization of a particular market, when interventions focused not on the basket as a whole but on one or more specific goods. Despite the many criticisms (Clark 1933; see the exchange of articles in the *Journal of Political Economy* between W. T. M. Beale, Jr., M. T. Kennedy, and Willis Winn [1942] on the one hand and Benjamin Graham [1943] and Frank D. Graham [1943a] on the other, with a reply by Winn [1943]), this reform cropped up repeatedly. It gave rise to a debate between Hayek and Keynes in the *Economic Journal* in 1943. A memorandum was submitted to the Bretton Woods conference (B. Graham and Hirsch 1952); the scheme was put forward again in the sixties by Hart, Kaldor, and Tinbergen (1964). More recently, Robert Hall (1982) proposed a unit of account comprising four goods of notable price stability, but his plan did not provide for the accumulation of stocks or for the convertibility of the monetary unit into the goods.

While these projects were peculiar and outside the mainstream, John Williams's sketch of his key currency plan (1935), drawn in greater detail in a later essay (1937), became one of the unofficial proposals circulating in advance of Bretton Woods (Horsefield 1969a, 17–8). The scheme was centered on the United States and Great Britain, which, maintaining domestic monetary stability, would presumably sustain a stable international monetary setup. Floating exchange rates would be resorted to in exceptional circumstances and for different reasons by both the center and the peripheral countries. Along the same lines, Hansen's idea of "a managed international monetary system" (1937a, 132) contains some embryonic elements of the Bretton Woods system, tempering the pursuit of domestic targets with the maintenance of international equilibrium through cooperation between exchange stabilization funds. Exchange stability could be preserved by using the gold stocks, and any short-run disequilibria could be overcome by corrective measures. If such measures were ineffective, there would emerge a long-term disequilibrium – a concept analogous to that of "fundamental disequilibrium" as in the IMF Articles of Agreement – and exchange rates would be allowed to vary (Hansen 1937a, 135–6).

In general, in the 1930s there was a widespread convergence on Keynes's position of 1923, which had been regarded as quite radical at the time. Gustav Cassel restated the crucial aspect as follows: "Clearly, the only way to a permanent stabilization of the world's monetary system is to make the supply of credit entirely independent of the gold reserves of central banks" (1936, 229). Among mainstream scholars, in fact, the system's commodity characteristic was increasingly discussed.[18] Criticism of the gold standard was no

[18] This is clear in the writings of Cassel, who in 1936, in contrast with his earlier publications, definitely rejected the gold standard. "I spent many years of hard work fighting for the restoration of an international gold standard. But when success seemed within reach, the forces of destruction again set in and swept away everything that had been accomplished. Careful examination of subsequent events has convinced me that a new attempt at restoration would be hopeless. But more than that: in the light of the experience that we now possess the shortcomings and defects of the gold standard appear to be so fundamental that the very idea of a return to such a system of money must be rejected as extremely hazardous; and we shall henceforth have to devote all our efforts to building up a new monetary system, entirely independent of gold" (1936, vi–vii). The refusal of an "automatic" monetary mechanism thus paved the way for a conception of stabilizing monetary policy; as Angell argued: "[M]ost students at the present day are agreed that monetary policy can and should be a continuous thing, designed not merely

longer revolutionary, especially once sterling had left the system in September 1931 and a new parity for the dollar had been set in January 1934. The transformation of the paradigm was described by Mlynarski:

The classical doctrine of the automatic standard was thus opposed by the conception of a managed currency. More and more economists were accepting the principles of the new school. Today Keynes appears to have the greatest number of adherents; according to him the gold parity should be changed from time to time. Foreign-exchange quotations should fluctuate within limits broader than those of the gold points, for instance within 5 percent of a given parity. The issue of bank notes should be severed from gold movements and controlled only from the point of view of stabilizing the purchasing power of money as the most important consideration. Without going into technical details, and without discussing the shortcomings or advantages of the new doctrine, it can be stated that it is a complete reversal of the Ricardian theory and hence quite revolutionary with regard to the classical doctrine. (1937, 272)

All the same, metallism still loomed large in the views of policymakers, the financial community, and the public, resulting in a gulf with the approach taken by economic theorists.[19] The great

---

to meet acute emergencies but also to prevent such emergencies from appearing, and in general to keep the tempo of economic activity on as even and rational a basis as possible. . . . That is, monetary policy should be planned and operated not only to deal with acute booms and collapse after they have occurred, but also to counteract as far as possible the less extreme fluctuations in which booms and collapse presumably originate, while at the same time securing continuously a reasonably full utilization of the existing factors and techniques of production" (1937, 52–3).

[19] This was pointed out, in a critical vein, by the conservative economist Charles Rist: "A wider and wider gap is opening every day between this deep-rooted conviction [that gold was the sole safe medium for conserving wealth] on the part of the public and the disquisitions of those theoretical economists who are representing gold as an outworn standard. While the theorizers are trying to persuade the public and the various governments that a minimum quantity of gold – just enough to take care of settlements of international balances – would suffice to maintain monetary confidence, and that anyhow paper currency, even fiat currency, would amply meet all needs, the public in all countries is busily hoarding all the national currencies which are supposed to be convertible into gold" (1934, 251–2). On the other hand, Cassel (1936, 230–4) described the limits and contradictions of the plans for the restoration of the gold standard put forward by study groups and international organizations, including the Bank for

variety of opinion was indeed a major factor in the stalemate that prevented the formulation of a well-grounded reform proposal. In the meantime, events imposed other policy choices, such as the abandonment of the gold standard or the introduction of exchange controls. Thus, Cassel considered the call for a return to gold as a mere formal homage to the gold standard, not the expression of any real intention. In the conclusion of his book, he emphasized the profound transformation of the system:

To summarize our conclusions: A restoration of the gold standard is not to be reckoned with. The belief in the gold standard may still live on for some years as a creed to which people pay lip-service. But for all practical purposes the gold standard is a thing that belongs to the past. We are actually passing through a period of transformation in which the foundations of a new and more reliable monetary system are being laid. This task is the concern of those who have their eyes turned towards the future. What has happened since 1928, when the first tentative restoration of the gold standard was accomplished, has fully justified the title of this work: the Downfall of the Gold Standard now stands out as the most prominent and definite feature of the economic history of our generation.
(1936, 257–8)

5.3. THE QUEST FOR SUPRANATIONAL MONETARY INSTITUTIONS

The rejection of the extreme models of monetary organiza-tion – the gold standard and flexible exchange rates – far from indicating a single direction of analysis, produced a fuzzy picture

International Settlements, the International Chamber of Commerce, and the League of Nations. In the Rhodes Memorial Lectures, in the midst of the depression, Cassel noted the attachment of those responsible for monetary policy to traditional ideas: "There are still many people, even in responsible positions, who do not understand that what has happened is something much more serious than a temporary abandonment of the Gold Standard, and who believe that the old system can be restored as soon as exchanges happen to return for a moment to their old level or to any other level believed to be desirable. This is a very superficial view. If the analysis which I have given in these lectures is correct we are confronted now with a complete breakdown of the old interna-tional Gold Standard system, including the very position of gold as a standard of value" (1932b, 88).

for mainstream economics.[20] The economists' task was a difficult one because it did not involve just the introduction of some remedial technical device but the design of a new set of rules from the ground up. The starting point of the analysis was the generally recognized defect of the interwar monetary experience, namely the lack of cooperation. Under the gold standard, cooperation was the natural outcome of the rules of the game, which were founded on a widely shared analytical framework. After the war, the progressive modification of the paradigm altered the implicit rules, distorting the key properties of the standard. These developments sapped the very basis of cooperation. Because there was no ready alternative model possessing the same properties, it is not surprising that the call for cooperation went unheard. Countries now pursued the stabilization of prices, output, and employment, as well as the liquidity of the banking system in the very short run,[21] but the weight given to such targets varied because the policymakers' theoretical approaches were not uniform. As Flandreau and Eichengreen remark:

The ideological underpinnings of the prewar gold standard no longer carried the same force. Proto-Keynesian ideas surfaced in a growing number

---

[20] The difficulties of theorists in devising innovative monetary arrangements was, according to Keynes, part of a general problem in economics. Analytical results should be sufficiently well-founded before translating them into effective policy measures: "[I]t is characteristic of economics that valuable and interesting work may be performed and steady progress made for many years, and yet that the results will be almost useless for practical purposes until a certain degree of exactness and perfection has been reached. Half-baked theory is not of much value in practice, though it may be half-way towards final perfection. Thus it would not be true to say that there has been sound instruction available [in the field of monetary theory], the conclusions of which practical men have neglected" (1930, Vol. 2, 406).

[21] The severe currency crises after 1929 posed another urgent problem. Hawtrey, pointing up the international nature of the depression and the inability of individual countries to tackle it, suggested establishing "an international lender of last resort": "If the central bank is to meet demands for accommodation in excess of its reserves it must itself borrow. The need arises for *an international lender of last resort*. Perhaps some day the Bank for International Settlements will be in a position to meet this need. But, as things are, the function can only be undertaken by a foreign central bank or by a group of foreign central banks in co-operation" (1932, 228; italics in the original).

of places. Policy makers in different countries interpreted the economic malaise in different ways and prescribed different policy responses, rendering concerted international action all but impossible.   (1997, 22–3)

The paradigm shift in response to the depression, setting the priority on domestic policy aims, thus demanded the overhaul of international monetary arrangements. Facing this daunting task, the research strategy was to fill the vacuum left by lack of cooperation either by buttressing the gold exchange standard or by more radical reform – that is, a supranational monetary authority. As we have seen, the former approach, while contributing a number of suggestions and intuitions, did not lead to a widely accepted construction. The most original thinkers took the second route, aiming at the establishment of an international body to govern the monetary system. Here we naturally focus on the most innovative and influential theorist of the day: John Maynard Keynes.

Keynes had led the way for mainstream monetary thinking with his *Tract on Monetary Reform* and again with the *Treatise on Money*. Even though the analytical basis of the *Treatise* was criticized on the grounds that the "fundamental equations" were tautological, the discussion of international finance addressed some essential points that would be at the center of the debate that preceded the Bretton Woods agreements. According to Keynes, although it was hard for an international standard to do without gold, the exclusion of the metal from the currency in circulation and its management by a supranational authority would permit an "ideal" system. The crucial problem of reconciling the discipline of a commodity standard with the flexibility needed to pursue domestic objectives[22] necessarily had a compromise solution, because countries would not sacrifice their own economic policy goals in order

---

[22] "This, then, is the dilemma of an international monetary system – to preserve the advantages of the stability of the local currencies of the various members of the system in terms of the international standard, and to preserve at the same time an adequate local autonomy for each member over its domestic rate of interest and its volume of foreign lending" (Keynes 1930, Vol. 2, 304).

to sustain the system (Keynes 1930, Vol. 2, 300–6). Broadening the fluctuation band of the price of gold to 2 percent would discourage capital mobility and create scope for maneuvering the short-term interest rate. In fact, the high capital mobility underlying an international standard had to be rejected because it would give rise to sudden adjustments that, in a context of rigidities and frictions, would have pernicious effects.

If we deliberately desire that there should be a high degree of mobility for international lending, both for long and for short periods, then this is, admittedly, a strong argument for a fixed rate of exchange and a rigid international standard. What, then, is the reason for hesitating before we commit ourselves to such a system? Primarily a doubt whether it is wise to have a Currency System with a much wider ambit than our Banking System, our Tariff System and our Wage System. Can we afford to allow a disproportionate degree of mobility to a single element in an economic system which we leave extremely rigid in several other respects? If there was the same mobility internationally in all other respects as there is nationally, it might be a different matter. But to introduce a mobile element, highly sensitive to outside influences, as a connected part of a machine of which the other parts are much more rigid, may invite breakages. (Keynes 1930, Vol. 2, 334–5)

At the factual level, this point of view was corroborated by contingent factors, such as the different reaction function of central banks, notably the Federal Reserve, and above all the rigidity of wages. Writing before sterling abandoned the gold standard, Keynes pragmatically suggested that an international standard should in any case be accepted, while postponing a system in which the value of gold would be regulated by a supranational authority and greater autonomy granted to domestic policies (Keynes 1930, Vol. 2, 330–8). When the *Treatise* was published, the first signs of the depression hinted at the repercussions of the high interest rates inherited from the war and an intensification of the deflationary process. The suggested cure was a highly expansionary monetary policy by the Federal Reserve in order to lower interest rates. In view of its greater international openness, the United Kingdom could not pursue such a policy and should instead have increased public investment (Keynes 1930, Vol. 2, 369–77).[23]

Although in the *Treatise* Keynes viewed the evolution of the international monetary system not as the outcome of a pre-arranged plan but rather as a gradual process, he outlined the design of a supranational managed money. Gathering up the threads of his analysis, in the last chapter he set out two proposals for reform (1930, Vol. 2, 395–402). One involved just a few innovations, some already suggested at Genoa: a ban on the circulation of gold, a greater role for foreign exchange reserves, and a 2 percent fluctuation band. The second was more radical, based on the creation of a supranational central bank that was to issue a currency that, together with gold, would be part of the reserves of the national central banks. This institution was to act like a central bank within a country, managing the interest rate and carrying out open-market operations to stabilize the relative price of gold and prevent international pressures on the price level. These proposals were not highly innovative, but the introduction of a supranational monetary authority represented an attempt, albeit not supported by convincing arguments (1930, Vol. 2, 374–7), to implement cooperation.

The redesign of the monetary system, whose defects were seen as the root cause of the depression, was addressed by the mainstream within the framework of the classical model based on the equilibrium hypothesis. Keynes made a frontal attack on this hypothesis and set out to refound economic theory. In "Poverty in Plenty: Is

[23] Pondering the possible effects of passivity, Keynes remarked: "If we leave matters to cure themselves, the results may be disastrous. Prices may continue below the cost of production for a sufficiently long time for entrepreneurs to feel that they have no recourse except an assault on the money-incomes of the factors of production. This is a dangerous enterprise in a society which is both capitalist and democratic. It would be foolish of us to come to grief at a time when the pace of technical improvements is so great that we might, if we choose, be raising our standard of life by a measurable percentage every year. It has been my rôle for the last eleven years to play the part of Cassandra, first on the Economic Consequences of the Peace and next on those of the Return to Gold; – I hope that it may not be so on this occasion" (1930, Vol. 2, 385).

the Economic System Self-Adjusting?" (1934), he answered in the negative and, counting himself among the "heretics," announced his intention of challenging the classics on their own ground, declaring that he had found the weak point in the orthodox model:

Now *I* range myself with the heretics. I believe their flair and their instinct move them towards the right conclusion. But I was brought up in the citadel and I recognise its power and might. A large part of the established body of economic doctrine I cannot but accept as broadly correct. I do not doubt it. For me, therefore, it is impossible to rest satisfied until I can put my finger on the flaw in that part of the orthodox reasoning which leads to the conclusions which for various reasons seem to me to be inacceptable. I believe that I am on my way to do so. There is, I am convinced, a fatal flaw in that part of the orthodox reasoning which deals with the theory of what determines the level of effective demand and the volume of aggregate employment; the flaw being largely due to the failure of the classical doctrine to develop a satisfactory theory of the rate of interest. (1934, 489; italics in the original)

Fully immersed in the preparation of the *General Theory*, in the first half of the 1930s Keynes published only a few short writings on monetary reform. Chairing a session of the Chatham House Study Group on the International Functions of Gold (Keynes 1931b), he made some remarks on central banks' gold policy, drawing attention to the role of creditor countries in the adjustment process. In particular, the massive accumulation of gold by France and the United States was just a symptom. It had little to do with gold as such and actually signaled a failure in international lending. This feature was regarded by Keynes as a central weakness of the monetary system, and mending it would hold a central place in all his future reform proposals, including the plan bearing his name.

In the final chapters of his essay *The Means to Prosperity* (1933a, 358–60), Keynes offered a blueprint that had several points in common with the one that emerged at Bretton Woods. Though based on gold, the plan was to introduce greater elasticity in the stock of reserves in order to stabilize the price level. An international

authority was to issue gold notes, which would be drawn by individual countries against the value of gold bonds of their respective governments, according to quotas set on the basis of the gold reserves
held at a certain date;[24] the voting power of each country was to
be proportional to its quota. The creation of gold notes and the
interest rate on bonds were to be fixed so as to stabilize prices. The
plan implied "a qualified return to the gold standard" (1933a, 362);
parity revisions would be permitted and the gold points allowed
to diverge by up to 5 percentage points in order to avoid sudden
large capital movements. The ultimate objective was to raise world
prices, and he contrasted his proposal with a generalized devaluation that would unduly benefit the countries with substantial gold
reserves.

Further reflections on these issues are contained in an article on
the future of exchange rates (1935). After stressing the difficulties
that the gold bloc policy put in the way of equilibrium exchange
rates, a necessary condition for implementing any reform, Keynes
discussed the problems of short-term fluctuations and persistent
disequilibrium. He reaffirmed the idea developed in *The Means to
Prosperity* of overcoming short-term fluctuations by controlling
the interest rate in order to support employment (1935, 365–6).
Persistent disequilibrium was to be overcome by adjusting the parity. This approach turned the principles underlying the system

[24] The preeminent role of gold in this scheme led some commentators to suggest that
Keynes had suddenly changed his opinion, a view that he rejected in a letter to the editor
of *The Economist* dated 20 March 1933. "I should like . . . to remind you that my recent
advocacy of gold as an international standard is nothing new. At all stages of the post-war
developments the concrete proposals which I have brought forward from time to time
have been based on the use of gold as an international standard, whilst discarding it as a
rigid national standard. The qualifications which I have added to this have been always
the same, though the precise details have varied; namely (1) that the parities between
national standards and gold should not be rigid, (2) that there should be a wider margin
than in the past between the gold points, and (3) that if possible some international
control should be formed with a view to regulating the commodity value of gold within
certain limits. You will find that this was my opinion in 1923 when I published my *Tract
on Monetary Reform* (see Chapter 5) and again in 1930 when I published my *Treatise
on Money* (see Chapters 36 and 38); just as it is today, as set forth in my articles in *The
Times* and in my pamphlet *The Means to Prosperity*" (1933b, 186).

upside down. It rejected the restoration rule, which was the basis of the commodity standard, and thereby permitted discretionary policy. Continuing to advocate a return to gold, like a report by the Bank for International Settlements (BIS) did, implied living "in an unreal world, a fool's world" (1935, 367). Keynes argued that a monetary restriction to defend the parity would diminish income and employment unless it led to a fall in nominal wages, which was unlikely. In conclusion (1935, 368), he put gold at the center of the system and excluded national reserves of assets in sterling or in a currency issued by the BIS. Thus, the proposal reflected the need for an anchor for the price level, but not a rigid one as under the gold standard. The introduction of a wide spread between the gold points, no longer linked to the cost of transferring the metal, would give policymakers room for maneuver in the short term. In the long run, in the face of a structural disequilibrium the gold parity could be altered.

Apart from Keynes's contributions to a new way of conceiving the monetary system, the *General Theory* produced a sea change in economics, constructing a model that allowed a role for activist economic policies. Although the book did not address the question of monetary institutions as such, the penultimate chapter, devoted to a revaluation of mercantilism and other heterodox theories, stressed the impossibility of pursuing domestic objectives under the gold standard and proposed an "autonomous" interest rate policy and an investment program for full employment (1936, 348–9). This analytical framework was to exert a strong influence on the preparatory work for Bretton Woods.

In conclusion, it is clear that developments in economic theory and in the monetary arrangements on the eve of the articulated reform process leading to the Bretton Woods conference were intertwined. The depression severely challenged the classical model and its equilibrium hypothesis, paving the way for the pathbreaking work of Keynes. Even within the classical framework, however, the disastrous crisis of 1929 shifted the focus of research toward the contrivance of policies that could prevent large income fluctuations. Whereas in the 1920s the main objective had been to stabilize the price level and restore an accordingly modified gold standard, in the 1930s the ultimate goal came to be forestalling massive unemployment and oscillations in output. Hence, the design of both economic policies and monetary arrangements was definitively turned upside down, and the paradigm change was recognized even by conservative economists.[25] The international monetary system came under scrutiny, because its defective operation was considered to have been a major factor in triggering and propagating the depression. Consequently, the center of gravity of economics shifted further away from the commodity standard.

The broad agreement on the need for new monetary arrangements, however, was not matched by any comparable consensus on the features of the reform. Mainstream economists suggested various technical devices to improve the operation of the gold exchange standard, while others called for an international monetary institution. Both approaches had their limitations. The changes in the rules of the game since the war had irremediably ruined the properties of the gold standard and impeded cooperation. Keynes, as we have seen, was deeply skeptical about cooperation, which he considered "a pious hope" (1923, 174). Yet a supranational monetary authority would face stubborn political constraints, related to the surrender of sovereignty. Thus, Hayek deemed this solution "a utopian dream"

---

[25] Presenting his case for a truly international monetary system, Hayek observed: "And although this would probably be denied by the advocates of Monetary Nationalism, it seems to me as if we had reached a stage where their views have got such a hold on those in responsible positions, where so much of the traditional rules of policy have either been forgotten or been displaced by others which are, unconsciously perhaps, part of the new philosophy, that much must be done in the realm of ideas before we can hope to achieve the basis of a stable international system" (1937, xiii). Moreover, Gregory noted: "The international gold standard has few friends to-day. The unparalleled depression of the last five years and the dangers and uncertainties of the present moment have seriously weakened its prestige and, since a large part of the world now possesses currency systems no longer linked with gold, one of its main intellectual supports has been destroyed. For one of the great justifications of the international gold standard was precisely that it *was* an international standard" (1934, 145; italics in the original).

(1937, 93). The criticisms of Keynes and Hayek, though opposite in direction, have a common basis. As radical thinkers, both rejected middle-of-the-road recipes, which are likely to lack coherence, and respectively argued for an entirely new centralized system or an unadulterated return to the classical gold standard.

In general, the essential purpose of monetary reform was to fill the void left by the defective working of the gold exchange standard. This objective was not attained, but these endeavors did prepare the ground for the drafting of the plans that would be discussed at Bretton Woods. Notwithstanding all but universal drive to reform the malfunctioning monetary system, however, commodity money still loomed large both theoretically and institutionally. Indeed, continued attachment to fixed exchange rates while the policy priority was shifted to domestic objectives gave rise to hybrid reform projects prone to inconsistencies. The Bretton Woods monetary order was thus the culmination of the evolutionary process that began after World War I, driven by the interplay of major shocks and advancement in economic theory. On the eve of World War II, therefore, the direction, though not the exact route, of the arduous advance toward monetary reconstruction was in the main already set.

6 PROVIDING FOR A NEW MONETARY ORDER

THE TRIPARTITE AGREEMENT OF 25 SEPTEMBER 1936 BETWEEN the United States, Great Britain, and France was the last pre-war attempt to remold international monetary institutions. The aim was to stop competitive devaluations, remove trade barriers, and return to multilateral trade. The agreement did not fully attain its purposes – at best, it inhibited the destabilizing conduct of the years preceding – but it did roughly outline the design for a new set of rules (Eichengreen 1992a, 379–82). In particular, it brought out the need to negotiate a new institutional framework based on exchange rate stability to enhance international trade. With the war, economists' interest in the topic waned and the debate petered out. Witness the papers presented to the American Economic Association in December 1940, which mostly treated past or current policy issues rather than novel monetary schemes. Academic discussion, in fact, developed only after the publication of the official reform projects in 1943; it was policymakers who were on the front line.

From the outbreak of hostilities, the belligerents posed the question of reconstructing the monetary system. In Germany, Walther Funk (1940), minister for the economy and president of the Reichsbank, suggested replacing the gold standard, the symbol of British hegemony, and London, the center of international finance, with a New Order headquartered in Berlin. As described by the Reichsbank's vice-president (Puhl 1940), the plan was to introduce a clearing mechanism among the countries of continental Europe. It envisaged wartime controls on current account transactions, to be relaxed at the end of hostilities to produce a multilateral exchange regime. In reality, German policy was to overvalue the mark, driving down the terms of trade of the satellite countries, and regulate trade through bilateral agreements (Ellis 1942, 199–200). Though it was called "multi-angular," the system ensured German supremacy, with very considerable advantages from economic relations with the countries under German dominion.

The reform proposals put forward by Britain and the United States in response to the New Order formed the point of departure for the Bretton Woods talks. The analysis that follows is conducted mainly from the standpoint of monetary theory, not diplomatic or political history.[1] Still, it is worthwhile recalling the steps leading up to the Bretton Woods conference. The first version of the Keynes Plan was released on 8 September 1941, just weeks after the signing of the Atlantic Charter, a joint declaration by Churchill and Roosevelt on the principles that would govern international economic relations after the war. Keynes himself had taken part in the talks on the charter (Kahn 1976, 5–6). White began drafting his plan around that same time. In early January 1942, the first version was circulated within the U.S. government. These initial contributions had a restricted circulation; not until after protracted discussion were both the plans published, in 1943.[2] The intense activity of

---

[1] For full reconstructions of that point of view, see Gardner (1969), Oliver (1975), Kahn (1976), Van Dormael (1978), Ikenberry (1993), and James (1996).

[2] As used here, the terms "Keynes Plan" and "White Plan" refer, respectively, to the official documents of 7 April 1943 and 10 July 1943, reprinted in Horsefield (1969b, 19–36, 83–96). In July 1942, the British Treasury unexpectedly came into possession of the U.S. plan; at the end of August, a copy of Keynes's proposal was sent to White (Horsefield 1969a, 16). The official projects were flanked by other plans put forward by government officials, university professors, and independent scholars (Horsefield 1969a, 16–8), inspired by the Tripartite Agreement or looking to the constitution of a fund to stabilize exchange rates and eliminate trade controls. Among the most noteworthy suggestions were those of Jacob Viner, who favored a modified gold standard that would permit changes in the price of gold approved by an international body; of Herbert Feis (1942), who called for the abolition of exchange controls, the stabilization of exchange

discussion and revision of the two plans culminated with the drafting of the basic document for the conference, the *Joint Statement
by Experts on the Establishment of an International Monetary
Fund*, released in Washington on 21 April 1944 and in London the
next day.

The three-year-long road to Bretton Woods was tortuous and
laborious. A lengthy series of versions of the reform proposals were
drafted in response to critiques bearing not only on their analytical
consistency but also on their political implications. The complexity
of the process was bound up with the exceptional nature of the
task: For the first time ever, a group of experts was designing a new
international monetary order.

6.1. THE REFORM PLANS

Intellectual work on international monetary arrangements got
under way immediately upon the outbreak of the conflict. As U.S.
Treasury Secretary Henry Morgenthau explained in his preface
to the White Plan, it would be a mistake to come to the end of
the war unprepared for the problems of reconstruction (Horsefield 1969b, 84). What is more, the swift and timely release of a
plan for international cooperation might actually contribute to the
war effort by strengthening the alliance against the Axis powers.
In the present section, the development of the Keynes and White
plans will be traced separately, preliminary to a comparative
examination.

Asked by British Minister of Information Harold Nicholson to
give a radio talk criticizing the German New Order and countering
German propaganda, Keynes ruled out any resuscitation of the
gold standard, because he considered Funk's rejection of gold to be
basically correct. Rather, the line was to improve the plan by putting

rates, and the establishment of a fund to enable countries to pay for imports or to discharge
debts; and of John Williams (1937) (described in Chapter 5, Section 2), whose scheme
had the shortcoming of discriminating between countries.

all countries in equal conditions. In his reply on 20 November 1940, Keynes wrote:

Your Department think that they are making a good joke at Funk's expense by saying 'gold will have no place in this brave new world' and quoting German propaganda to the effect that 'gold will no longer control the destinies of a nation' etc. Well, obviously I am not the man to preach the beauties and merits of the pre-war gold standard. In my opinion about three-quarters of the passages quoted from the German broadcasts would be quite excellent if the name of Great Britain were substituted for Germany or the Axis, as the case may be. If Funk's plan is taken at its face value, it is excellent and just what we ourselves ought to be thinking of doing. If it is to be attacked, the way to do it would be to cast doubt and suspicion on its *bona fides*. (CW 25, 2)[3]

In this initial phase, Keynes did not draft a detailed alternative plan and only set out several of the general principles, some of them political in character, suggested both by his theoretical work and by the crises of the interwar years. At the end of the war, German economic recovery would have to be sustained in order not to leave the country open to Soviet expansionism (CW 25, 9–13). The idea was to avoid repeating the errors of Versailles by instituting, among other things, an immediate aid program for the former belligerents, the European Reconstruction Fund.

On his return from the United States in August 1941 following the talks for the Atlantic Charter, Keynes drafted two memoranda. One was a general paper on the reform of monetary institutions,

---

[3] In a later document, "Proposals to Counter the German 'New Order,'" Keynes reaffirms the validity of the German approach but calls for applying it correctly, not for the purpose of exploiting other nations. "I have, therefore, taken the line that what we offer is the same as what Dr Funk offers, except that we shall do it better and more honestly. This is important. For a proposal to return to the blessings of 1920–33 will not have much propaganda value. The virtue of free trade depends on international trade being carried on by means of what is, in effect, *barter*. After the last war *laissez-faire* in foreign exchange led to chaos. Tariffs offer no escape from this. But in Germany Schacht and Funk were led by force of necessity to evolve something better. In practice they have used their new system to the detriment of their neighbours. But the underlying idea is sound and good" (CW 25, 8–9; italics in the original). References to Keynes's *Collected Writings* are annotated here as CW followed by the volume number.

the other the original version of his plan, "Proposals for an International Currency Union" (CW 25, 21–40). The first, after pointing to the contradiction between the dysfunctions of the system in the 1920s and 1930s and the notion of an "automatic" adjustment mechanism,[4] attributed the success of the gold standard to the role of London as a financial center in shifting the burden of adjustment from the debtor to the creditor country. Noting the failure of the solutions tried after World War I, Keynes recognized the originality of Schacht's idea of doing without an international currency, thus eliminating the problems created by the monetary mechanism. What was needed, therefore, was "refinement and improvement of the Schachtian device" (CW 25, 24), bringing the creditor countries into the adjustment process in order to remedy the main defect of the interwar monetary mechanism. Another defect, destabilizing capital movements, would be tackled by regulation. Keynes was well aware that, owing to its novelty and the need for greater cooperation, his plan might not be readily accepted (CW 25, 33). From the standpoint of modern theory, his Clearing Union proposal actually involved extending to the international context a fundamental principle of monetary evolution – a cheaper way of executing transactions – as well as the search for macroeconomically optimal solutions. The goal was to eliminate the gold standard's high adjustment costs and the other drawbacks by using the "principle of banking," as was done at the domestic level.

---

4 Thus, Keynes disparages the classical adjustment mechanism, which is viewed as the origin of protective measures. "To suppose that there exists some smoothly functioning automatic mechanism of adjustment which preserves equilibrium if only we trust to methods of *laissez-faire* is a doctrinaire delusion which disregards the lessons of historical experience without having behind it the support of sound theory. So far from currency *laissez-faire* having promoted the international division of labour, which is the avowed goal of *laissez-faire*, it has been a fruitful source of all those clumsy hindrances to trade which suffering communities have devised in their perplexity as being better than nothing in protecting them from the intolerable burdens flowing from currency disorders. Until quite recently, nearly all departures from international *laissez-faire* have tackled the symptoms instead of the cause" (CW 25, 21–2).

The second memorandum transposed this analytical framework into a set of clauses that, notwithstanding subsequent modifications, already contained the essential points of the future Keynes Plan. National central banks deposit reserves with an International Clearing Bank, which performs the classic central bank functions. Although they can institute exchange controls on residents' transactions, the national central banks must make their credit balances available to other central banks. Exchange rates with the currency issued by the clearing bank, defined in terms of gold, are fixed. The central banks can pay gold into their clearing accounts but cannot withdraw it. Each is assigned a quota corresponding to its maximum permissible overdraft. A country may devalue by up to 5 percent if its debit balance exceeds a quarter of its quota; if the debit balance exceeds half of the country's quota, the Governing Board may require devaluation. Conversely, surplus countries are allowed or required to revalue; in the case of a surplus that exceeds the full amount of the quota, the excess must be deposited in a special contingency fund.

The two memoranda did not elicit much response within the Treasury, but they did stimulate comment by a number of economists: Kahn, Meade, Hawtrey, and later Robbins and Robertson (CW 25, 40–2). Hawtrey in particular called attention to the inadequacy of the 5 percent limit on exchange rate variations and to the lack of a mechanism for stabilizing the purchasing power of the unit of account and penalizing debtors. This criticism eventually became so recurrent that the Keynes proposal was tarred as inflationary.[5]

---

[5] In July 1942, in a letter to Keynes, Harrod stressed the need for tougher sanctions on countries accumulating debt (CW 25, 157 note 2). Rolf Lüke (1985) traces the core idea of the Keynes Plan back to the plan for a "Clearing House" presented by Hjalmar Schacht at an international conference in February 1929. The plan failed because of American opposition, motivated by its supposedly inflationary nature; this was the same objection raised to the Keynes Plan: "[O]ne very important clause, which was not contained in the written draft but revealed to the author by Shepard Morgan, was that Germany itself would have no access to Clearing House credits. Except that a 'Bank for International Settlements' was subsequently founded, Schacht's plan was never realised, the reason, as Shepard Morgan pointed out, being precisely this clause. The American delegation saw in

Over the next year and a half, revision would produce a series of versions. With respect to the original draft, the definitive Keynes Plan was more detailed and made some technical and terminological modifications,[6] but it was based essentially on the same principles.

Right at the start, the plan emphasized the independence of national economic policy and the need for the monetary system not to interfere with it (Horsefield 1969b, 19). The idea was to restore stability in international monetary relations under a fixed exchange rate regime but leave considerable maneuvering room to policymakers. The mechanism was intended to return to multilateral trade, stable exchange rates (by preventing competitive devaluations), a money supply not vulnerable to the volatility of the gold market or the actions of countries holding substantial reserves, contribution of creditor countries to the adjustment process, and an international institution that was technical but not political. To avoid leaving himself open to the charge of excessive monetary creation, Keynes devised a series of increasingly rigid limitations for debtors, imposed a charge of 1 (or 2) percent on a country's average balance, whether credit or debit, in excess of a quarter (or a half) of its quota, and also provided for a universal, proportional reduction of quotas should there be "an excess of world purchasing power" (Horsefield 1969b, 25). The essence of the plan was to avoid

it a device on the part of Schacht to expose Germany's neighbour and creditor countries to inflation, by which Germany, the only country unaffected, would correspondingly benefit. This was the same 'inflationary' argument which is regarded as being responsible for the failure of the Keynes Plan 14 years later" (1985, 73).

6 In the second draft, the International Clearing Bank's currency was called the "grammor"; in the third, the "bancor" (CW 25, 61, 72; according to Horsefield, 1969a, 18, the terms appear in the first and fourth versions, respectively). The grammor, a unit of account equivalent to one gram of gold, was the basis of one of the plans set out at the Paris monetary conference of 1867, which called for the introduction of a universal currency (Haines 1943, 122–3). After its publication, Keynes described his plan before the House of Lords on 18 May 1943 and asked for suggestions for the name of the unit of account (CW 25, 271). He liked "mondor," coined by Viner, whom he told that he had gotten more than a hundred proposed names for the international currency (CW 25, 321). Robertson's candidate was "*Winfranks* – a compliment to the [Prime Minister] and the President, with a suggestion of victory, of the continuity of monetary history, and of the ancient unity of Europe under Charlemagne" (CW 25, 302; italics in the original).

sharp changes in the money stock during the adjustment process by allowing countries in temporary difficulty to draw on the Clearing Union's lines of credit. This would prevent the operation of the monetary system itself from causing contractions in output. Capital controls would ensure the conditions for effective economic policies. The accusation that the plan would undermine national sovereignty was rejected, because the renunciation required was not much different from that inherent in trade treaties. Transposing the model of domestic banking systems to the international setting, the plan emphasized the benefits of eliminating "hoarding":

In short, the analogy with a national banking system is complete. No depositor in a local bank suffers because the balances, which he leaves idle, are employed to finance the business of someone else. Just as the development of national banking systems served to offset a deflationary pressure which would have prevented otherwise the development of modern industry, so by extending the same principle into the international field we may hope to offset the contractionist pressure which might otherwise overwhelm in social disorder and disappointment the good hopes of our modern world. The substitution of a credit mechanism in place of hoarding would have repeated in the international field the same miracle, already performed in the domestic field, of turning a stone into bread.

(Horsefield 1969b, 27)

The Keynes Plan embodied an advanced state of monetary organization based on the clearing principle. However, this idea was not quite original (see footnote 5), and, besides, the plan had several weaknesses. The main problem lay in pursuing activist economic policies with the adjustable peg. Controls on capital movements were supposed to make the plan consistent, but their efficacy is debatable. Then, the possible conflict between expansionary policy and exchange rate stability, not to mention the emergence of a one-way bet for speculators, could lead to the cumulation of payments imbalances, because repeated devaluation was not allowed. Moreover, one of the essential aims of the reform, namely the elimination of the adjustment asymmetry underlying the interwar malfunctions, does not seem guaranteed.[7] Under the gold standard, symmetry is intrinsic to the system because gold acts as the nth currency, forestalling Mundell's redundancy problem. The price level is determined in the gold market; gold is the anchor of the system and the source of policy discipline. In the International Clearing Union, however, the constraints on policymakers could prove ineffective, insofar as the "impersonal" rules of the gold standard are supplanted by sanctions imposed by an authority, which may not be enough to enforce economic policy discipline on a nation. Hence, the system could prove not to be viable. The inflationary potential of the Keynes Plan, therefore, lay not so much in any particular defect as more generally in the latent conflict between policymakers' room for maneuver and fixed but adjustable exchange rates, which might not be solved by the Clearing Union's rules.

These analytical observations are mirrored in the institutional design. In a system born of an agreement and run by an international body, there is the problem of sharing power, which tends to gravitate to just a few member countries. The problem with extending the "principle of banking" to an international context is the lack of a supranational governmental authority.[8] This limitation is political, but it carries major economic implications in that the sovereignty vacuum voids the disciplinary power required to guarantee viability. Keynes seems to have been aware of this problem

---

[7] The Keynes Plan introduced penalty charges on excess creditor balances, but this was hardly relevant, as in both plans penalty charges were "so inconsequential that they are likely to have only symbolic importance" (Viner 1943, 197).

[8] Contrasting domestic with international monetary arrangements, Koichi Hamada remarked: "The domestic monetary system in a single country rests on the national consensus. This system evolved through a long process in which the seigniorage rights to issue money gradually became concentrated in the hand of a nation state along with the development of banking systems. On the other hand, political power is only partly concentrated in the European Community or other monetary unions. Since no 'world government' exists, the world monetary regime rests directly and explicitly upon the consensus among the nations. This situation has an analogy in international law where the power relationship is still often explicit in resolving conflicts of interests, while in domestic law it is mostly behind the veil of rule and order" (1977, 14–5).

because, in the second version of his plan, he noted the need for additional rules to permit the "principle of banking" to be applied internationally and, especially, to avoid the uncontrolled expansion of debit and credit balances.

In only one important respect must an International Bank differ from the model suitable to a national bank within a closed system, namely that much more must be settled by rules and by general principles agreed beforehand and much less by day-to-day discretion. To give confidence in, and understanding of, what is afoot, it is necessary to prescribe beforehand certain definite principles of policy, particularly in regard to the maximum limits of permitted overdraft and the provisions proposed to keep the scale of individual credits and debits within a reasonable amount, so that the system is in stable equilibrium with proper and sufficient measures taken in good time to reverse excessive movements of individual balances in either direction.   (CW 25, 45)

The limitation in question also brings out the conflict between fixed exchange rates and the independence of economic policy, which was to be one of the factors in the eventual collapse of the Bretton Woods order. The product of three decades of thought by Keynes, the International Clearing Union was an effort to reconcile domestic economic policy flexibility with stable international monetary relations. Though just as radical as his earlier reform proposals, the Clearing Union was more favorably received, because the design was underpinned by the entire apparatus of the *General Theory*.

The innovative Keynes Plan contrasted sharply with the conservative nature of the White Plan. The first draft in April 1942 expressed an expansionist vision that was eventually watered down, but the essential outlines of the final proposal were already present: an international stabilization fund and a bank for reconstruction and development, the payment of quotas in gold and government bonds, and the possibility of modifying exchange rates to correct a "fundamental disequilibrium" (Horsefield 1969b, 43). The text, lacking in originality, lays out the rules for the fund in excruciating detail, and its tenor is tiresome indeed for the reader.[9] Unlike the Keynes Plan, which did not change substantially by comparison with the version sent to Morgenthau in August 1942, the U.S. plan underwent a series of revisions, especially after White's meetings in London in October (Horsefield 1969a, 30–2). In December, a new draft introduced the "scarce currency clause," a momentous breakthrough in the negotiations (Harrod 1951, 543–5).

In a paper presented at the American Economic Association meeting in January 1943, White (1943) set out a four-part program for postwar monetary reconstruction, focusing on the general principles rather than the details. The emphasis was on the role of international consultation and of an international agency to provide for financing facilities and exchange rate changes to face both the emergency at the end of the conflict and future imbalances. At the same time, the Treasury's approach to monetary reform grew steadily more conservative under the influence of internal political factors; thus, White played down the more innovative features of his plan (Gardner 1969, 77).[10] Accordingly, it is best to focus on the definitive version released on 10 July 1943.

[9] Keynes's reaction to the first draft of the White Plan, as expressed in two letters to Richard Hopkins and Frederick Philips dated 3 August 1942, was negative on the substance but more optimistic on future prospects: "[T]he Harry White scheme...is a tremendous labour to read and digest in full. It obviously won't work. But nothing could be more encouraging than the general attitude shown and the line of approach indicated"; "I have also been making a study of the Harry White document. Seldom have I been simultaneously so much bored and so much interested....The general attitude of mind seems to me most helpful and also enlightening. But the actual technical solution strikes me as quite hopeless. He has not seen how to get round the gold standard difficulties and has forgotten all about the useful concept of bank money. But is there any reason why, when once the advantages of bank money have been pointed out to him, he should not collect and re-arrange his other basic ideas round this technique?" (CW 25, 158–9).

[10] During the gestation of the plan, in May 1943 the United States invited representatives of forty-six countries to submit comments. Meanwhile, the negotiations with the United Kingdom proceeded, and at a meeting at the British Embassy in Washington on 23 June White set forth four conditions deemed necessary to obtain congressional approval: "(1) the United Kingdom must not alter its exchange rate until after the Fund had begun operations (later interpreted as requiring the exchange rate for sterling to be fixed at $4=£1); (2) the commitment of the United States must be limited to $3 billion as a maximum, and it might have to be limited to $2 billion; (3) the Fund must be based on initial subscriptions from its members and not on the principle of bank overdrafts; and

The purpose of the International Stabilization Fund was to avoid the problems of the interwar period. The proposal was to stabilize exchange rates, overcome temporary payments imbalances, and create propitious conditions for world trade, eliminating bilateralism and other trade restrictions. The members would pay quotas in gold or their own currency, totaling at least $5 billion. The Fund's monetary unit was to be the "unitas," defined as an amount of gold equivalent to ten dollars. Exchange rates, which would be allowed to fluctuate within limits established by the Fund, could be adjusted only to correct a "fundamental disequilibrium" in the balance of payments and with the approval of a majority of three-quarters of the voting rights. The accumulation of a creditor position was governed by the "scarce currency" clause: The Fund would move to buy the scarce currency from the other members and devise a method to share the supply, at the same time calling on the country to discourage accumulation of gold and currencies by its residents.

It has often been observed (Eichengreen 1989, 263–4) that the differences between the British and American plans reflected not only conflicting views of the adjustment mechanism but a divergence of interests. Britain was worried primarily about unemployment, which had been especially acute, and by the size of the sterling balances of the sterling bloc countries against massive wartime imports. The United States, given its strong competitiveness, had built up a very substantial creditor position and held a good part of world gold reserves. These contrasts unquestionably affected the architecture of the two plans. The present work, however, examines the analytical differences that are relevant to understanding the structure and limitations of the reforms proposed.

The objectives of the two plans were similar: multilateral trade, fixed exchange rates, symmetry in the adjustment process, and overcoming of temporary imbalances at an acceptable cost in

(4) the United States must be able to veto any proposal to change the value of the dollar or of unitas" (Horsefield 1969a, 48).

employment and output. The instruments differed. The Keynes Plan sought to overcome the liquidity shortage produced by the slow and cumbersome operation of the gold standard with a clearing system offering overdrafts to any country in case of need. But the United States rejected this credit facility (see footnote 10). The English banking technique of the overdraft, in which the borrower takes the initiative of going into debt, was unfamiliar to the Americans, who were used to lodging the power to extend loans with the bank. Accordingly, in the White Plan the quotas were to be effectively paid in, while in the Keynes Plan they served merely to set the ceilings on the countries' debit and credit positions, purportedly to satisfy the property of symmetry. In the U.S. proposal, this was to be ensured by the scarce currency clause, whose operation was complicated and less immediate;[11] the British scheme was more flexible, aiming at a greater involvement of the creditor country in the adjustment process, although the treatment of creditors was rather supple.

The plans differed in other important respects. Under the Keynes Plan, debtor countries could reduce the currency parity in terms of bancor – in some cases, could be required to.[12] By contrast, the

---

[11] According to Eichengreen (1989, 266–7), the scarce currency clause was actually designed to deal with the dollar shortage; and once that emergency was settled, the clause was never used.

[12] Still, Keynes always viewed devaluation as exceptional. Thus, on 22 January 1942, answering Sir Richard Hopkins' "Critical Observation" on the third draft of his plan, Keynes remarked: "I myself greatly doubt the utility of sudden exchange depreciations to meet sudden developments. Broadly speaking, the factor governing the exchanges in the long run is the level of money wages relatively to efficiency in one country as compared with another. This is not as a rule anything which changes very suddenly. The causes of sudden difficulties are very rarely, I should have thought, properly dealt with by exchange depreciation, which may easily do more harm than good" (CW 25, 105–6). This concept was also expressed in a comment (Keynes 1943, 186) on Hayek's (1943) call for a commodity reserve currency and in a letter to Viner on 9 June 1943: "My own feeling about exchange rates is that we should aim at as great stability as possible and that exchange depreciation is not at all a good way of balancing trade unless the lack of balance is due to a particular cause. This particular cause is the movement of efficiency wages in one country out of step with what it is in others. One needs flexibility of rates to meet that contingency and, apart from that contingency one should generally speaking aim at stability" (CW 25, 323).

White Plan admitted exchange rate changes only in special circumstances to correct a "fundamental disequilibrium," but it left the notion undefined. Furthermore, the British plan emphasized controls on capital movements, which took up all of Section VII, while in the U.S. document they were mentioned in passing as an exception to the general principle of eliminating all restrictions on foreign exchange transactions.

Finally, the Americans did not accept a distinctive feature of the Keynes Plan: the introduction of an international currency that would have lessened the importance of gold. Except for defining the bancor as a unit of account, gold would have no other essential function: Indeed, the aim of the Keynes Plan was precisely to sever all ties to the gold standard.[13] This radical innovation worried the Americans, who feared that it would be hard for politicians to accept (Horsefield 1969a, 30) and could never win congressional approval. The White Plan took a more traditional approach, stressing the principle of free trade and anchoring the system to gold. The U.S. aversion to foreign exchange controls formed part of this vision, which was in line with the country's competitive advantage and its net international creditor position. Thus, Keynes's opinion that the first version of the White Plan was really a variant of the gold standard was not unfounded. However, the defects of the gold exchange standard were now flanked by the strains engendered by

[13] Contrasting his own scheme with an early version of the White Plan, Keynes remarked: "[T]he proposed Stabilisation Fund . . . makes no attempt to use the banking principle and one-way gold convertibility and is in fact not much more than a version of the gold standard, which simply aims at multiplying the effective volume of the gold base. Nearly all the consequences aimed at could be equally well attained by halving prices in every country, or, more simply still, by devaluing all exchanges in terms of gold, so that they would maintain their relative values, but everyone's gold reserve would go twice as far as before in meeting adverse international balances. This is the basic mistake of the plan. Put this way, one sees how inadequate it is to solve the real problem. The scheme is only helpful to those countries which have a gold reserve already and is only helpful to them in proportion to the amount of such gold reserve. If, however, a country has only a little gold and, therefore, needs much support, the scheme provides on the contrary that it shall receive only a little support. To him that hath it is given" (CW 25, 160).

the greatly enhanced role of economic policy thanks to the influence of the *General Theory*. After the depression, policymakers' overriding concern for employment was fundamental to the design of the international monetary system.[14] In both projects, the pursuit of several different objectives generated inconsistencies that were reflected in the loopholes found in the rules of the game. If we are to understand the dysfunctions the Bretton Woods system was to suffer, we must begin with this observation.

6.2. THE DISCUSSION OF THE BRITISH AND AMERICAN PROPOSALS

The publication of the plans aroused interest in the academic world, prompting various sorts of comment – analytical, pedagogical, and historical.[15] In what follows, we consider only the analytical responses, focusing on the critiques that highlight their relative consistency and limitations.

Most economists brought out the defects of both plans, albeit sometimes in partisan fashion. The negative assessments of the Keynes Plan were put forth mainly by Americans, those of White by Britons. A notable exception was Jacob Viner (1943). His

---

[14] Thus, referring to unofficial reform proposals, Kindleberger noted: "[T]he various authors do not explicitly rely on expansion or contraction of money incomes as a method of adjustment – such as are called for under the 'gold standard,' which has been politically repudiated on this account" (1943, 386 note 1). And Harry White, stressing the need for activist domestic policies, remarked: "Foremost among these policies should be the elimination of unemployment" (1943, 387). In this connection, Richard Gardner stressed the influence of Keynes's ideas on the U.S. Treasury: "Morgenthau, White, and their subordinates were not believers in *laissez-faire*; they shared the belief of most New Deal planners that government had an important responsibility for the successful direction of economic life. To some extent they were under the influence of the new formulations of Keynesian economics. They sought to make finance the servant, not the master, of human desires – in the international no less than in the domestic sphere. In their view the events of the 1920's and early 1930's had discredited private finance. They considered government control of financial policy the key to the objectives of high employment and economic welfare" (1969, 76).

[15] Examples of pedagogical and historical essays respectively are Schumacher (1943) and Haines (1943, 121), who attributed "the first proposal for an international money" to Gasparo Scaruffi, an Italian economist writing in 1582.

penetrating comments caught several weaknesses of both schemes: the lack of a check on inflation, the ineffectiveness of exchange controls, and the danger of exploitation of creditor countries in the Keynes Plan and the White Plan's resemblance to the gold exchange standard. However, refraining from destructive criticism, he recognized the need for a novel institutional framework that combined the best of both proposals (1943, 215).

This positive attitude is hard to find in the rest of the profession. Criticisms were plentiful and often to the point, anticipating some of the flaws of the postwar monetary system. Concerns were voiced not only by conservative economists who set the new schemes against the gold standard as a natural benchmark, but also by those – the great majority – who rejected the return to gold and highlighted the interwar problems of uncontrollability of the money supply, asymmetry of the adjustment mechanism (due to the surplus countries' failure to abide by the rules of the game), destabilizing capital movements, and the impact of wage rigidity on employment (Lutz 1943, 3–4; Robinson 1943, 161–2). Above all, the reform proposals were judged artificial, consisting of measures that were ad hoc if not actually incoherent. According to Frank Graham, the plans "reveal a confusion of purpose, and a lack of consistent principle, which are likely to result only in frustration or disaster" (1943b, 1).[16] In Graham's view:

The primary defect of both the Keynes and the White plans, and of the compromise between them, is that their authors favor fixity of exchange rates in neglect of domestic monetary policies and, conscious of the disruptive effects to be expected in this situation, present measures of half-hearted coercion of such states as are recalcitrant in their adhesion to some

---

[16] In his conclusions, Lutz maintained: "It is interesting to step back and to look at the plans as a whole. Unlike the classical economists, most modern economists do not favor solutions of economic problems which are based on principles. Instead they advocate, in each concrete instance, measures devised *ad hoc* which, if ingenious from a technical point of view, may contradict other measures devised in other fields. The result is that the pattern of economic policy of modern governments is far from being a model of logical consistency" (1943, 20–1).

undefined national monetary policy which, it is fondly hoped, will more or less miraculously emerge as the "norm." (1943b, 21)

In the Keynes Plan, Lutz argued (1943, 13–4), this potential conflict could foster expansionary monetary policy, thus leading to frequent devaluations. Actually, this objection is not quite correct, because in the British scheme devaluation could be resorted to only once, unless the board consented to repeat it. Regardless of its formal accuracy, though, this criticism points to the more general question of the inadequacy of the rules of the game to assure viability. In this respect, Viner raised the problem of restraining borrowing accumulation which, if unsolved, would lead to the failure of both plans:

If these restraints should prove effective in checking borrowings but ineffective in inducing correction of the factors responsible for the disequilibrium, the agency would become inoperative and we would be back in a world of defaults, of frozen balances, and of unilateral exchange depreciations. Neither plan, therefore, will have succeeded in its objectives if the over-all borrowing limits it provides are reached or even approached.

(1943, 201)

Reconciling exchange rate stability with monetary policy autonomy was the task of the international monetary organization. However, unless all members renounced their independence and conformed their policies to the stance of the dominant country – that is, "that country which, somehow, manages to corral the bulk of the world's gold" (F. Graham 1943b, 12) – the entire structure is unstable. And neither plan provided for effective measures to this purpose.

A further, related issue in both schemes is the one-way bet offered to speculators in a fixed but adjustable exchange rate regime, a point that was reiterated by Frank Graham (1940a; 1943b, 7–8) and also raised by Friedrich Lutz (1943, 13). These limitations thus foreshadow the root problems of the Bretton Woods system. In fact, according to Frank Graham, the British and American proposals share the main features of the fixed exchange rate regime of the late 1920s and of the Tripartite Agreement of 1936: "Both the Keynes and the White plans are hybrids of these unsuccessful parents. The fruit of their own marriage shows all the weaknesses to be expected from the inbreeding of defective stocks" (1943b, 14).

Besides these general comments, there were many specific criticisms. The White Plan was treated as tantamount to the gold exchange standard. Frank Graham, noting the preeminent role of the United States in the future system, highlighted the eventual hindrances to parity changes:

The fact that the "unitas" (which is Dr. White's name for the international monetary unit he would set up) is, except against an all but unanimous vote to the contrary, to be kept unchanged in dollar and in gold value, would seem to mean, in effect, that, in his plan American monetary policy would be the "norm." After a short period of transition is passed, moreover, great difficulties are to be put in the way of a change in the gold value of the currency of *any* adhering country. The "new" system, if adopted, would then (aside from a few dubious frills and a still more dubious bias toward control of capital movements) be not much else than a reversion to the traditional international gold standard. One wonders why such a reversion was not proposed in the first place and gets the impression that the plan is designed to cajole an adhesion to that standard by countries that would not otherwise adopt it. (1943b, 13 note 11; italics in the original)

According to Schumacher (1943, 25), the American scheme, if it was meant to resurrect the gold exchange standard, entailed a policy design that did not allow full employment. In addition to the cumbersome machinery and relatively opaque objectives (Lutz 1943, 16; Robinson 1943, 167),[17] criticism was also leveled

---

[17] Comparing the two proposals, Lutz remarked: "The Keynes plan has the advantage of a simpler structure and shows, clearly, the nature of the economic phenomenon behind the transactions of the international institution. It also avoids the quite unnecessary trouble, imposed upon the member states by the White plan, of going through the procedure of paying in contributions" (1943, 6). According to Joan Robinson: "Unlike the British statement, which makes the intentions of each of its proposals clear, the American document contains merely a set of rules, without explanations, and has to be read in the spirit of a detective story" (1943, 167). Finally, see Schumacher's lapidary

at the proposed solution to the accumulation of creditor positions (Robinson 1943, 170). When a currency became "scarce," the Fund would ration it, but this contradicted the spirit and the letter of the plan, which was against the retention of controls (Lutz 1943, 15; Robinson 1943, 167; Schumacher 1943, 22–4). The most obvious solution, Lutz suggested (1943, 16), was inflation or an appreciation of the currency. In this respect, Viner (1943, 204–5) noted that the majority required to approve a change in parity (four-fifths in the first version of the White Plan, three-fourths in the final one) would make such changes virtually impossible, so that the exchange rate regime would be even more rigid than under the gold standard. The treatment of creditors was controversial. Joan Robinson (1943, 167) went so far as to contend that creditor countries would be less severely penalized under the Keynes Plan, which would not restrict the several alternatives open to them.

The point here, however, is a different one: While Keynes wanted to design a symmetrical system, White was intent on imposing more stringent rules on debtors. In any case, as Lutz observed (1943, 17), neither provided any mechanism to prevent policies from generating a fundamental disequilibrium. The Fund or the Clearing Union was to overcome temporary balance-of-payments crises with lines of credit, reinstating the stabilizing function played, under the gold standard, by capital movements. Yet gold was not at all the basis of the new system; indeed, it was "quite unnecessary or even a nuisance under both schemes" (Lutz 1943, 20). Its presence, in reality, is explained by the need not to run counter to the interests of gold producers and of the United States, with its massive gold reserves. The resemblance to the gold exchange standard simply reflected the features of the adjustment mechanism in a fixed exchange rate

comment: "Many of the [American] Plan's provisions are somewhat difficult to decipher in their significance, and the authors of the memorandum have done little to explain what motives have led them to their specific recommendations. It may not be unfair to suggest that they themselves were perhaps not always aware of the technical and economic consequences of their own scheme" (1943, 28–9).

regime. Both plans, in fact, and especially that of Keynes, entailed a progressive detachment from commodity money, assigning economic policy a crucial role in achieving full employment. Capital controls would ensure the consistency of the design. However, the main change in the monetary system, namely the loss of credibility bound up in the transition from the gold to the gold exchange standard, was not taken into account.

The Keynes Plan, too, was broadly criticized. The most common objection was that it was inflationary. Lutz (1943, 7–10) contended that if a monetary expansion was equal in all countries, thus not creating external payment imbalances, the rules of the Clearing Union would not restrict it. Several economists (de Vegh 1943, 538–41, 546; Lutz 1943, 7–8; Viner 1943, 200–1) noted the large total amount of the quotas, at least $25 billion, and called attention to the mechanism producing its automatic increase – namely, unrestricted access to borrowing regardless of the creditworthiness – and the heavy postwar demand for credit that could be expected.[18] The Americans' concern was that they would have to defray excessive costs during European reconstruction, being bound by the decisions of the new international body. This fear accompanied their rejection of the bancor. Technically, the Clearing Union did provide for a series of measures to prevent the excessive buildup of debtor positions,[19] but these were thought to be insufficient or ineffective. Thus, Lutz (1943, 12–3) pointed to two drawbacks to the

[18] In his letter to Viner dated 9 June 1943, Keynes recognized that countries would not accept an unlimited liability to be net creditors; at the same time, he noted the difficulty of finding an alternative solution, deeming the scarce currency clause "rather obscure" (CW 25, 322).

[19] At a conference in Chicago on 26 August 1943 attended by the members of the board of directors of the federal reserve banks, Robertson tried to clear the field of these American worries: "It is arguable that the proudest day in the life of the Manager of the Clearing Union would be that on which, as a result of the smooth functioning of the correctives set in motion by the Plan, there were *no* holders of international money – on which he was able to show a balance sheet with zero on both sides of the account" (1943, 359; italics in the original).

devaluation required of a country whose debtor position exceeded half its quota for more than two years. First, the measure would have to be taken while the debt was still increasing, not when it had stabilized, after the new point of equilibrium had been reached. And second, as Cassel had already observed and Friedman would underscore, the perception of a state of crisis would give speculators a one-way bet. In this regard, Frank Graham (1943b, 13–4) and de Vegh (1943, 543), respectively, warned about the cumulation of exchange rate disequilibria and the perverse effects of devaluation.

More generally, the resistance to an innovative system like Keynes's was bound up, on the political plane, with special interests. Robertson (1943, 355–60) considered the bancor so essential that its elimination jeopardized the viability of the entire scheme, but he also noted the inadvisability of presenting other countries with a reform imposed by the United States and the United Kingdom. And, as we have seen, Frank Graham raised the problem of exercising the discretionary power deriving from the abandonment of commodity money by the dominant country. The two plans, in fact, did not discuss the adaptation of other countries' monetary policy to that of the dominant country, except in their treatment of the rules for restoring payments balance. In this connection, as Keynes had foreseen the coming hegemony of the United States, the greater flexibility of the British plan was also due to the need to temper the effects of anchoring to U.S. monetary policy.

These considerations are also relevant theoretically. Whereas a commodity standard, *de facto*, deprives the individual country of monetary sovereignty, the evolution toward a managed currency allows the exercise of discretionary power but at the same time undermines the system's credibility by accentuating an element of volition, control of which is in the hand of a government authority. In response to the failure of the system of the 1920s and 1930s, the reform proposals drafted new rules, transferring to an international body a portion of monetary sovereignty that was relatively limited in the American scheme, more substantial in the British.[20] The essential point remained resolving the inherent inconsistency between independent monetary policy and fixed exchange rates. While the White Plan made only modest changes with respect to the gold exchange standard, the Keynes Plan offered the radical innovation of the clearing principle. This was the core of Wicksell's pure credit system (1906, 87–126), which had been anticipated by Mill (1848, 524–5) and has now been resumed by the new monetary economics, highlighting the distinction between money and an accounting system of exchange (Fama 1980). The International Clearing Union was such a system; the bancor, the unit of account defined in terms of gold, was its peg. Yet its viability was dubious, in that discretionary policies for full employment could come into conflict with the equilibrium of the Clearing Union. True, the Keynes Plan did consider the risk of "creating excessive purchasing power and hence an inflation of prices" (Horsefield 1969b, 34), but its rules could have proved insufficient if the mechanism for disciplining policymakers was not effective or credible. Aware of this crucial problem, Keynes wanted the new international authority to wield broad powers and assigned the International Clearing Union a role that would make it "a genuine organ of truly international government" (Horsefield 1969b, 35).

[20] Keynes envisaged a broader role for the International Clearing Union, not restricted to the monetary sphere, assigning it duties involving relations with other international agencies for economic development, for defense, and for the control of commodity markets. "The Clearing Union might become the instrument and the support of international policies in addition to those which it is its primary purpose to promote. This deserves the greatest possible emphasis. The Union might become the pivot of the future economic government of the world" (Horsefield 1969b, 33). Aware of the possible objections, he deemed the renunciation of sovereignty required under his plan as comparable to that imposed by trade treaties. Moreover, members could withdraw from the agreement whenever they wished (Horsefield 1969b, 36). The extension of the Clearing Union's tasks was criticized by Viner (1943, 213) because it would endanger its primary function of monetary stabilization.

Besides the political difficulties of achieving this aim, however, the necessity of providing for an effective adjustment mechanism was inescapable. In this respect, neither plan offered a well-defined recipe, and the Keynes Plan, in particular, left the issue open to different solutions. This is the essence of the substantial criticisms of the proposals, showing just how complicated it was to design a consistent, viable monetary reform. Noting the search for compromise in both schemes, Lutz predicted problems once the transition period was over.

The two plans discussed in this paper are an illustration of the point [the inconsistency of economic policy]. They avoid clear-cut solutions such as the gold standard, or a paper standard, or one single Central Bank for all countries would offer. Free exchange markets but also foreign exchange control, fixed exchange rates but also currency depreciation (and in addition perhaps a small dose of deflation), the use of gold as international currency but without its having any role as an integral part of the mechanism of international adjustments; all these ideas are merged into one plan. It is unlikely that such a combination will work satisfactorily. It seems more probable that one of the mutually inconsistent ideas worked into the plans will win out. As it stands, the least desirable, foreign exchange control, would seem to have the best chance. The plans have great advantages for the period immediately following the war inasmuch as they provide reserves of international currency, for those countries which will need them to finance an import surplus, and offer a method of avoiding complete chaos in the foreign exchange market. They have, moreover, the merit of bringing before the public an important problem which deserves extensive discussion. But they do not give a solution which can be regarded as satisfactory for the long run. (1943, 21)

6.3. ALTERNATIVE MODELS OF MONETARY ORGANIZATION ON THE EVE OF BRETTON WOODS

Among the many comments on the British and American proposals, the criticism of the International Clearing Union as being identical to the gold standard (de Vegh 1943, 536, 549 note 4) would appear paradoxical, given Keynes's explicit call to abandon that system. As he stated in the first draft of his plan, he wanted to create an innovative setup by "discarding the use of a currency having international validity" (CW 25, 23). However, the unwritten rules of the gold standard provided for an international monetary and financial network centered in London[21] that, as far as the transactions technology is concerned, had the same main features as the Clearing Union. Thus, de Vegh's remark is no paradox at all in that, as we suggested at the end of Chapter 5, extreme solutions produce clear-cut results, having some basic characteristics in common. Of course, the gold standard was grounded on principles – metallism and the equilibrium hypothesis – that Keynes refuted in making full employment the key economic policy goal. In the aftermath of the depression, the *General Theory* necessarily weighed heavily on any possible approach to monetary reform (see footnote 14), although the White Plan and other schemes as well did not entirely sever the link with the commodity standard.[22] Hence, on the eve of

[21] The operation of this network was masterfully analyzed by Hawtrey (1929a). Emphasizing the relationship between gold flows and changes in the stock of credit, he noted: "The nineteenth century credit system is not to be interpreted as consisting of a number of countries each exercising independent control over credit within its own limits, and being led by the influence of gold movements to accommodate its credit policy to that of the others. It is rather to be regarded as a centralised system responding to a leader. The center was London and the leader the Bank of England.... The world credit movements were initiated in London, and tended to spread to all other centres without further action. Only if some resistance arose against the tendency to spread, was any action by authorities outside England called for. Undoubtedly the need for such action was not infrequent. Undoubtedly also the action taken by the Bank of England was often dictated by occurrences in other countries. The Bank was not so autocratic as to be able to disregard credit movements starting abroad, especially when they approached or attained the magnitude of financial crises. But so far as any intentional or systematic regulation of credit was concerned, no one else attempted to take the lead. Credit policy was in the hands of the Bank of England" (1929a, 70–2).

[22] Needless to say, the restoration of the gold standard was now rejected by most economists. For this point of view, Viner wrote that return to gold "seems to me to be day-dreaming, and, considerations of national prestige aside, the dream is not a wholly pleasant one. An unregulated international gold standard would put the world into a monetary straitjacket which would block the adoption of desirable as well as of foolish policies" (1943, 195). Nonetheless, there were still a few die-hard conservatives, like Edwin Kemmerer (1944), who unyieldingly advocated the gold standard.

the decisive negotiations leading to the Bretton Woods conference, two alternative models characterized the state of the art, the innovative Keynes Plan on the one hand, the more traditional projects on the other.

The essential aspects of these contrasting views emerge in an illuminating debate between Hayek and Keynes. Making a case for the commodity currency, Hayek (1943) recalled the advantages of the gold standard – the creation of an international currency without subjecting individual countries to a supranational authority, its automatic mechanism, and hence the predictability of monetary policy, and the stabilizing character of changes in the money supply – and its defect, namely the slowness with which the gold supply could adapt to the demand. The commodity reserve currency would retain the advantages while obviating this drawback.[23]

Unoriginal though it was, Hayek's piece elicited a reply from Keynes (1943), who seized the occasion to clarify the significance of his plan. His proposal offered new solutions to the two defects of commodity money, namely the uncontrollability of the money supply beyond the short run and the adverse impact of adjustment on employment. On the first point, the Clearing Union would work on the velocity of circulation and not, as under Marshall's tabular standard, Fisher's compensated dollar, or Hayek's commodity reserve currency, on the volume of money. On the second, the plan would enable every member to conduct its own wage and price policies. If a substantial deviation from equilibrium occurred, the country would have to revise its policies or, if that proved impracticable, modify the exchange rate.[24] This measure would be

[23] An analogous claim is set forth in the first draft of the Keynes Plan, aiming "to sketch out ... an ideal scheme which would preserve the advantages of an international means of payment universally acceptable, whilst avoiding those features of the old system which did the damage" (CW 25, 32).

[24] In reply to Frank Graham (1944b), Keynes repeated the ideas set forth in his comment on Hayek. Though he did not oppose the tabular standard in principle, he advocated finding the most politically opportune way of linking national currencies to an international currency with an "orderly, yet elastic method," in particular avoiding external pressure on wages and attacks on the interest of gold producers (Keynes 1944, 429).

allowed in case of a misalignment of the country's efficiency wage (see footnote 12), which was Keynes's conception of a fundamental disequilibrium. Unlike the gold standard, therefore, the plan left ample maneuvering room to economic policy.

> The fundamental reason for thus limiting the objectives of an international currency scheme is the impossibility, or at any rate the undesirability, of imposing stable price-levels from without. The error of the gold-standard lay in submitting national wage-policies to outside dictation. It is wiser to regard stability (or otherwise) of internal prices as a matter of internal policy and politics. Commodity standards which try to impose this from without will break down just as surely as the rigid gold-standard.
>
> (Keynes 1943, 187)

Keynes's own reading of his project confirms its close connection with the *General Theory*, the intent being to overturn the monetary system so that instead of a constraint it could be a tool for pursuing full employment. This is a further advance on the concept developed in the *Tract*, namely that the rigid rules of the gold standard should be bent to make room for policy action and increase social welfare.[25] Apart from its impact on the architecture of postwar monetary institutions, this approach also strengthened the definitive acceptance of a full-fledged managed money and, eventually, accelerated the transition to fiat money.

The spread of Keynes's thought at a time of major international monetary imbalances raised the question of consistency between the reestablishment of fixed exchange rates and the imperative of pursuing domestic policy objectives. The issue at stake is reflected in the fuzziness of the adjustment mechanism in both plans, which led to widespread conjecture as to which solution would eventually prevail: exchange controls, tariffs, economic policy reversal, exchange

---

[25] As Keynes had vigorously advocated detachment from commodity money since World War I, his emphasis on the introduction of monetary rules, noted by Allan Meltzer (1989), needs to be rightly interpreted. Keynes's intention was not to bind policymakers but, on the contrary, to broaden their range of action. The rules of the International Clearing Union were designed to guarantee its viability, certainly not to constrain the conduct of central banks.

rate changes. True, both projects spelled out a hierarchy among the possible adjustment channels, the British proposal being more conducive to expansionary policies and parity changes, the American relying on stricter discipline.[26] Yet both displayed heterogeneous elements due to the pursuit of conflicting objectives and thus hardly represented a well-grounded blueprint for monetary reform.

The contrast with the gold standard is eloquent. Underlying its successful performance was a coherent set of rules hinging on the all but universally accepted classical model, which also allowed a certain degree of flexibility through the escape clause of suspending convertibility. The rules of the game were enforced not by treaty but by countries' optimizing behavior. Because ultimately the theoretical framework is what provides the basis of policy design and of international arrangements, consensus on a consistent paradigm is essential to the smooth working of the monetary system.[27] On the other hand, the presence of rival approaches accentuates the surrender of sovereignty to an international organization. The coexistence of discordant models, producing diversity in policy response and heightening uncertainty, calls for broad powers of enforcement to enhance the system's viability. Thus, under the gold standard, an extreme case of full adherence to an equilibrium model, there was no need to renounce any sovereign power, let alone establish an international body. At the other extreme, in the highly variegated economic and monetary theory of the early 1940s, with the growing distrust in the equilibrium hypothesis, substantial

---

[26] As Viner remarked: "It seems to me indeed that if the White plan were to be put into successful operation, it would result in fact if not in form in an international gold standard, strengthened, moreover, by additional legal sanctions international in character, reinforced by the establishment of additional facilities for international short-term credits, and improved in its functioning by virtue of the supervisory activities of the new international monetary board" (1943, 207).

[27] This point was clearly perceived by Keynes, who saw its sheer novelty as a possible weakness in his plan. Thus, in the first draft he noted: "[The plan] is also open to the objection, as the reader will soon discover, that it is complicated and novel and perhaps Utopian in the sense, not that it is impracticable, but that it assumes a higher degree of understanding, of the spirit of bold innovation, and of international co-operation and trust than it is safe or reasonable to assume" (CW 25, 33).

and effective powers had to be assigned to an international authority.

Monetary reconstruction, then, came at the crossroads of the emergence of an alternative paradigm following the disruptive shock of the depression. The message of the *General Theory* took time to be absorbed by the profession.[28] The coexistence of diverse approaches in this transitional period was reflected in the two plans that, while sharing objectives, used different instruments and left the solution to a number of several problems open. One should never forget that the architects of the postwar monetary system faced the daunting task of constructing a new order *ex nihilo*, while the several forces at work – intellectual, social, political – were all but certain to produce reform proposals that were patchy, hybrid, perhaps even inconsistent.

---

[28] In a well-known letter sent to George Bernard Shaw on 1 January 1935, Keynes wrote: "To understand *my* state of mind, however, you have to know that I believe myself to be writing a book on economic theory which will largely revolutionise – not, I suppose, at once but in the course of the next ten years – the way the world thinks about economic problems" (CW 13, 492; italics in the original). On the supposed revolutionary character of the *General Theory*, see Laidler (1999, Chapter 11).

7 THE BRETTON WOODS AGREEMENTS

The IMPELLING OBJECTIVE OF RECONSTRUCTING THE INTERNAT-
ional monetary system provided the driving force for fram-
ing an agreement starting from the quite different approaches of
the Keynes and White plans. The sheer diversity of these proposals required a major effort, both analytical and at the negotiating
table, to arrive at a shared solution, but the goal was pursued with
determination and confidence. Setting out the main features of the
International Clearing Union before the House of Lords on 18 May
1943, Keynes noted: "I have not the slightest doubt in my own
mind that a synthesis of the two schemes should be possible" (CW
25, 279).

The round of intense negotiations, which a year later produced
the Joint Statement of 21 April 1944, was decisive. In fact, that
document contained all the essential elements of the Articles of
Agreement approved at Bretton Woods just three months on. The
numerous, punctilious discussions served to narrow the distance
separating the British and American positions and produce a draft
that could be acceptable to other nations as well. In a sense, the
road to the Joint Statement was the real negotiation over the postwar monetary order: The Bretton Woods conference settled many
questions of detail, but essentially adopted that blueprint.

7.1. THE JOINT STATEMENT AND THE ORGANIZATION
OF THE CONFERENCE

Work on a synthesis of the British and American proposals started soon after their publication. While revised drafts of the White Plan were issued in May and June, before the final version was released on 10 July, the Americans held meetings in Washington with a number of countries. The greater bargaining power of the United States weighed from the very start and conditioned developments after the Bretton Woods conference as well. Indeed, the negotiations were marked by the contrast between the scant political clout of the British delegation, despite its great expertise, and the political predominance of the American delegation.[1] Aware of the American supremacy, Keynes did what he could to get the reform through even if he had to see his plan progressively set aside.[2] An

---

[1] The difference in personality between Keynes and White could not have been greater. In Richard Gardner's vivid description: "What powerful and contradictory forces were at work in this association! The sources of friction were obvious enough. Both were proud, sensitive, and self-confident to the point of arrogance. Not much else did they have in common. White was an ambitious middle-class boy who had made good; Keynes an urbane product of cultured academic stock. The first set little store by social conventions; the second was the product of a society where manners were the mark of a man. One bore a deep resentment of the advantages that heredity could bestow; the other possessed the well-bred Englishman's easy self-confidence. Veterans of the Anglo-American negotiations recall how, in the midst of some controversy, White would address Keynes as 'your Royal Highness,' sitting back with an ironic smile to watch the latter's ill-disguised irritation. It was certainly a wonder that these two could get along together at all.... Occasionally bitterness would creep in. Keynes would take White out of his depth; White would feel, but not admit, his intellectual inferiority; he would say something to remind Keynes that he, not Keynes, represented the stronger party in the negotiations. There would be angry words; papers would be thrown on the floor; one of them would stalk out of the room. The other negotiators would stay to patch up the quarrel. The next day the same procedure would be repeated. Eventually a tentative agreement would be reached, which could be submitted to the respective Governments for approval. In this way, slowly, almost imperceptibly, there emerged the terms of the financial compromise" (1969, 111–2). Horsefield (1969a, 55–6) sketches a similar portrait of the two protagonists.
[2] Writing to Roy Harrod on 27 April 1943, Keynes anticipated the course of the negotiations: "I fully expect that we shall do well to compromise with the American scheme and very likely accept their dress in the long run. But I am sure that it would be premature to do so at present. For one thing, their plan is very far from being a firm offer. The real risk, I always have thought, is that they will run away from their own plan, let alone

examination of the official documents and the material available in the *Collected Writings* gives an immediate idea of this effort to smooth over the disagreements[3] and reach an acceptable compromise, an uncomfortable task for the scholarly mind. As Donald Moggridge, the editor of Volumes 25–6 of the *Collected Writings* observes, Keynes, in a letter to David Waley "added after the word 'diplomacy' . . . '– the meanest occupation known to man'" (CW 26, 117 note 33).

White, instead, pursued the American policy of relatively conservative reform, something not unlike the gold exchange standard, which would serve the interests of the United States, which held almost 60 percent of the world's gold reserves at the end of 1945, a share that would rise to nearly 75 percent at the end of 1949, exceeding 22,000 metric tons.[4] From the outset, the United States had intended to dominate the discussion. At the end of a series of meetings with some twenty-five countries, White warned Keynes (CW 25, 335–8) of the mistake of presenting to Congress a proposal that risked rejection. A politically acceptable plan had to have

ours. By continuing to press ours, there is at least a little chance that they may develop some patriotic fervour for their own" (CW 25, 268).

3 In particular, in his House of Lords speech Keynes dispelled U.S. concerns about having to shoulder a large burden: "There is one important respect in which the British proposals seem to be gravely misunderstood in some quarters in the United States. There is no foundation whatever for the idea that the object of the proposals is to make the United States the milch cow of the world in general and of this country in particular. In fact the best hope for the lasting success of the plan is the precise contrary. The plan does not require the United States, or any other country, to put up a single dollar which they themselves choose or prefer to employ in any other way whatever. The essence of it is that if a country has a balance in its favour which it does not choose to use in buying goods or services or making overseas investment, this balance shall remain available to the Union – not permanently, but only for just so long as the country owning it chooses to leave it unemployed. That is not a burden on the creditor country. It is an extra facility to it, for it allows it to carry on its trade with the rest of the world unimpeded, whenever a time lag between earning and spending happens to suit its own convenience. I cannot emphasise this too strongly. This is not a Red Cross philanthropic relief scheme, by which the rich countries come to the rescue of the poor. It is a piece of highly necessary business mechanism, which is at least as useful to the creditor as to the debtor" (CW 25, 276–7).

4 After reading the final version of the White Plan, Keynes remarked: "Some of its provisions are drafted with gross selfishness in the interests of a country possessing unlimited gold" (CW 25, 316).

four features: (1) a limited financial commitment, not exceeding $3 billion; (2) quotas partly in gold; (3) a link between quotas and veto powers; (4) an agreement on the exchange rates of the leading countries (see Chapter 6, note 10). The Articles of Agreement essentially contained all of these ingredients, even the first, considering that they provided for quotas totaling $8.8 billion, compared with the $26 billion proposed by the British (Eichengreen 1989, 265–6). Keynes saw that the American demands conflicted with his plan, but he chose to play down the differences.

In September 1943, with the start of formal Anglo-American talks in Washington, the negotiations took a new turn. Both delegations, as Keynes wrote to Louis Rasminsky, were now actively pursuing a common objective "in an atmosphere singularly free from unnecessary controversy or obstacle" (CW 25, 340).[5] Eventually, however, contrasts emerged, and the British gradually yielded on most issues. Despite numerous discussions, some topics remained controversial, such as the conditionality of members' access to Fund resources (Horsefield 1969a, 67–75). While the United States assigned the Fund the right to stave off drawings if a country's economic policies were considered harmful from an international viewpoint, the British stuck to the idea of leaving the borrowing decision to members, subject only to the limitations set forth in the agreed clauses. Robertson (1943, 358) made this point to Fed officials and Keynes, in his letter to Viner, emphasized the "increase of confidence" to be accorded to countries, regarding it "as perhaps one of the major contributions that the plans can make to future stability;" thus, the Fund should not exercise a "grandmotherly" influence (CW 25, 333, 404).

---

5 This positive impression is confirmed by Keynes in a letter to Jacob Viner shortly before his return to England: "In the opinion of all of us we have made really enormous progress towards a common view, and whilst there are still outstanding points of difference, my own expectation is that they will not be unduly difficult to settle after we have got back to London" (CW 25, 332). For a detailed reconstruction, the reader is referred to Horsefield (1969a, Chapter 3).

Once the Joint Statement was near completion, Keynes and White hastened its publication for fear that mounting criticism in both countries might block the road to reform.[6] In the British version, the text was preceded, on Keynes's insistence (CW 25, 436), by "explanatory notes" (Horsefield 1969b, 128–31) that minimized the differences with the proposed Clearing Union. Anyway, except for the claim by Eichengreen that the British won important concessions with regard to exchange rate variations and exchange controls (1989, 263–7), the outcome has usually been judged as basically conforming to the White Plan. This is correct with regard to the stipulations of the accord but is a reductive reading of Keynes's influence, because it disregards the impact of his contributions to the prevailing paradigm.

A distinction must here be drawn between the design of the reform and its implementation. Throughout the negotiations, there was no conflict about the theoretical approach to reconstructing the monetary system. After the disruptive shock of the Great Depression and the appearance of the *General Theory*, full employment was the overriding target of policymakers on both sides of the Atlantic.[7] This shared vision and analysis helped the lengthy negotiating process to its successful completion and was reflected in the new monetary arrangements: The Joint Statement would stipulate that "the maintenance of a high level of employment and real income...must be a primary objective of economic policy" (Horsefield 1969b, 131). On the other hand, the details of the

---

[6] In a letter to White, on 18 March 1944 Keynes wrote: "On this side the Chancellor of the Exchequer is being constantly pestered by Members of Parliament with questions as to when they can hear more. There is obviously a good deal of restiveness, which can be largely explained, I think, by the lack of news. It is obvious that the proposals are most likely to be attacked on this side on the ground that, however we dress them up, they are no better than a revised gold standard, and they will be charged with submitting this country to the same yoke, from which it had escaped with so much difficulty but with so much ultimate relief in 1931" (CW 25, 429).

[7] In this connection, White himself has often been described as a Keynesian with reference to his views on macroeconomic policy and international finance (Boughton 2002, 2004; Vines 2003, 350–1). See also Chapter 6, note 14.

Bretton Woods architecture were driven more by the tactical moves of the two sides than by strategic design; and tactics were dictated by politics.

In the spring of 1943, to avoid jeopardizing the entire reform, White modified his stance to reflect the conservative make-up of the new Congress (see Chapter 6, Section 1). This shift in the American position would emerge in the discussion of innumerable specific questions. One example is White's aim of putting the dollar alongside gold at the center of the postwar international monetary system, which had been constantly opposed by Keynes.[8] Van Dormael's detailed account of Bretton Woods shows how White, avoiding a general debate by assigning the task of solving the problem to a small group of technicians headed by himself, managed to have the Final Act read not "gold" but "gold and US dollars" (Van Dormael 1978, 200–3). In this and in countless other cases, the solution resulted from the negotiating ability and, above all, the bargaining power of the parties. The balance thus tipped toward the Americans, although the British were able to secure some substantial concessions.[9] Tactics were motivated by the political interests of the parties involved; strategy reflected theory and thus Keynes's

---

[8] At the meeting in Atlantic City in June 1944, Keynes firmly opposed giving the dollar a special status. The Americans apparently did not discuss the subject. However, as Armand Van Dormael noted: "[T]hough the Statement of Principles, as it was submitted to the Bretton Woods Conference, clearly stated that 'The par value of a member's currency ... shall be expressed in terms of gold,' White knew that the international bankers were extremely anxious to see the dollar become the international currency of the future" (1978, 201).

[9] As Harold James remarked: "In order to be able to satisfy the political requirements of the time, the proposed settlement had to include not just a sustainable economic vision but also appropriate concessions to the powerful interests involved in the negotiations. The United States had a profound conviction of the merits of trade liberalization and an abhorrence of the bilateral trade and manipulated exchange rates that had been operated by National Socialist Germany. The United Kingdom, on the other hand, wanted to find a mechanism to protect itself against the immediate impact of the trade liberalization required by the United States. The goal of the monetary mechanism for likely debtor countries (such as Britain) would be to prevent the buildup of large surpluses by others and to include penalties or deterrents for likely long-term creditors. The surplus countries should take a part of the adjustment: otherwise the world would find itself repeating the deflationary experience of the 1920s" (1996, 30).

paramount message. In the longer run, the influence of Keynes's thought progressively gained momentum: As will be seen in the next chapter, the dominance of Keynesian economics would be a decisive factor in the evolution of the Bretton Woods monetary system.

In general, the negotiators' efforts to reach an agreement[10] made compromise all the more characteristic of the accord, so that the effective operation of the system depended strictly on interpretation. With regard to conditionality, for instance, Richard Gardner remarked: "One could not be sure from the wording of the Articles themselves whether the British or the American view on this subject would finally prevail" (1969, 114). And Keynes, in his address to the House of Lords on 23 May 1944, presented the outcome of the negotiations as advantageous to Britain. He acknowledged that "certain features of elegance, clarity and logic in the Clearing Union plan . . . have disappeared," but he considered the Joint Statement "a considerable improvement on either of its parents" (CW 26, 10) and stressed its advantages: maintenance of exchange controls during the postwar transition, restoration of convertibility in connection with London's role as a financial center, increase in the stock of reserves, creditor countries' sharing of the burden

---

[10] The huge amount of work that went into drafting the reform is recalled by Keynes in the conclusion of his speech to the House of Lords on 23 May 1944 explaining the main properties of the Joint Statement: "The proposals which are before your Lordships are the result of the collaboration of many minds and the fruit of the collective wisdom of the experts of many nations. I have spent many days and weeks in the past year in the company of experts of this country, of the Dominions, of our European Allies and of the United States; and, in the light of some past experience I affirm that these discussions have been without exception a model of what such gatherings should be – objective, understanding, without waste of time or expense of temper. I dare to speak for the much abused so-called experts. I even venture sometimes to prefer them, without intending any disrespect, to politicians. The common love of truth, bred of a scientific habit of mind, is the closest of bonds between the representatives of divers nations" (CW 26, 20–1). And White, in the opening paragraph of his article in *Foreign Affairs*, remarked: "Perhaps no economic measure has ever received the careful consideration, extensive discussion and painstaking labor that went into the formulation of the proposal for an International Monetary Fund. The preparations for the United Nations Monetary and Financial Conference were a model of democracy in action" (1945, 195).

of adjustment, and an international organization as a forum for discussing and preventing problems. In putting domestic purposes before the stability of the exchange rate, the reform overturned the old monetary order: Economic policy was aimed not at maintaining the parity of the currency, as in the gold standard, but at full employment. This epochal change reflects the impact on the monetary system of Keynes's contributions, as he himself observed, over "the last twenty years" (CW 26, 16):

[T]his plan is the exact opposite of [the gold standard]. The plan in its relation to gold is, indeed, very close to proposals which I advocated in vain as the right alternative, when I was bitterly opposing this country's return to gold. . . . The plan not merely confirms the dethronement [of gold] but approves it by expressly providing that it is the duty of the Fund to alter the gold value of any currency if it is shown that this will be serviceable to equilibrium. In fact, the plan introduces in this respect an epoch-making innovation in an international instrument, the object of which is to lay down sound and orthodox principles. For instead of maintaining the principle that the internal value of a national currency should conform to a prescribed *de jure* external value, it provides that its external value should be altered if necessary so as to conform to whatever *de facto* internal value results from domestic policies, which themselves shall be immune from criticism by the Fund. Indeed, it is made the duty of the Fund to approve changes which will have this effect. That is why I say that these proposals are the exact opposite of the gold standard. They lay down by international agreement the essence of the new doctrine, far removed from the old orthodoxy. (CW 26, 17–19)

Opposition to the monetary reform was strong in both countries. In Great Britain, the ideas of radical economists, most notably Thomas Balogh, in favor of bilateralism and controls, reinforced the stance of conservative financial circles defending the role of sterling in the Commonwealth. In the United States, the political debate was even fiercer, especially during the parliamentary hearings on the Articles of Agreement (Gardner 1969, 129–43). Before the conference, however, White was not worried by Republican opposition because, as Keynes explained in a letter to Richard Hopkins on

25 June 1944,[11] this would lead the Democratic Party to support the reform.

The preparations for Bretton Woods (Horsefield 1969a, Chapters 4, 5) began in April 1944. On 25 May, with President Roosevelt's assent, Treasury Secretary Henry Morgenthau invited forty-four nations to participate in the conference, which would open on 1 July.[12] Seventeen of the attendees gathered at a preliminary meeting in Atlantic City in the second half of June to try to eliminate the most glaring disagreements between Britain and the United States. No definitive text was drafted, however, because, as Keynes wrote to Hopkins (CW 26, 61), White did not want to present the countries and the members of the U.S. delegation who were not at Atlantic City with a finished document that had only to be rubber-stamped.

On the appointed day, 730 participants, three times more than expected, gathered at the Mount Washington Hotel in Bretton Woods, NH, which had been closed for two years and was reopened to host the conference. The conference, which lasted until 22 July, created three committees: on the Fund, on the World Bank, and on international financial cooperation, chaired, respectively, by White, Keynes, and Eduardo Suarez of Mexico. The agenda was daunting, and the conditions under which the delegates labored were far from ideal.[13] The conference turned out five hundred documents totaling

---

[11] "An effort is being made to get a plank of the Republican platform opposing international collaboration on the Monetary Plan. White expresses himself as not too much concerned at this. Indeed he thinks it might lead to the Democratic party taking a much more definite stand in favour. The staging of the vast monkey-house at Bretton Woods is, of course, in order that the President can say that 44 nations have agreed on the Fund and the Bank and he challenges the Republicans or anyone else to reject such an approach. I should say that this tactic is very likely to be successful" (CW 26, 63).

[12] In addition to the official delegations, a representative of Denmark was also invited in a personal capacity inasmuch as a Danish government in exile had not been formally established (Horsefield 1969a, 79).

[13] Keynes offers vivid testimony concerning the atmosphere: "It is as though ... one had to accomplish the preliminary work of many interdepartmental and Cabinet committees, the job of the ... draftsmen, and the passage ... of two intricate legislative measures of large dimensions, all this carried on in committees and commissions numbering anything up to 200 persons in rooms with bad acoustics, shouting through microphones, many of those

some twelve hundred pages. However, most of the disagreements were dealt with in informal meetings among the major countries. In this regard, contacts between the United States and the Soviet Union in early 1944 had brought out divergences on several matters. The Soviets wanted to reduce their contribution, strengthen the veto, avoid giving the Fund the right to fix the exchange rate of the ruble, and reduce the gold payments of the occupied countries. These divergences were discussed and resolved with White and the U.S. Treasury so that the Soviet Union participated in the conference and signed the Final Act, but did not ratify the treaty. In the end, the Soviets were unwilling to disclose the country's economic data and join an institution that would be dominated by the United States. Even within the Western bloc, the agreements ushered in a phase not of collaboration but of conflict. The discussion went beyond the interpretation of the key clauses, such as Article VIII on convertibility and its implications for sterling balances (Gold 1981), and also dealt with purely practical issues, such as the location of Fund and Bank headquarters, their organization, and economic arrangements.[14]

present... with an imperfect knowledge of English, each wanting to get something on the record which would look well in the press down at home, and... the Russians only understanding what was afoot with the utmost difficulty.... We have all of us worked every minute of our waking hours... all of us... are all in" (quoted in Horsefield 1969a, 92). Among other things, Keynes's already precarious health grew worse, as Lionel Robbins noted in his diary: "[T]hroughout the Conference we have all felt that as regards Keynes's health we were on the edge of a precipice. There was one evening of prostration at Atlantic City, two the first week here, three last week, and I now feel that it is a race between the exhaustion of his powers and the termination of the Conference" (CW 26, 97 note 25).

[14] These problems gave rise to heated talks, an examination of which goes beyond the scope of the present work; the most important episodes will be briefly mentioned. According to Keynes, the new institutions should be based in two different cities, London and New York. The question was not settled at Bretton Woods. The Americans proposed that the Fund and the Bank be based in the country with the largest quota. However, the British succeeded in having the decision deferred until the first meeting. In March 1946, in Savannah, the United States, with the support of China and several South American countries, secured approval of Washington as the headquarters of both organizations, causing resentment among the British and numerous other delegations. Keynes commented in a report that he wrote during his return voyage on the *Queen Mary*: "These methods, however, were felt to be distasteful by many, including several of the Americans, who sympathised with and apologised to us behind the scenes, and created for

Without going into the technicalities incorporated in the Articles of Agreement, the outcome of the conference should be seen against the backdrop of the system's transformation following the demise of the gold standard. The Bretton Woods arrangements were intended to restore symmetry to the adjustment mechanism and multilateralism to international trade in a regime of fixed exchange rates while maintaining capital controls in order to give each country reasonable leeway for full employment policy. In reality, the new international monetary order had a number of weaknesses, chiefly relating to the conflicts between its main objectives, and it eventually accelerated the move toward fiat money. Born of a blueprint drafted by experts, the project was without precedent, presupposing at least an identity of approach, a generally accepted theoretical paradigm. But even this was not enough to guarantee the validity of the ultimate outcome, which was determined by the balance of power between the leading actors. The result was a compromise, a hybrid that was less coherent than the original proposals. The Keynes Plan and the White Plan both offered cleaner solutions, respectively an innovative clearing scheme and a revised gold exchange standard; the mutual concessions resulted in an agreement whose provisions were open to diverse interpretations, so much so as to jeopardize the very consistency and viability of the resulting system.

7.2. THE POST-CONFERENCE ACADEMIC DEBATE

No sooner had the proceedings ended than a wide-ranging debate on the Bretton Woods agreements began, witness the symposium

a time a disagreeable atmosphere, though the cloud gradually lifted towards the end" (CW 26, 222). In a letter to Kahn dated 13 March 1946, Keynes lamented the management approach imposed by the Americans, based on a padded staff and very high salaries designed to gain the acquiescence of many member states, especially the South Americans (CW 26, 217–25). According to Sir George Bolton's account, during the voyage Keynes wrote a fierce article condemning the American policy, but Row-Dutton and Bolton himself convinced him to destroy the text so as not to jeopardize Britain's interests (Kahn 1976, 28–9).

published in the *Review of Economic Statistics* (November 1944), the collection of papers edited by Murray Shields (1944), and numerous articles in leading journals in the later 1940s. Leaving aside the defense of the agreements by some of the protagonists (Bernstein 1944, 1945; Bourneuf 1944; White 1945),[15] the conference results were analyzed from both the political and the technical point of view. The former will not be examined here, but it is worth spending a few words on the sharpening tension between the United States and Britain. Recurring objections to the new system – fear of having to shoulder most of the financial burden, easy access to the Fund's excessive resources, the inadequacy of the adjustment mechanism – led the United States to pressure Britain to proceed with the convertibility of sterling and accept a loan to cope with postwar difficulties. On the other hand, the British stressed the absence of stringent obligations for creditor countries and the Fund's limited resources and opposed the immediate application of the new rules (Mikesell 1949, 395 note 2). In the end, American prevalence had serious repercussions on the British economy.

On the technical plane, early comments focused rather on specific aspects than on the structure of the novel monetary construction, because the final compromise was more elusive than the original British and American proposals, making it hard to assess a monetary reform whose actual operation would result from future interpretation. The uncertainty was further heightened by postwar imbalances and the attendant effects of the transition. Hence, until a clearer picture emerged from the full-fledged implementation, commentators were prudent in appraising the Bretton Woods monetary order. One crucial point was soon raised, however: the

---

[15] Edward Bernstein, who would be director of the Fund's Research Department from 1946 to 1958, was an *éminence grise* within the American delegation, as Keynes observed in a revealing letter to Wilfrid Eady on 3 October 1943: "Both the currency scheme and the investment scheme are, I think, largely the fruit of the brain not of Harry [White] but of his little attaché, Bernstein. It is with him rather than Harry that the pride of authorship lies. And when we seduce Harry from the true faith, little Bernstein wins him back again in the course of the night" (CW 25, 364).

compatibility of full employment, unanimously considered as the keystone of economic policy design, with external equilibrium. Condliffe remarked:

The great issue of international economic collaboration is to find methods by which domestic policies aiming at high-level employment may be reconciled with freer international trade and investment. Means must be found whereby domestic policies do not restrain international cooperation while the necessity for balancing payments in and out of national economies does not introduce instability into domestic employment. (1944, 166)

This problem was central to the Bretton Woods debate. Halm (1944, 172) left its solution to the experience of the Fund's board rather than to rigid formulae, while Schumacher and Balogh (1944, 83–4), from a radical position, questioned the consistency of the new monetary arrangements with both full employment and essential imports, criticizing the premature waiver of controls. Tackling the subject from the perspective of international adjustment, Triffin (1947a, 55–63) stressed the distinction between worldwide cyclical fluctuations and fundamental disequilibria affecting one or a few countries, which would be solved respectively by appropriate domestic policies and exchange rate variations. The success of Bretton Woods then required employment policies in lieu of the gold standard rules. Indeed, the pursuit of full employment was viewed as a condition for overcoming exchange controls, expanding trade, and ensuring international equilibrium, thus contributing to the smooth working of the new system (Fellner 1945, 265–6; Nurkse 1947, 569). Haberler (1947, 88–90), however, criticized Triffin's distinction for its misinterpretation of the classical theory, which also confined automatic or induced price changes to the adjustment of structural rather than temporary disequilibria, and for its disregard of the reciprocal influences between cyclical and fundamental disequilibrium. Two further issues emerged: asymmetry and the difficulty of defining "fundamental disequilibrium."

First, while deficit countries were allowed to devalue, revaluation was hardly contemplated, given the need to avoid deflation. The scarce currency clause should have solved the surplus problem, but it was regarded as a temporary measure, not a restoration of equilibrium (Halm 1944, 173), conflicting with a main purpose of the reform: restoring the multilateral dimension of trade. Thus, the asymmetry that had plagued the monetary system in the interwar years was not removed. Furthermore, as Jacob Viner (1944, 238) and Frank Graham noted, the Bretton Woods rules, designed to avoid deflation, actually were prone to inflation, with the effect of penalizing the most virtuous countries:

Deflation and depression were so impressed on the consciousness of the drafters of the legislation that they completely failed to take into account the evils of *inflation* with the result that, probably in innocence, they put punitive legislation into effect against such countries as might then pursue a policy of monetary rectitude and in favor of those on an inflationary junket. Since the currency of a country which merely fails to keep pace with general inflation in the outside world will, under fixed exchange rates, always tend to become a "scarce currency," such a country would, under the statutes of the Fund, be subject to discriminatory action penalizing its export industries and forcing it to inflate to the degree prevalent abroad. These provisions, therefore, not only violate the professed purpose of our recently established international economic institutions to promote free, multilateral, non-discriminatory, trade, but they put a premium on progressive, and universal, inflationary practices. (F. Graham 1949, 12; italics in the original)

Second, the economists' attempts to define fundamental disequilibrium produced more questions than answers, thus making the issue even more controversial. Purchasing power parity theory would have provided a suitable analytical tool; but despite the popularity it had enjoyed after World War I, it was widely criticized. The focus shifted to the flow of international reserves. Haberler identified an actual deficit in the balance of payments as "an objective, unambiguous, and observable criterion" (1944, 181) and countered the argument of Nurkse (1944, 126), also taken up by Hansen (1944), that this was not a sufficient criterion because, as the U.K. experience in 1925–30 showed, a country may attain balance of payments equilibrium by means of restrictive policies but then suffer unemployment. The same point was raised by Triffin (1947a, 75–8) in relation to the case of Belgium after the devaluation of the pound in September 1931, again prompting Haberler's critical assessment (1947, 97–8). In reality, these punctilious discussions did little to advance understanding of the issue at stake.[16] Bewildered by the problem of hitting both internal and external targets, the debate failed to arrive at a solution. This came many years later from Robert Mundell (1962).[17]

Given the fundamental compromise characterizing the agreement, the effectiveness of the adjustment mechanism remained an open question, strengthening the impression that the new

[16] Raymond Mikesell's remark – "Indeed, fundamental disequilibrium has never been defined in fewer than ten pages" (1994, 18) – is indicative of the intricacies surrounding the concept in question. In an article published in 1947, Mikesell, then an economist at the U.S. Treasury involved in work related to Bretton Woods, recounted the interpretation that passed current among negotiators: "Although fundamental disequilibrium is not defined in the Fund's *Articles of Agreement*, it was evident from the discussions which preceded the formal drafting of the agreement that the term refers to a sustained imbalance in a member's current international accounts. Properly interpreted, such an imbalance would be one which was not offset by long-term borrowings and would be accompanied by a sustained loss of international reserves or continued borrowings from the Fund or from other sources of short-term credits"; and in a footnote attached to this passage, he added: "From a study of the unpublished minutes of the pre–Bretton Woods negotiations, . . . it is clear that the principal criterion for rate alterations in the minds of the authors of the text of the Fund agreement was the existence of a disequilibrium in the current international accounts of the member requesting a change" (1947, 503–4).

[17] Before the Bretton Woods conference, Keynes (1943) had given his own interpretation of fundamental disequilibrium in a comment on Hayek (1943) (see Chapter 6, Section 3). Calling for an independent economic policy aimed at domestic objectives, Keynes confined exchange rate adjustment to specific instances of long-run disequilibrium. In particular, a divergent trend of a country's price level or of wages relative to efficiency impervious to corrective measures should be tackled by a change in parity. Keeping cyclical and structural disequilibria on different analytical planes, Keynes refrained from clear-cut definition of fundamental disequilibrium and set the problem in a more general perspective (Cesarano 2003b). In this connection, see David Vines (2003) on Keynes's reliance on fiscal rather than monetary discipline to solve domestic imbalances.

monetary architecture lacked coherence. Thus, even those sympathetic to the reform took a cautious stance. In his contribution to a volume edited by Murray Shields,[18] Jacob Viner pointed out the ambiguity of the scheme, setting the goal of exchange rate stability while sanctioning exchange rate variation "as a normal procedure for relieving pressure on international balances" (1944, 235). Exchange rate changes were generally seen as the main means of long-run adjustment, because barring resort to tariffs or controls full employment excluded deflationary policy and left no other tool to correct a persistent disequilibrium. Other authors were more optimistic about the successful operation of Bretton Woods as long as all the available policy tools were used. For Nurkse, relying on international liquidity and the Fund's resources in the short run, trade policy in particular circumstances, and exchange rate adjustment in the long run, "the new system of international currency and trade is quite capable of being operated so as to allow scope for national policies aimed at high and stable levels of employment and at the same time to promote the flow of international trade" (1947, 577). The panoply of economic policies deployed after the Great Depression could reconcile the commitment to full employment with the smooth working of the new monetary scheme, which, however, should eschew rigid, predetermined recipes.[19]

In general, the influence of Keynesian economics on the analyses of Bretton Woods was very substantial from the start, as clearly

---

[18] The essays included in that book were, with the exception of Viner's, mostly descriptive rather than analytical. The participants to the symposium, albeit taking position either against (Kemmerer) or in favor (Hansen) of the accord, did not probe the implications of Bretton Woods much in depth.

[19] In this regard, Triffin contended: "The new weapons should not be scrapped indiscriminately – an objective on which general agreement would, anyway, be impossible – but harmonized and integrated, through international consultation, into the implementation of internationally defined monetary objectives. This would increase their national effectiveness, as well as ensure their international usefulness. Progress along this path will be made incomparably easier by the creation of the International Monetary Fund. . . . The Fund's philosophy should not be frozen, especially at this early stage, into the rigid, ready-made formulas which have so often contributed to the sterility of previous efforts at international economic collaboration and organization" (1947b, 323–4).

appears from the contributions to the 1947 *American Economic Review Papers and Proceedings*. As Abba Lerner noted: "The outstanding feature of this session is the extent of agreement.... The agreement between Mr. Smithies, Mr. Nurkse, and nearly all the other discussants stems from the recognition of this error [that somehow full employment was being maintained all the time] and the integration of the free trade issue with the employment problem. As such it has great promise for future public policy" (1947, 592–3). In fact, there was only one discordant voice in the discussion, Elmer Wood, who acknowledged the need to avoid deflation but warned against internal disequilibrium and unemployment brought about by exchange controls or exchange rate variations. To smooth out the negative effects of the search for internal and external stability, Wood argued, the adjustment process should rely on a certain degree of flexibility in the real economy, as happens between the different regions of the United States. This is a most interesting point because it relates to the problem that, more than a decade later, would originate the literature on optimum currency areas. Anticipating the seminal contribution of Robert Mundell (1961), Lerner answered the question at once and identified labor mobility as the optimality principle.

There is such a principle. Where there is mobility of labor, and for this purpose it is real and not just legal mobility which is relevant, there is no need for an exchange adjustment to restore equilibrium between a deficit area and a surplus area. This is because the unemployed in one area where there is a depression can go to the other area, where there is a boom, and get a job. (1947, 594)

If labor mobility were lacking, then according to Lerner exchange rate change would remain the best solution, over the alternatives of price level variation, depression, or trade restriction.

Economists were generally sympathetic to the Bretton Woods accord, albeit in different shades, with only a few harsh critics. Even a skeptical scholar like Henry Simons, though doubting the usefulness of the Bretton Woods agreements, called for their ratification, foreseeing a possible role for the Fund in monetary and fiscal policy coordination. Running counter to the mainstream, however, Simons emphasized monetary stability, not full employment, as the key condition for success:

Finally, I should stress the importance of domestic monetary stability. Our tariff aside, there is perhaps no greater proximate obstacle to close economic co-operation with our friends than their uncertainty about the future commodity-value of our currency. Given a really stable dollar, the task of restoring orderly international finance and decent commercial policies would be vastly simplified. A severe or prolonged American deflation is, if only for obvious reasons of domestic politics, utterly improbable; but vigorous leadership on minimal rules or objectives for domestic fiscal policy is needed to reassure the English – needed and lacking for the peace as it has been for the war. . . . Moreover, the requirements of an orderly world economy are not much better served by finance-be-damned schemes for domestic full employment than by prescriptions of relentless budget balancing or of radical devaluation – not to mention cotton-export subsidies. (1945, 295)

Supporters of the Bretton Woods system, though aware of its possible technical weaknesses, looked at the new arrangement from a broader perspective, highlighting the need to rebuild the international monetary system and fill the void created by the monetary disorders of the 1930s. Viner (1944, 235–8), for instance, was critical of exchange controls and preferred revaluation to trade restriction when a currency has become "generally scarce." Nevertheless, he refuted the main objections against Bretton Woods raised in the United States (1944, 238–43) and regarded the opposition of bankers as blatantly conflicting with their own objectives (1947a, 295). He saw the accord as a first, necessary step toward restoring stable international economic relations. For Viner, the kernel of the agreement was the members' commitment to exchange rate stability and free exchange markets in exchange for the U.S. pledge of financial aid. The institutional framework was instrumental to these objectives, in that it set up rules for fair treatment of debtor countries[20] and, more generally, enhanced the reorganization of the international economy in "harmony... with liberal nineteenth-century doctrine" (Viner 1947b, 97).

However, the quest for monetary reconstruction along lines suggested by Simons and Viner was impeded by growing skepticism about the efficacy of market mechanisms in view of the depression. This frame of mind could be described no better than in the following remarks by Lloyd Metzler. Asking whether there was a unifying principle linking the new theories of international trade, he answered in the affirmative, but added:

The connecting idea, however, is essentially negative. Historically, the interwar period will probably be remembered as a period of retreat from the price system, when all sorts of temporary or provisional measures were adopted to regulate economic activity. The market mechanism had broken down and no one seemed to know quite why or just what to do about it. This was perhaps even more true of the international mechanism than of domestic markets, and to a very great extent the theoretical developments reflected the empirical. (1948, 253)

A case in point was "elasticity pessimism," which implied a deterioration in the trade balance following a devaluation, orienting economic policy toward controls. Bloomfield (1947, 582–3) counted Balogh, Hansen, Kalecki, Lerner, and Tinbergen among the "pessimists," but he did not agree with them and linked the efficacy of devaluation to the length of the period considered. In any case, advocacy of controls was tempered by recommendations that they should be eliminated as soon as possible inasmuch as they could not cure structural imbalances, which instead required an adjustment of the exchange rate (Nurkse 1947, 573–4).

[20] "Both agencies [the Fund and the Bank] have the all-important merit that the dealings of debtors will be with a multinational agency which will have the obligation to refrain from serving narrowly national purposes and which will not readily find within the limitations of powers set by their charters the means to violate the obligation, even if, perchance, the will to do so should arise. In so far as their resources permit, these agencies will enable economically and politically weak countries to receive financial aid without thereby becoming entangled in the political net of a great power" (Viner 1947b, 103).

Strictly related to this antimarket conception was the dollar shortage, a central issue in the postwar debate. The forecast that the United States would run a large and persistent payments surplus was based on the inefficacy of the adjustment mechanism. On the one hand, the classical approach had been rejected, because the burden of adjustment would fall mostly on output, not prices. Besides, the central bank could sterilize the inflow of gold, drastically reducing its effects, as in the early 1930s. On the other hand, in the Keynesian approach equilibrium was surely not reestablished unless the growth in income due to export expansion was accompanied by an increase in investment (Metzler 1948, 219–20). In both cases, the ineffectiveness of the adjustment process was aggravated by "compensatory" monetary and fiscal policies. Thus, Mikesell remarked: "[T]here exists no dependable mechanism by means of which deep-seated maladjustments in the structure of world trade can be removed" (1947, 502).

Notwithstanding these perplexities and the predominance of the Keynesian paradigm, there were a few attempts to rehabilitate the classical model, but they went largely unheeded. Rendigs Fels (1949) pondered the reasons for the success of the gold standard before the First World War and hypothesized that in the longer term an increase in the stock of gold has effects on income and prices in concomitance with an expansionary phase of the cycle. Accordingly, the classical adjustment mechanism was not ineffective at all, because it preserved its validity in the long run. Lloyd Metzler noted that "the pendulum has now swung too far in the anti-classical direction" (1948, 254), while confining the relevance of classical theory to resource allocation; international adjustment would instead be fulfilled by exchange rate variations. The arch-defender of classical thought, however, was Frank Graham. Focusing on certain analogies of the Bretton Woods system with the Tripartite Agreement of 1936, Graham stressed the irreconcilability of a fixed exchange rate regime with independent monetary policy and vehemently criticized the new monetary order:

It would seem that, after all this, we might have learned that we cannot both have our cake and eat it. We should know that we must either forgo fixed exchange rates *or* national monetary sovereignty if we are to avoid the disruption of equilibrium in freely conducted international trade or the system of controls and inhibitions which is the only alternative when the internal values of independent currencies deviate – as they always tend to do – from what was, perhaps, a correct relationship when the fixed rates of exchange were set up. Yet the old error was, to all intents and purposes, again repeated in the International Monetary Organization which did not much curtail national monetary sovereignty. It is true that some concessions were made to the consequent demand for flexibility in exchange relationships. But there is, nevertheless, a strong bias in the statute toward the ideal of rates maintained unchanged for an indefinitely lengthy period, and not even the slightest provision for the adoption, by the various participating countries, of the congruent monetary policies without which a system of fixed exchange rates simply does not make sense. (1949, 6; italics in the original)

Graham attacked the prevalent view, which stressed the intractability of the dollar shortage because of elasticity pessimism, and explained it as due simply to the undervaluation of the dollar. Divergent monetary policies in a fixed exchange rate regime and meddling with the price system produced disturbances and trade distortions substantial enough to undermine the international adjustment mechanism. Bretton Woods suffered the same defects and so was doomed to fail.[21]

[21] Graham concluded: "In the establishment of the International Monetary Fund in 1945 we had not learned the obvious lessons of the inter-war period and had forgotten that the days of the sacred repute of gold had long since passed away. The Fund, therefore, not only repeated the errors of most of its predecessor organizations but has added noxious features never before embodied in any international agreement. All this is the result not of malevolence but of a stubborn refusal to face facts. Uncoordinated national monetary policies, non-discriminatory, multilateral, trade on the basis of free enterprise, and exchange rates fixed, even provisionally, cannot be made to mix. We must choose between them. If we insist on fixed exchange rates we must proceed immediately to the coordination of national monetary policies on a covenanted basis or we shall lose our bone in pursuit of a shadow. If a covenanted coordination of national monetary policies is held to be impracticable, the sooner we abandon any effort to keep unchanging exchange relationships between the various national currencies the better it will be for

Frank Graham was an isolated voice as Keynesian thought spread. Quite surprisingly, however, in this intellectual atmosphere Keynes himself warned against rejecting classical theory outright. In his last article (1946), noting the upward pressure on U.S. prices, he questioned the forecast of a dollar shortage over the next five or ten years, citing the specie-flow mechanism and, more generally, the forces that determine equilibrium in classical theory (Cesarano 2003a, Section 2). Classical economics had to have some validity; otherwise, the success of the gold standard up to 1914 would be inexplicable.

> In the long run more fundamental forces may be at work, if all goes well, tending towards equilibrium, the significance of which may ultimately transcend ephemeral statistics. I find myself moved, not for the first time, to remind contemporary economists that *the classical teaching embodied some permanent truths of great significance, which we are liable to-day to overlook because we associate them with other doctrines which we cannot now accept without much qualification.* There are in these matters deep undercurrents at work, natural forces, one can call them, or even *the invisible hand,* which are operating towards equilibrium. If it were not so, we could not have got on even so well as we have for many decades past. (Keynes 1946, 185; italics added)

Free trade, the special objective of the United States, was essential for the classical adjustment mechanism to be effective.[22] While recognizing the usefulness of trade controls and exchange rate

---

all concerned. This will require the reform, or demise, of the International Monetary Organization" (F. Graham 1949, 14–5).

[22] Endorsing the American proposal for a conference on trade liberalization, Keynes warned against embracing too radical a theoretical stance: "We have here sincere and thorough-going proposals, advanced on behalf of the United States, expressly directed towards creating a system which allows the classical medicine to do its work. It shows how much modernist stuff, gone wrong and turned sour and silly, is circulating in our system, also incongruously mixed, it seems, with age-old poisons, that we should have given so doubtful a welcome to this magnificent, objective approach which a few years ago we should have regarded as offering incredible promise of a better scheme of things" (1946, 186). Moggridge (2001) has reconstructed the vicissitudes of the publication of Keynes's last paper. It should also be remembered that Viner, too, disputed the forecasts of a dollar shortage (1944, 240 note 6).

variations in the short run, Keynes called attention to the limits of these expedients and, reaffirming the importance of the classical adjustment mechanism, praised the recent international agreements for combining both kinds of measures:

I must not be misunderstood. I do not suppose that the classical medicine will work by itself or that we can depend on it. We need quicker and less painful aids of which exchange variation and overall import control are the most important. But in the long run these expedients will work better and we shall need them less, if the classical medicine is also at work. And if we reject the medicine from our systems altogether, we may just drift on from expedient to expedient and never get really fit again. The great virtue of the Bretton Woods and Washington proposals, taken in conjunction, is that they marry the use of the necessary expedients to the wholesome long-run doctrine. It is for this reason that, speaking in the House of Lords, I claimed that "Here is an attempt to use what we have learnt from modern experience and modern analysis, not to defeat, but to implement the wisdom of Adam Smith." (1946, 186)

In his conclusion, however, Keynes was cautious about the success of the new monetary order, given the uncertainties and glaring contrasts of the modern economy.[23] And in his speech at the inaugural meeting of the Fund in Savannah he reminded his audience of the fragility of international institutions, so often exploited by the dominant countries to advance their own agenda, urging that the international nature of the Fund and the World Bank be safeguarded. Confidence in an organization depended on its being free from partisan interests; otherwise, politics would prevail.

The Savannah address thus shaded Keynes's unfailingly positive judgment on Bretton Woods. The new scheme might possibly

---

[23] "No one can be certain of anything in this age of flux and change. Decaying standards of life at a time when our command over the production of material satisfactions is the greatest ever, and a diminishing scope for individual decision and choice at a time when more than before we should be able to afford these satisfactions, are sufficient to indicate an underlying contradiction in every department of our economy. No plans will work for certain in such an epoch. But if they palpably fail, then, of course, we and everyone else will try something different" (Keynes 1946, 186).

prove inadequate, but the effectiveness of the classical adjustment mechanism should be relied on to ensure long-run stability.

Economists' responses to Bretton Woods in the 1940s, as we see, ranged from uncompromising criticism to almost full backing. Underlying these variegated opinions were different theoretical models. Cautious supporters, while sensitive to the need to rebuild the monetary system on a new analytical basis, pointed out weaknesses. The optimists, espousing a decisively innovative theoretical stance, trusted in domestic policies to foster economic growth and maintain international equilibrium. The academic spectrum tended to be in favor of the agreements. Fundamental critics were a small minority, the main figure being Frank Graham. Relying on classical economics, he did not advocate a reshaped, resurrected version of the gold exchange standard but flexible exchange rates to solve the inherent inconsistency between monetary independence and a fixed exchange rate. Recalling the one-way bet offered to speculators (see Chapter 5, Section 2), he revealed a fatal weakness of Bretton Woods that everybody else failed to detect (1949, 9–10).[24] In fact, supporters were confident that the defects of the interwar monetary arrangements had been remedied and that the potential conflict between fixed exchange rates and activist economic policies could be defused by the provisions of the agreement.[25] The complexity of this task would be at the root of the difficulties and the eventual crisis of the new monetary order.

---

[24] A glaring example is the following statement by Nurkse: "The object of the International Monetary Fund is to keep exchange rates stable in the short run but to permit step-by-step adjustments of rates from time to time, as and when the trend of international payments requires it. The method of exchange adjustment can under the new system be used in a way entirely compatible with the objectives of internal as well as external equilibrium" (1947, 575).

[25] As Triffin noted: "The experience of the thirties has demonstrated the pitfalls of monetary isolation along purely national lines and the difficulties of reconciling domestic stability and prosperity with international disequilibrium. The Bretton Woods agreements, without returning to the full subordination of national monetary policies to the single goal of exchange stability, have sought to re-establish some mechanism designed to protect the international economy against autarchic excesses in the monetary field" (1947a, 54).

7.3. THE SIGNIFICANCE OF THE TREATY AND ITS DEMISE

The ideal of reconstructing the international monetary system motivated the painstaking labors of the Bretton Woods negotiators. The traumatic experience of the depression and the new paradigm introduced by Keynes's *General Theory* loomed large in the agreements. Hence, the "spirit of the treaty," to use McKinnon's graphic expression (1993, 13), was to introduce sufficient flexibility in monetary arrangements to allow for domestic policy objectives. Shielded by capital controls, policymakers could stabilize employment and the price level, using exchange reserves and the Fund's resources to tackle short-run payments difficulties, while exchange rate changes were expressly envisaged in case of structural disequilibria.[26] This represented a major break with the past in formally rejecting the restoration rule and embracing a diametrically opposite model. The keystone of the monetary system was no longer maintenance of the fixed parity, as in the gold standard, but the pursuit of full employment.

At Bretton Woods, the departure from the commodity standard made a quantum jump to a new institutional framework that reflected Keynes's work. The gold standard had been grounded in the classical equilibrium model and evolved spontaneously; the new system was grounded in the analytical apparatus of the *General Theory* and born of an international agreement. In fact, given the mistrust of the equilibrium approach, the vacuum produced by the collapse of the gold standard could only be filled by new rules that put cooperation in the place of the old "automatic" mechanism. White underscored two premises at the heart of the Bretton Woods system: "The first is the need for stability, order and freedom in

---

[26] Metzler noted that full employment policies, preventing major output fluctuations, would reinstate the classical adjustment mechanism because equilibrium was restored by changes in the terms of trade, achieved via changes in exchange rates. "Indeed, in a world of high and stable employment, movements of exchange rates are virtually the only more or less automatic means of influencing international trade without resorting to direct controls" (1948, 221–2).

exchange transactions. ... The second is that stability in the international exchange structure is impossible of attainment without both international economic coöperation and an efficient mechanism for implementing the desire for such coöperation among the United Nations" (1945, 196). These objectives posed the challenging task of creating a set of rules as consistent, enforceable, and credible as the gold standard. To give just one example, the essential role of mainly private capital movements in the adjustment mechanism was a natural feature of the gold standard because of the high credibility stemming from the restoration rule. In reconstructing the monetary order, then, reviving the involvement of creditor countries became, as Keynes had repeatedly emphasized, a central objective, but the new arrangements lacked the credibility of the gold standard.

The Bretton Woods agreements reinstated fixed exchange rates, but allowed for modifying them under particular circumstances, so as not to hinder activist economic policies. The new monetary framework was intended especially to avoid deflation and maintain full employment. Yet from the beginning, the spirit of the treaty was betrayed and the Bretton Woods game was actually played under the rules of a fixed exchange rate regime, imposing much stricter discipline than the architects had intended. All countries conformed at once, doing away with the innovative scheme born at Bretton Woods.

This step backward according to McKinnon (1993, 37), poses "a major historical puzzle," which he explains in two ways: the establishment of the European Payments Union based on the dollar as the unit of account and the quest for an external nominal anchor by European countries and Japan to enhance policy credibility. Other factors, too, buttress this explanation. First of all was the U.S. concern for disciplining other Fund members. The fear of becoming, as Keynes put it, "the milch cow of the world" (see footnote 3) was paramount throughout the negotiations and even after the signing of the agreements, witness the congressional debate (Gardner 1969,

129–43). White offered this near caricature of the American sentiment: "It has been asserted that the Fund is only a device for lending Unites States dollars cheaply and that the money will be wasted or lost; that other countries just want to get our dollars, and that there is nothing to stop them from quickly draining our dollars from the Fund" (1945, 201). In defense of the accord, he went on to list the provisions limiting access, while Walter Gardner of the Fed underlined the need for domestic restriction in case of external imbalances due to inflation.[27] During the talks, the Americans had sought consistently to bend the outcome toward more stringent rules.

The U.S. stance was thus congruent with the other countries' objectives, all the more that, in postwar continental Europe, policymakers were not yet fully receptive to Keynes's message. Rather, they wanted clear-cut rules that could restore a stable monetary framework. True, managed money had by now been widely accepted, recognizing Keynes's early argument that the Fed prevented gold inflows from exercising their effects and thus "a dollar standard was set up on the pedestal of the Golden Calf" (1923, 198), but this pedestal was still there, inasmuch as central bankers continued to entertain the idea that gold possessed some ultimate, distinctive properties and remained the basis of the system. Emerging from the war with negligible gold reserves, the main continental European countries accumulated gold for the next two decades. Hence, the central bankers' revealed preferences were not discordant with the tenets of a commodity standard and, in particular, with a fixed exchange rate regime, traditionally viewed as a formidable defense against government interference. Milton Friedman, in a little-known 1953 paper, highlighted the sheer conservatism of

---

[27] "The management of the International Monetary Fund can properly insist that countries which are developing deficits in their international balance of payments because of inflation should not periodically come to it for permission to alter their rates of exchange. Rather they should take measures to stop the inflation" (Gardner 1945, 284–5).

central bankers and their attachment to the gold standard, underscoring the shortcomings of the Bretton Woods construction:

The central bankers of the world...and numerous other proponents of a fully operative gold standard are fervent defenders of the price system in most other manifestations. Yet they oppose its application to exchange rates because they cling to the shadow of rigid rates in the hope of getting the substance of external restraints on domestic monetary policy. The result has been support for a system which makes the worst of both worlds. The postwar system of exchange rates, temporarily rigid but subject to change from time to time by governmental action, can provide neither the certainty about exchange rates and the freedom from irresponsible governmental action of a fully operative gold standard, nor the independence of each country from the monetary vagaries of other countries, nor the freedom of each country to pursue internal monetary stability in its own way that are provided by truly flexible exchange rates. This postwar system sacrifices the simultaneous achievement of the two major objectives of vigorous multilateral trade and independence of internal monetary policy on the altar of the essentially minor objective of a rigid exchange rate. (1953b, 217)

Thus, not only the operational requirements of the European Payments Union (EPU) but also the cultural background of most central bankers contributed decisively to turning the monetary system away from the spirit of Bretton Woods. Indeed, after the winding up of the EPU in December 1958, gold accumulation continued unabated in Europe (except Britain) and by the mid-sixties had more than doubled.

The prevalence of this attitude among central bankers is corroborated by the growing importance attributed to the Triffin dilemma, which was not entirely justified.[28] As McKinnon (1993, 18) noted, in a pure dollar standard official dollar claims were demand determined and, because they were no longer strictly related to domestic money growth, had no impact on the rate of inflation. Hence, the

---

[28] According to Eichengreen (1992, 203), this issue had been raised as early as in 1929 by Mlynarski and then rediscovered by Triffin (1947a). However, it did not attract policymakers' attention until the publication of Triffin's book (1960).

buildup of dollar reserves would not harm the viability of monetary arrangements as long as the U.S. price level was stable; and it was. From 1960 to 1967, when policymakers were most sensitive to the Triffin dilemma, inflation averaged 1.7 percent, even less than in the preceding decade when it was 1.9 percent.[29] However, central bankers did not see Bretton Woods as a pure dollar standard but rather as a system hinged on the dollar's convertibility into gold. The steady expansion of official dollar holdings while the U.S. gold stock declined was thus viewed as a fatal flaw.

A combination of factors, then, contributed to dissolving the spirit of the Bretton Woods treaty and the swift establishment of a system much akin to the gold exchange standard. The deep concern of the United States over possible lack of discipline by other countries met with the conservative stance of European central bankers, who saw fixed exchange rates as the prerequisite for a viable monetary order. The operational requirements of the European Payments Union acted as a catalyst for a fixed exchange rate regime and policies consistent with it, reflecting the central bankers' analytical background and established modes of behavior. Policymakers clung to a view of the monetary system that ran counter to the message of Bretton Woods, instituting more rigid arrangements whose fundamental fragility was revealed by the rising pressures of the 1960s.

[29] A good part of the overall inflation of the 1950s was due to the 8.1 percent price rise in 1951; the average rate over 1952–9 was only 1.5 percent, but the rate achieved in 1960–7 was just marginally above that (data are from the *International Financial Statistics Yearbook, 1980*). Furthermore, according to the statistical evidence shown by Bordo (1993, 7), the average U.S. inflation rate was the lowest among G7 countries during Bretton Woods (2.4 percent in 1946–70; G7 mean: 3.6 percent) and in the subperiod following convertibility (2.6 percent in 1959–70; G7 mean: 3.9 percent).

8 BRETTON WOODS AND AFTER

THE EVOLUTION OF THE MONETARY SYSTEM IS GOVERNED BY THE interaction between advances in economic theory and major shocks. This hypothesis is corroborated by the articulated process that led from the downfall of the gold standard to the Bretton Woods agreements and then to the sudden abandonment of the spirit of the treaty. A detailed examination of the actual working of Bretton Woods, however, is beyond the scope of the present work. This concluding chapter thus focuses exclusively on the factors behind the system's eventual collapse and the prospects for the development of the international monetary system.

The Bretton Woods conference was unique to monetary history. It designed a new monetary order from scratch. John Ikenberry, for one, noted:

The Bretton Woods agreements, negotiated largely between Britain and the United States and signed by forty-four nations in 1944, were remarkable in a variety of ways. First, they represented an unprecedented experiment in international rule making and institution building – rules and institutions for post-war monetary and financial relations. Second, the Bretton Woods agreements were the decisive step in the historic reopening of the world economy. Agreement was reached, at least in principle, whereby the world economy would abandon regional currency and trade groupings in favor of a liberal multilateral system. Third, Bretton Woods created an entirely new type of open system – something that the capitalist world had not seen before. The Anglo-American agreements established sophisticated rules that would attempt to reconcile openness and trade expansion with the commitments of national governments to full employment and economic stabilization. At its heart, the Bretton Woods accord was an unprecedented experiment in international economic constitution building. (1993, 155)

The task was as ambitious as it was difficult. The Bretton Woods architects aimed for a consistent framework that could overcome the problems of the interwar years, but as we have seen the policymakers' laggard theoretical approach and a series of significant events thrust the design back toward the gold exchange standard, whose defects were eventually aggravated by the call for activist economic policies. In essence, the increasing rigidity of the Americans about the actual rules of the game found its counterpart in the conservative position of other countries, thus turning the system away from the spirit of the treaty. In this respect, theory was crucial, in that the emergence of antithetical approaches produced inconsistencies that proved fatal to the Bretton Woods construction.

This failure offers several lessons for the future of monetary institutions. On a general plane, the difficulty of devising plans of monetary reform contrasts starkly with the smoothness of market-led processes of monetary evolution, like the gold standard. When the rules of the monetary system have to be designed by experts, the soundness and consistency of the paradigm chosen is essential to viability. A weak or backward theoretical apparatus or the presence of alternative models will likely give rise to imbalances and serious crises. In this connection, the demise of Bretton Woods is illuminating in that it originated from conflicting, incoherent approaches to monetary economics and institutions. Gathering up the threads of this work, Bretton Woods can be seen as a last, vain attempt to revive a monetary order still linked to commodity money, the culmination of the complex interplay of the advance of economic theory and the disruptive shocks to the major economies and the monetary system between the world wars. The failure of this endeavor paved the way to fiat money, an unparalleled break in twenty-five hundred years of monetary history.

8.1. THE CRISIS OF THE POSTWAR MONETARY ORDER

The operation of the Bretton Woods system reflects the factors that brought about the abandonment of the spirit of the treaty. Following the course to convertibility set by the European Payments Union, countries found themselves constrained by the fixed exchange rate regime, which was perfectly consistent with the need to enhance the credibility of economic policies and with the American desire for financial discipline in other countries. Underlying these developments was the central bankers' cultural background still attached to the commodity standard, as is shown by the large-scale accumulation of gold by the main continental European countries and the importance ascribed to the Triffin dilemma. In this regard, the difference between those who put the inception of the dollar standard in the late sixties, and specifically in March 1968 with the end of the Gold Pool (Williamson 1985, 77; Bordo 1993, 74), and those who date the change to 1950 (McKinnon 1993, 15–6) is revealing because it stems from two distinct perspectives on Bretton Woods: the institutional, reflecting the central bankers' views in line with the letter of the accord,[1] and the theoretical, pointing out the conditions for viability in a system in which gold was losing its role. The slow adjustment of policymakers to changes in monetary arrangements, like the shift to the gold exchange standard after the First World War, was repeated after World War II, when the accelerating transition to fiat money was simply not understood. The mid-1960s were a watershed in the life of Bretton Woods: Before it, while the center country mostly stuck to the rules of the game, the others caused disequilibrium by constantly increasing their gold reserves; afterward, expansionary monetary and fiscal policies in the United States touched off the effects of those cumulative imbalances.

---

[1] As John Williamson wrote: "Bretton Woods ratified the gold-exchange standard, it did not legislate a dollar standard" (1985, 75).

The fixed-rate dollar standard required the United States to stabilize the price level and maintain fiscal discipline as well as a net international creditor position, while remaining passive in the foreign exchange market and keeping U.S. capital markets open to foreign governments and private parties. Until the mid-sixties, the United States essentially abided by these rules; in particular, it had met the basic condition of anchoring the world price level. In 1950–67, the U.S. inflation rate was the lowest of all the G7 countries, averaging 1.8 percent (G7 mean: 3.1 percent), and showed the lowest standard deviation: 1.9 (G7 mean: 3.1; *International Financial Statistics Yearbook, 1980*). At the same time, central bankers, failing to perceive the diffusion of the dollar standard and the underlying model, stepped up gold accumulation and put the system under undue pressure. Without a new conception of the monetary mechanism based on total detachment from commodity money, then, not even the most virtuous conduct by the center country could keep the new monetary order functioning.

That this inadequate conception was not confined to arch-conservative policymakers in continental Europe but was widely held also in the United States is indicative of the confusion in assessing monetary arrangements in the postwar years. In 1965, as the link with gold was steadily weakening and the dominant role of the United States had become a plain fact, Jacques Rueff emphasized the problem of the "solvency" of the dollar, pointing out the unstoppable deficit in the U.S. balance of payments and the seigniorage gained by the United States.[2] Rueff's opinion, far from

---

[2] The growing imbalances of the Bretton Woods system were graphically described in a long passage by Jacques Rueff that is worth quoting in full: "I wrote in 1961 that the West was risking a credit collapse and that the gold-exchange standard was a great danger for western civilization. If I did so, it is because I am convinced – and I am very emphatic on this point – that the gold-exchange standard attains to such a degree of absurdity that no human brain having the power to reason can defend it. What is the essence of the regime, and what is its difference from the gold standard? It is that when a country with a key currency has a deficit in its balance of payments – that is to say, the United States, for example – it pays the creditor country dollars, which end up with its central

singular and unconventional, was not at odds with the mainstream, the only difference lying in the solution proposed: While he suggested raising the price of gold and returning to an undiluted gold standard, the great majority, and most notably Triffin, called for an increase in international liquidity through the creation of new reserve assets. Yet everyone pointed to the dollar's convertibility into gold as the critical factor undermining confidence in the system. Thus, interviewing Rueff, Fred Hirsch remarked: "Many of us largely agree with your criticisms of the gold-exchange standard, which interestingly are much the same kind of criticisms as are made from the other wing by Triffin." And Rueff answered: "You have first named my friend Triffin. I must say that we are in full agreement on the diagnosis. We differ on the remedy, but the diagnosis is the same" (1965, 4).

These widely held tenets, however, were not immune from criticism. Despres, Kindleberger, and Salant (1966) contested the consensus view and put forward a diametrically opposite "minority view," according to which the U.S. capital market provided liquidity and banking services to both private agents and foreign governments so that the worry over American gold losses and external disequilibrium was unfounded. Had central bankers recognized these principles, the hasty conversion of dollars into gold and the consequent disruption of capital flows would have ceased:

[T]he point is that they [dollar holdings] not only provide external liquidity to other countries, but are a necessary counterpart of the intermediation which provides liquidity to Europe's savers and financial institutions. Recognition of this fact would end central bank conversions of dollars into gold, the resulting creeping decline of official reserves, and the disruption

bank. But the dollars are of no use in Bonn, or in Tokyo, or in Paris. The very same day, they are re-lent to the New York money market, so that they return to the place of origin. Thus the debtor country does not lose what the creditor country has gained. So the key-currency country never feels the effect of a deficit in its balance of payments. And the main consequence is that there is no reason whatever for the deficit to disappear, because it does not appear. Let me be more positive: if I had an agreement with my tailor that whatever money I pay him he returns to me the very same day as a loan, I would have no objection at all to ordering more suits from him" (1965, 2–3).

of capital flows to which it has led. (Despres, Kindleberger, and Salant 1966, 528)

The paper by Despres et al., which appeared not in some obscure academic journal but in *The Economist*, cast light on the subject, showing a new way of looking at the monetary system. Already in the early 1950s, Milton Friedman (1953a, 191–2) had pointed out the declining role of gold in postwar monetary arrangements, arguing for flexible exchange rates and treating gold like any other commodity. Restating this position a few years later, Friedman stigmatized the backwardness of economists on the issue:

Only a cultural lag leads us still to think of gold as the central element in our monetary system. A more accurate description of the role of gold in U.S. policy is that it is primarily a commodity whose price is supported, like wheat or other agricultural products, rather than the key to our monetary system. (1960, 81)

The economist's box of tools for tackling the growing instability of Bretton Woods was not empty, then, but these original ideas clashed head-on with the mainstream and were mostly regarded as curiosities. The minority view failed to shake the consensus, which considered the growth of dollar assets as a serious problem undermining confidence in the dollar and called for the correction of the U.S. balance-of-payments deficits and the creation of new instruments of international liquidity. Paradoxically, the alleged shortcomings of the system had already been disposed of by the role played by the United States as the nth country in Mundell's redundancy problem, thus filling the void that sapped the viability of the postwar monetary order. But all countries, including the United States, failed to recognize these developments, showing policymakers' sheer lack of understanding of how the system actually worked.[3] As Despres et al. contended, the confidence problem

---

[3] In this regard, Ronald McKinnon remarks: "The alternative solution [to detailed negotiations among all N countries] to the redundancy problem is both simple and elegant. If a natural candidate exists, assign one of the N countries to be the passive Nth country,

stemmed from a misleading policy stance. On the other hand, private investors, fully grasping this policy design, did not lose confidence in the dollar and reacted accordingly.

> Such lack of confidence in the dollar as now exists has been generated by the attitudes of government officials, central bankers, academic economists, and journalists, and reflects their failure to understand the implications of this intermediary function. Despite some contagion from these sources, the private market retains confidence in the dollar, as increases in private holdings of liquid dollar assets show. Private speculation in gold is simply the result of the known attitudes and actions of governmental officials and central bankers.... Although there has been private speculation in gold against the dollar, it has been induced largely by reluctance of some central banks to accumulate dollars. (Despres, Kindleberger, and Salant 1966, 526–7)

Underlying the policymakers' destabilizing behavior was their boundless trust in a monetary construction resting on the keystone of gold. In fact, the large-scale accumulation of gold in Europe was due not to the one-way bet on a rise in the price of gold but to the central bankers' *Weltanschauung*, which blinded them to the substantial transformation of the monetary system. This was the view not just of a few conservatives but of the mainstream. With hindsight, the consensus in Europe and the United States was defective, while the analyses of Friedman, Despres, and Mundell more correctly account for the main features of the postwar monetary setup. Yet these insights remained unheeded, so the gap between the evolution of monetary arrangements and the policymakers' obsolete paradigm widened into a gulf that eventually drove the system to irreversible crisis.

The special role of the United States arose spontaneously, driven by market forces behind the diffusion of a vehicle currency that,

and leave the other N-1 countries responsible for setting their par values and balance-of-payments targets independently. That corresponds precisely to the 10 rules for the Fixed-Rate Dollar Standard from 1950 to 1970. But this was the monetary order from which the United States was trying to escape!" (1993, p. 26).

from a theoretical point of view, mirrors the origin of money (Menger 1892; Jones 1976). The information-producing mechanism inherent in the development of an exchange medium is replicated at the international level, leading all countries to converge on the use of a single currency internationally. The smoothness of this market-led process contrasts with the difficulty of designing reform schemes based on a supranational money, like the Keynes Plan, arising from the problem of sharing sovereignty (see Chapter 6, Section 1 and note 8).

The spread of an international money is a quite resilient phenomenon because, as Paul Krugman (1984) has shown, it involves an element of circularity: The use of a currency as a vehicle itself reinforces that currency's usefulness. Hence, only a particularly disruptive shock can alter the equilibrium and usher in a new international money. Throughout history, the currencies of the dominant powers have succeeded one another as international monies: the Roman-Byzantine monetary order, which lasted twelve centuries; the Venetian ducat of the late Middle Ages; Spanish domination in the early Renaissance, later challenged by the Dutch; and sterling three centuries later (Mundell 1972, 92–5).

For nearly three millennia, monetary turning points ultimately stemmed from the political decline of the dominant power. Strong governments could prevent competition in coinage and enforce seigniorage by inflicting cruel punishment (in medieval times, counterfeiters were boiled alive). On the other hand, in particular situations characterized by the absence or weakness of an imperial power, currencies circulated *ad pensum*. The maintenance of a pure commodity standard for very long periods, however, requires strict fiscal discipline. Moreover, unless new mines are discovered, it brings a deflationary bias that, as wages are sticky downward, negatively affects output and employment. Thus, as Keynes (1936, 306–9) remarked, in the course of history the most frequent solution to deflationary pressure was changing the monetary standard, not pushing down wage rates, which explains the secular rise in the price level.[4] In this connection, Keynes considered the relatively stable price movements of the nineteenth century as the outcome of especially favorable circumstances. The gold standard, the culmination of a process that began in the 1660s and in which coins were exchanged *ad pensum* (Mundell 1995, 21), represented a successful yet exceptional experience.

This brief historical digression suggests that the emergence of an international money is normally accompanied by the extraction of seigniorage by the dominant power that issues it. In the Bretton Woods monetary setting, the increasing role of the dollar put the question of seigniorage back in the spotlight, although inflation in the United States remained relatively small and stable until 1967. In this regard, several considerations are in order.

Despite the clash of opinions, majority and minority alike considered price stability in the United States essential to the viability of the system. Of course, to judge whether it is actually observed, the rule needs to be precisely specified. In recent times, the countries experimenting with inflation targeting have adopted various criteria: a 2–3 or 1–3 percent range (Australia and New Zealand); a 2 percent target + or − 1 percent (Canada and Sweden); and a 2 percent target supplemented by a reporting procedure when inflation moves away from the target by more than 1 percentage point in either direction (United Kingdom). For the European Central Bank, price stability has an upper bound of 2 percent. All in all, although it is pointless to single out "the" inflation rate that defines price stability, the 1.8 percent rate observed in the United States from 1950 to 1967 would satisfy even the strictest of today's standards.

Moreover, at least since David Hume (1752a), a case has been made for slightly increasing prices as a stimulus to output. A decreasing price level would have the opposite effect. Thus, the difficulty of precisely hitting a given rate of change of the price level would make a zero inflation target inadvisable, because it would run

---

4 Feliks Mlynarski (1936a) made the same point (see Chapter 4, Section 1, note 9).

the risk of deflation. And after the depression, deflation was deemed a most dreadful eventuality by both economists and policymakers, so theoretical arguments for a decreasing price level were ignored until Friedman's seminal contribution (1969a). Meanwhile, rejecting deflation, an inflation rate below two per cent could hardly be regarded as undermining the system's viability. Rather, the problem originated with the inadequate, confusing approach to the working of the postwar monetary order.

Had policymakers embraced an alternative analytical framework, reflecting the transformation of monetary arrangements toward a dollar standard, even the thorny issue of seigniorage might have proved more manageable. The United States, as the center country of the system, provided the rest of the world with liquidity services and took care of the viability of the fixed exchange rate system, partaking of the nature of an international public good. This applies to the unit-of-account function of money and, in particular, to the role of the dollar in invoicing international trade and pegging official parities. The unit-of-account function was likened by John Stuart Mill (1848, 483) to "a common language," one of the advantages of the use of money. Albeit the classics, and Mill is no exception, held that the essential function of money, from which all the others originate, is the medium-of-exchange function, the different functions reinforce one another, fostering the diffusion of the vehicle currency.[5]

---

[5] The issue reflects the multifaceted nature of money and, more generally, the complexity of monetary theory. In this connection, the change of approach in Keynes's trilogy is crucial. While the opening sentence of the *Tract* underlines the medium-of-exchange function, the very beginning of the *Treatise* stresses the unit-of-account function and, finally, the *General Theory* highlights the store-of-value function. This brings in a further aspect of the complexity of monetary theory in that the threefold functional distinction elicits different concepts of the "price of money" – witness the clash between Milton Friedman and James Tobin on monetarism. Friedman states: "For the monetarist/non-monetarist dichotomy, I suspect that the simplest litmus test would be the conditioned reflex to the question, 'What is the price of money?' The monetarist will answer, 'The inverse of the price level'; the non-monetarist (Keynesian or central banker) will answer, 'the interest rate.' The key difference is whether the stress is on money viewed as an asset with special characteristics, or on credit and credit markets, which leads to the

Of course, in a world of fiat money the vehicle currency is virtually costless and seigniorage cannot be thought of as a fee charged to users. Nonetheless, under the fixed-rate dollar standard the center country bore a different kind of cost – namely, a rigorous monetary and fiscal stance. Indeed, the extra degree of freedom giving rise to Mundell's redundancy problem, far from allowing the nth country wide discretion on economic policy, entailed the responsibility of maintaining a stable price level to anchor the system. Given the dominance of Keynesian economics, this was a truly binding constraint involving a significant cost.[6] Had these features been recognized as distinctive of the dollar standard, countries might have been less sensitive to seigniorage, viewing it as the price paid to the United States for bearing the cost of forsaking greater flexibility in economic policy. It is also worth noting that the amount of seigniorage was small, given the low U.S. inflation rate and the limited share of dollar holdings in the form of monetary base.

There was, instead, a general failure to grasp the substantial changes in the monetary system and their implications for the emerging dollar standard. This conservative attitude put the monetary framework under increasing strain. From the mid-1960s, the United States implemented a conspicuous fiscal expansion,[7] which

analysis of monetary policy and monetary change operating through organized 'money,' i.e., 'credit,' markets, rather than through actual and desired cash balances" (1976, 316). And Tobin retorts: "Friedman's own litmus paper test, 'What is the price of money?' is fun at cocktail parties. But some of my friends are good enough capital theorists to question the question. They can recognize *both* the purchasing power value of a dollar bill and the per annum opportunity cost of holding a dollar bill rather than some other asset. Others are good enough Marshallians or Walrasians to reject Friedman's favorite money–credit dichotomy. They suspect that 'monetary policy and monetary change' operate *both* through credit markets and through 'actual and desired cash balances'" (1976, 335; italics in the original).

[6] The abandonment of the Keynesian paradigm came much later, years after Milton Friedman's presidential address to the American Economic Association (1968a). The pathbreaking character of this contribution was not fully appreciated until the stagflation of the 1970s, which Friedman's analysis had actually explained in advance.

[7] U.S. monetary policy, however, had already become more expansionary at the beginning of the 1960s (Niehans 1976). In the same period, capital movements began to be liberalized and the official dollar liabilities held by foreign central banks passed U.S. gold reserves in 1964.

contrasted with the monetary and fiscal discipline, consistent with the fixed exchange rate regime, pursued by the other countries.[8] This divergence in economic policy strategies combined with the poor understanding of the transition toward a dollar standard to make the crisis inevitable. Indeed, the fact that "in the 1960s, intense schizophrenia afflicted the managers of the system" (McKinnon 1993, 19) is explained by the policymakers' misperception of the changing monetary environment and of the real rules of the game, giving them the sensation of being virtually powerless to buttress the Bretton Woods system.[9]

The diminishing role of gold, the consequent loss of relevance of the Triffin dilemma, and the functions performed by the United States as the center country of the system were all elements that slipped by practically unnoticed, and even if perceived they were not entirely understood. Policymakers, focusing on the wrong problems and the wrong model, set off cumulative imbalances that led to the undoing of the system. All in all, there was an inadequate grasp, by mainstream economists as well, of the novel factors at work, so that, failing the adoption of correct measures, the system drifted ineluctably toward a transition to fiat money.[10]

[8] The United Kingdom was an exception. The peculiarity of the British position has been noted, in a different context, by McKinnon: "This theorizing on the need for more exchange rate flexibility was prompted by numerous sterling crises in the 1950s and 1960s – which reflected attempts by the British government, under the strong influence of British Keynesians, to be more inflationary than the confines of the dollar standard allowed. But Britain was not typical" (1993, 23).

[9] In this connection, Niehans (1978, 165) points out the incorrectness of the remedies called for by the United States to redress the system – that is, the revaluation of European currencies and more expansionary policies in Europe: The former would have decreased the price of gold in terms of European currencies, thus hastening the gold drain; the latter, by raising the level of world prices and the European price level relative to the American price level, would have heightened disequilibrium. For Niehans, the right solution was an increase in the price of gold accompanied by noninflationary policies, underlying an interpretation of Bretton Woods akin to the gold exchange standard. This was hardly workable, however, because, apart from the unpalatability of dollar devaluation, during the previous half century the system had moved away from the commodity standard and the dominance of Keynesian economics had produced a further jump in that direction.

[10] Recalling the rising international role of the dollar since the 1920s, Mundell noted: "Initially the dollar borrowed prestige from gold. But as with the pound and the guilder

Viewed from a historical perspective, then, Bretton Woods emerges as the last stage of the move to fiat money, a change in kind rather than in degree that economists did not fully perceive until it was completed. The slowness of this transformation accounts for the hybrid nature of Bretton Woods, combining the novel quest for activist economic policies with the traditional attachment to fixed exchange rates.[11] Seen in this light, the enigma of Bretton Woods emphasized by Eichengreen (see Chapter 1, Section 1) – namely its substantial success but short life – can be solved. In the aftermath of World War II, reconstruction sharply raised growth rates. At the same time, gold accumulation by a number of countries was not a source of imbalance because the United States held huge gold reserves and maintained price stability. These beneficial yet ephemeral effects lasted until the central bankers' failure to grasp the transition to the dollar standard met with the expansionary policies of the United States and rising capital mobility, so that the system's actual and perceived constraints – fixed exchange rates and the convertibility of the dollar into gold – stretched the fabric of the whole structure. Thus, the short-term benefits laid the basis for an accumulation of imbalances that would prove intractable.

To keep the system viable, the center country should have maintained price stability and a sound fiscal policy while the rest of the world, severing the obsolete link to commodity money, should

---

before it, the dollar itself assumed a role distinct from the relation it had with respect to gold. With or without gold the dollar has taken on a vitality of its own internationally, a fact not well understood by many economists several years ago who, quite rightly, had recognized the importance of gold convertibility but not the steady transformation away from the need for it" (1972, 96).

[11] In this regard, the different recipes suggested by those who deemed the postwar monetary order not inherently faulty but requiring more appropriate rules reflect the stretching of the Bretton Woods hybrid in two opposite directions – gold exchange standard and pure dollar standard – yielding two different solutions: an increase in the price of gold accompanied by noninflationary policies (Niehans 1978, 165) and a stable price level in the United States together with demonetization of gold (McKinnon 1993, 39). In the 1960s, these solutions, one seeming too conservative and the other too radical, did not appeal to the mainstream. Hence, neither approach was embraced and Bretton Woods was doomed.

have been willing to consider seigniorage as the price for the center country's forgoing activist economic policies. These conditions, however, could hardly be met because they clashed with the dominance of Keynesian economics and with the misperception of the substantial transformation of monetary arrangements. These conflicting forces put the new monetary order under increasing strains, which finally destroyed it.

8.2. THE ROLE OF THEORY

The influence of economic theory in shaping the main features, molding the operating rules, and ultimately deciding the fate of the monetary system is especially clear in the case of Bretton Woods, which was the first monetary order designed by experts. The contrast between the laggard view of the monetary mechanism and the diffusion of Keynesian economics, as we have seen, produced severe imbalances that sapped the new construction. The smooth working of monetary arrangements, in fact, depends not only on the soundness of the prevailing paradigm but also on the absence of rival approaches. Yet coexistence of a variety of models is not uncommon in economics, where, as in all social sciences, the phenomena under study are potentially affected by a large set of variables whose influence cannot entirely be excluded. To build a model, the economist must select a few variables, but a slight change in the selection can lead to distinct, often conflicting hypotheses. The main problem, then, is to single out the assumptions most relevant to account for the questions at hand and make correct predictions.

With regard to the Bretton Woods experience, except for Frank Graham economists underestimated the difficulty of reconciling the objectives of the new monetary setting – free multilateral trade, fixed exchange rates, and full employment – as well as the one-way bet brought about by the adjustable peg. In this connection, though capital controls were imposed as a precondition to borrow, their long-run efficacy in stifling the one-way bet is doubtful. Underlying the postwar monetary reconstruction, there were two parallel strands of economic theory, relating to the operation of the monetary mechanism and the equilibrium properties of the economy. On the one hand, the unanimous call for reestablishing fixed parities was consonant with the classical equilibrium approach. The ideal of irrevocable parities was so intrinsic to metallic standards that in 1887 Marshall predicted: "[T]he time will come at which it will be thought as unreasonable for any country to regulate its currency without reference to other countries as it will be to have signalling codes at sea which took no account of the signalling codes at sea of other countries" (quoted in Viner 1943, 193). The success of the gold standard then seemed to represent a considerable advance, putting an end to the monetary disorder of earlier centuries. On the other hand, in the aftermath of the depression, Keynes's *General Theory* provided the foundation for the quest for full employment. However, these approaches, which bear on the central analytical issues of monetary arrangements – the nature of money and the effects of changes in the money supply (see Chapter 1, Section 2) – were patently incompatible.

The conflict did not emerge at once, given the widespread support for fixed parities, recalling the overall stability during the gold standard as contrasted with the instability of flexible exchange rates after World War I. Even Keynes, the arch-opponent of the gold standard, was an adamant supporter of fixed exchange rates, although he clarified the conditions for changing parities in case of structural disequilibrium (Keynes 1943) and, in his last published paper (1946), revived the classical price-specie-flow mechanism to account for long-run international adjustment. In any case, despite these brilliant intellectual acrobatics, the pursuit of full employment in a fixed exchange regime was an inherent inconsistency of the new monetary order, which was accentuated in the 1960s, in the heyday of Keynesian economics, and eventually proved to be fatal. Thus, David Laidler, recalling the importance of Keynes's contributions as the groundwork of the expansionary policies implemented before and after World War II, remarked:

[O]n the theoretical front, Keynes' (1936) *General Theory* was widely read as providing a foundation for the discretionary fiscal policies that had come more and more into favour in the years preceding its publication. After World War 2, most advanced economies relied primarily on such policies to achieve their domestic goals.... The monetary authorities and governments of many of those same economies also tried to have their monetary cake and eat it too by adopting adjustable-peg exchange rate mechanisms. Under the Bretton Woods system, monetary policy was to be tied to a fixed exchange rate, and to that extent be rule guided, but only so long as this did not interfere with the pursuit of domestic employment goals. If it did, then the rule was to be changed to create room for monetary policy to accommodate the discretionary fiscal measures needed to hit the latter. This system came under severe strain in the 1960s, and collapsed at the beginning of the 1970s. The factors that brought the Bretton Woods System down, and continued to plague the international monetary system in the 1990s, are the tendency, recognised as we have seen for two hundred years now, of external and internal monetary problems to arise together, their need for opposite remedies, and the reluctance of so many politicians and central bankers to face these facts of economic life, and make a choice between the systematic pursuit of *either* domestic *or* exchange rate stability." (2002, 26–7; italics in the original)[12]

The problems marring the viability of Bretton Woods can be brought out from another perspective, that of the role of gold. After World War I, policymakers sought to restore the gold standard, but the more original economists proposed different arrangements suited to activist economic policies. In his notes for a speech to the National Liberal Club in December 1923, Keynes described the

---

[12] Laidler's closeness to Frank Graham's position (see the quotation on p. 179), underscores the modernity of Graham's approach. In this connection, Lauchlin Currie (1936) had argued for activist monetary policies, under both fixed and flexible exchange rates, in order to prevent instability stemming from uncontrolled capital flows. To forestall these costs, discussed by White (1933), Currie favored controls on capital movements.

progress of monetary theory as "one of the biggest jumps forward ever achieved in economic science" (CW 19, 160). The core idea was to bend the rules of the gold standard, in which policies and the economy as a whole adapted to the fixed parity, in order to stabilize the price level, output, and employment: "Now even if gold was stable over long periods, it cannot deal with short periods. For the cure for short period fluctuations depends on being able rapidly to expand or contract the volume of money" (CW 19, 160–1). But these propositions were quite radical at that time and had a negligible impact on the background of monetary authorities. Notwithstanding the spread of managed money, central bankers rejected the gold exchange standard and remained wedded to the gold standard. As Feliks Mlynarski noted:

The banks which apply the pure gold standard – in other words, those which do not include foreign exchange in their fundamental or secondary reserves – enjoy a higher prestige than those which apply the gold exchange standard. The former are regarded as a higher, the latter as a lower type of bank. The belief prevails that the first class has greater power and greater resources. Such a classification is devoid of scientific justification. Nevertheless it exists, and the Central Banks must reckon with it. As a result of it, banks tend to abandon the gold exchange standard as soon as the economic position of the country has improved and as soon as fairly large reserves have been amassed for the support of the currency. Thus the gold exchange standard is regarded as a transitory system, and Central Banks which have already accumulated considerable foreign exchange reserves endeavour to increase their stock of gold in order to raise their prestige thereby. Frequently, they do this without any real need. (1931, 89)

In the wake of the depression, the international monetary system came under scrutiny, with a focus on the problems created by the large-scale accumulation of gold in France and the United States. But gold remained important, symbolizing the discipline inherent in fixed exchange rates. Practical metallism was a die-hard policy principle that, resisting the evolution of monetary institutions away from commodity standards, survived in the shape of fixed parities. Hence, gold retained its place in the Bretton Woods accord. The cancellation of the role of gold by a group of experts after twenty-five hundred years of commodity money was almost inconceivable.

As noted in the previous section, however, Milton Friedman (1953a) boldly argued for a free gold market and flexible exchange rates, anticipating the monetary setup of two decades later. Acknowledging the exhaustion of gold's monetary functions, he called for flexible exchange rates and, later, for a domestic rule to ensure monetary discipline. But his analysis went unheeded. Policymakers' concern for confidence in the dollar, the Triffin dilemma, and the liquidity of the system continued unabated, paving the way to the collapse of Bretton Woods and the emergence of fiat money.[13] Friedman's felicitous intuition is a clear instance of choosing the right assumptions for modeling and of the lag characterizing the spread of original ideas. Keynes made the latter point in the often-quoted closing passages of the *General Theory*, where he emphasized the importance of economic theory, rather than of vested interests, in influencing the course of events.[14] Interestingly,

---

[13] In all the vast literature on Bretton Woods (see Chapter 7, Section 2), no mention is made of the possible development of fiat money. The tendency toward "independent monetary management on a national scale" (Triffin 1947a, 54) was recognized, but not a definitive break with the commodity standard. Actually, the only reference to the transition to fiat money was by Benjamin Graham (1947, 305–6), talking about the U.K. and the U.S. experience in the 1930s. Also, as early as 1949, Frank Graham (see Chapter 7, note 21) forecast the downfall of Bretton Woods, highlighting the demise of gold and the inconsistency of fixed parities with independent monetary policies.

[14] "[T]he ideas of economists and political philosophers, both when they are right and when they are wrong, are more powerful than is commonly understood. Indeed the world is ruled by little else. . . . I am sure that the power of vested interests is vastly exaggerated compared with the gradual encroachment of ideas. Not, indeed, immediately, but after a certain interval; for in the field of economic and political philosophy there are not many who are influenced by new theories after they are twenty-five or thirty years of age, so that the ideas which civil servants and politicians and even agitators apply to current events are not likely to be the newest. But, soon or late, it is ideas, not vested interests, which are dangerous for good or evil" (1936, 383–4). Keynes made a similar remark in his letter to George Bernard Shaw in January 1935 (see Chapter 6, note 28).

Hayek stressed the same concepts in analyzing the implications of the prevalence of managed money for international stability (see Chapter 5, note 8) where, in the final page, he remarked: "I do believe that in the long run human affairs are guided by intellectual forces" (Hayek 1937, 94).

The whole Bretton Woods story, from the painstaking design of the system to its demise, offers corroboration. As we argued in Chapter 7, the supposed lack of influence of Keynes's contributions on the postwar monetary reconstruction appears unfounded. Although the Keynes Plan quickly appeared too radical to be accepted, the treaty was imbued with the message of the *General Theory*. Furthermore, even if the game was played by the old gold exchange standard rules, the objective of full employment was now essential. Actually, it was the clash between the center country's Keynesian policy stance and the fixed exchange rate regime that struck the fatal blow to the Bretton Woods monetary order. Indeed, most of the explanations for the system's collapse – the structural flaws, such as the gold exchange standard and fixed but adjustable parities; the U.S. failure to stabilize prices after 1965; and the industrial countries' reluctance to adopt the American policy and their concentration on their own goals (Bordo 1993, 83) – can be traced to the undisputed dominance of Keynesian economics and the employment objective.

The Bretton Woods rules reveal only the specific aspects of a more general problem caused by wrapping a rigid institutional arrangement, similar to the gold exchange standard, in an approach that blossomed into the maintenance of full employment. In particular, it was thought that the return to fixed exchange rates would reestablish a smoothly working system, but it was inherently at variance with activist economic policies. This conflict, only latent in the gold exchange standard, became blatant when the *General Theory* came to hold sway.

Perhaps the real contribution of Bretton Woods was its idealistic stimulus for the liberalization of international trade, a principle already enshrined in the Atlantic Charter. Progress along this road was necessarily slow and, so far as multilateral trade was concerned, was in any case achieved through other organizations, such as the European Payments Union. The success of the 1944 agreements was only seeming; the shakiness of its foundations led the new international monetary system into an inextricable crisis.

8.3. THE INTERNATIONAL MONETARY SYSTEM IN PERSPECTIVE

The end of the Bretton Woods monetary order was a watershed in world monetary history. Definitively removing the residual role of gold after twenty-five hundred years, it led to the emergence of fiat money. This epochal transformation shifts the focus of analysis from the exchange rate regime to the money object and the basic properties of monetary arrangements. Following the demise of fixed exchange rates, the current monetary setting has often been defined as a "nonsystem," in view of the contrast between its unstructured nature and Bretton Woods or the gold standard. This assessment, however, may merely refer to the absence of formal rules, certainly not to the lack of a model, which is in fact readily identifiable in the theory of competitive money supply (Klein 1974), applied to an international context.[15]

Benjamin Klein challenged the case for monopoly in money issue, showing that this is founded on indistinguishability between currencies. In a world of imperfect information, if product quality cannot be evaluated by the goods' physical characteristics, consumers rely on brand names. Fiat money is a case in point. Quality and brand name relate respectively to price stability and predictability. Brand name is a capital asset for the issuer, who invests resources optimally to increase the present discounted value of his profit stream. Because future money supply paths are unknown

---

[15] The extension of Klein's hypothesis to international monetary arrangements is examined in detail in Cesarano (1999b).

(otherwise, brand names would be valueless identification marks), agents estimate the probability of deception by the issuers and their eventual gains, thus determining the equilibrium value of the brand name capital.

Klein's intellectually appealing hypothesis may be hard to apply to a domestic setting because market forces would lead to the selection of one currency. And even conceiving the circulation of several monies within a country on purely abstract grounds, a further difficulty is that the viability of the scheme depends on having flexible exchange rates to make Gresham's Law inoperative. The post–Bretton Woods developments, instead, breaking all ties with commodity money and spreading flexible exchange rates, ushered in a scenario that exactly fits Klein's model, one in which each country issues its own, perfectly distinguishable, fiat money. The large, lasting fall in the inflation rate in the past quarter century, as contrasted with the inflationary spurt of the 1970s, corroborates the competitive money supply hypothesis. On this theory, high confidence money drives out low confidence money because consumers evaluate the predictability of money's future exchange value. Hence, in a competitive setting, there is an incentive for price stabilization even in the absence of rules. A country can gain from raising seigniorage revenue but at the cost of depreciating its brand name capital. Thus, it faces a dynamic optimization problem that also includes noneconomic objectives, such as political hegemony for the issuer of the vehicle currency and participation in a financial and economic community for others.

Monetary stability in a fiat money world may appear somewhat surprising, given the absence of constraints on countries' behavior, but it is the product of competition. On the other hand, the stability of the gold standard stemmed from strict rules of the game, taking control of the money supply out of the hands of the authorities and equalizing price trends across countries. It may seem odd, if not downright paradoxical, that diametrically opposite arrangements produce similar results, yet it is simply an instance of the general principle that clear-cut models of monetary organization are superior to hybrids. Indeed, as we shall see, large-scale innovation and sharp competition in the payments industry may transform monetary arrangements so deeply as to revive some central properties of commodity standards.

In the international economy, the one-to-one correspondence between countries and currencies is not just a manifestation of national sovereignty but also an implication of monetary theory. The essential role of money as an information-producing mechanism allowing the decentralization of exchange entails the circulation of a single medium of exchange, which in order to minimize accounting costs (Niehans 1978, 121) coincides with the unit of account. Underlying the development of a monetary economy is a market-led process that converges toward a single currency. At the dawn of monetary history, the government may have commanded a higher reputation in certifying the quantity and quality of the money commodity, soon learning the possibility of extracting seigniorage. Thus, the early appropriation by governments of the issuing function is congruent with the sizeable welfare gains of the introduction of money. Indeed, the essential properties of money are so pervasive and resilient that, as Friedman and Schwartz (1986, 44) note, no resort to alternative currencies is observed during periods of strongly increasing prices. Excepting major hyperinflations, the welfare gains generated by the circulating money are so high that people, even in the presence of huge costs of holding it, do not shift to a different currency.

Given the tendency of monetary sovereignty and political sovereignty to coincide under the centripetal forces of an exchange economy, in the international scenario countries act like maximizing agents in search of the optimal monetary arrangements and policy design. After the demise of fixed exchange rates, a country may consider the alternative of participating in a monetary union. However, the analytical groundwork underlying the calculus of participation – the theory of optimum currency areas – remains controversial. The traditional approach, static in character and based on price and wage rigidity, suggests several optimality criteria corresponding to exogenous characteristics of the economy. The variegated and partially conflicting nature of these criteria betrays the weak foundations of the traditional approach,[16] which in reality is an application of Tinbergen's theory of economic policy, where the extension of the currency area is the instrument of the optimization problem. As such, it clashes with the new classical macroeconomics, and in particular with the Lucas critique, because it disregards the agents' response to policy measures.

This modern research program suggests an equilibrium approach to optimum currency areas (Cesarano 1997; Frankel and Rose 1998; Alesina and Barro 2002), in which agents weigh the impact of national borders as of any other policy. The equilibrium approach overturns the received view, in that optimality is the outcome of individual maximizing behavior, not of exogenously given features. Within a country, the agents' information set is larger, because knowledge of institutions, market regulations, language, and the like increases the availability of data and the model's explanatory power. The costs and benefits of internal migration, for instance, are much easier to assess than those of international migration, where wider wage differentials are needed to prompt expatriation. Labor mobility, therefore, is not an exogenous quality of the economy but the product of rational behavior. This principle also applies, in different degrees, to other optimality criteria – openness to trade, the similarity of cycles, and the implementation of fiscal policies – which are thus endogenous to the currency area, not inborn features of the economy.

---

[16] In this connection, Paul Krugman criticized the "loose-jointed theory" (1993, 3) that matches the costs of lost monetary independence with the benefits of fixed rates, emphasizing the lack of a model of the microeconomics of money to analyze the latter. And Niehans, in his textbook, remarked: "Optimum currency areas are still a concept in search of a theory" (1984, 294). The analysis of this subject is based on Cesarano (1997); other topics dealt with later in this section – that is, the optimum quantity of money and the effectiveness of monetary policy – draw on Cesarano (1998b; 1998c).

In general, the efficacy of the adjustment mechanism is greatest within national borders, where equilibrating forces are enhanced: The effects of interregional money flows are inescapable (Mundell 1961, 660), a common legal and institutional framework exists, the larger information set reduces uncertainty in decision making, and fiscal transfers are possible. In an equilibrium model, under the extreme assumptions of a full-information, frictionless world, the issue would entirely vanish. But, of course, we do not live in such a world, so countries may not actually correspond to optimum currency areas. In this connection, the Economic and Monetary Union in Europe is peculiar and provides an interesting case study inasmuch as, running counter to the historical record, monetary unification has preceded political unification. The introduction of a common fiat money between sovereign states, still divided by national borders, is a singular experiment, at odds with the high degree of flexibility and integration underlying an equilibrium setting.

Optimum currency areas, however, is but one concept of optimality. Money is a multifaceted phenomenon, analyzable from several perspectives yet maintaining an underlying unity.[17] Parallel to the progress of monetary theory, the evolution of monetary arrangements is spurred by the search for less costly payments media and conditioned by the state of technology,[18] which are both intertwined with the growth of the banking industry. The interplay of these different factors crops up in implementing the optimum quantity of money. The rule set forth in Friedman's seminal contribution (1969a) – a rate of deflation equal to the rate of time

[17] In this respect, Milton Friedman noted: "Monetary theory is like a Japanese garden. It has esthetic unity born of variety; an apparent simplicity that conceals a sophisticated reality; a surface view that dissolves in ever deeper perspectives. Both can be fully appreciated only if examined from many different angles, only if studied leisurely but in depth. Both have elements that can be enjoyed independently of the whole, yet attain their full realization only as part of the whole" (1969, v).

[18] A good example is the introduction of steam-powered stamping presses that, hampering counterfeiting, fostered the diffusion of the gold standard in England in the early 1800s (Redish 1990).

preference bringing the nominal interest rate down to zero and real money balances to the satiation level – was soon criticized because, with money and bonds yielding the same return, the bond market would disappear. The origin of this problem (Cesarano 1998c) is that while the stock marginal utility of money can be driven to zero by increasing real cash balances through deflation, its flow marginal utility – that is, the utility of an additional dollar spent – remains positive. The weakness of the Friedman rule is that it sets the analysis of fiat money as a free good in general equilibrium theory, not in a model of a monetary economy. However, although the informational role of money can be played by a valueless instrument like paper money, it still retains positive purchasing power and flow marginal utility. Thus, driving the stock marginal utility of money to zero, instead of satiating people with cash balances, makes the demand for money insatiable.

This impediment may be overcome by payment technology. If tangible media of exchange vanish and are replaced by an accounting system run by banks (Fama 1980), we no longer have an asset commanding a liquidity premium, hence no interest rate differential between bonds and money. But this setup falls foul of Wicksell's problem of price level indeterminacy, whose solution requires central bank control of a nominal quantity (Patinkin 1961, 113–6). Fama's suggestion (1980, 55) of introducing currency might convey the misleading idea that, except for its greater efficiency, the new monetary setting would then be analogous to the present one. In an accounting system of exchange, however, the sole rationale for a constant stock of currency[19] is to make the price level determinate, a technical requirement like fixing the unit of account in the gold standard. This requirement is necessary to viability; thus, radically different in nature from other monetary rules, it should be less exposed to pressures to break it.

---

[19] Consistent with the Friedman rule, the stock of currency may be allowed to increase if the growth of the economy brings about a greater than optimal deflation rate.

A highly advanced exchange system, therefore, may paradoxically reinstate some of the central properties of ancient commodity standards. In a world of nontangible money, to ensure price level determinacy each country issues a given quantity of a fiat instrument, connected to the others by fixed parities with no fluctuation margins. As in the gold standard, an escape clause may allow a country to suspend the rule in exceptional circumstances, changing the quantity of currency once and for all.

The various topics touched upon in analyzing the consequences of Bretton Woods – the competitive money supply, optimum currency areas, and the optimum quantity of money – though seemingly unrelated, are actually bound together by the concept of equilibrium. Thus, competitive equilibrium forces prevented an inflationary drift after the demise of commodity money, even in the absence of binding monetary rules. Also, the equilibrium hypothesis underlying individual maximizing behavior heightens the effectiveness of the adjustment mechanism inside a country, fostering the optimality of a currency area within its political borders. And, finally, the welfare economics proposition on the optimum quantity of money might be implemented by future technological progress in the payments industry, driven by the search for a less costly medium of exchange. In application, these topics concern the efficiency of monetary arrangements and are, albeit at a lower level of abstraction, variations on the same theme: the theory of economic policy. In investigating monetary reforms, therefore, the conditions for their effectiveness must be considered.

In this respect, the availability of information is crucial. Assuming that information is neither complete nor entirely unavailable but is a scarce commodity optimally allocated like any other good, then in order to revise their expectations individuals must get a net benefit from gathering and processing information. If the model's explanatory power increases with the amplitude of policy measures (the effect on the price level of doubling the money stock can be more precisely predicted than that of a 1 percent variation), the cost and benefit of treating information are a negative and positive function respectively of policy amplitude: The smaller the policy action, the less individuals are induced to revise their expectations, because this involves a net loss. Thus, agents' responsiveness and the efficiency of predictions depend on the amplitude of the policy action (Cesarano 1998b). This hypothesis, focusing on the dimension of the agents' information set relative to that of policy measures, explains the effectiveness of moderate policy actions. Beyond the critical point at which the cost and benefit functions of processing information cross, a change in exogenous or policy variables triggers agents' response and thus produces only nominal effects. In this connection, the empirical evidence presented by Lucas (2003) in his presidential address to the American Economic Association is consistent with this conjecture. Looking at the U.S. experience over the past fifty years, Lucas rules out the possibility of a sizeable improvement in the economy's performance because the gain from removing consumption variability through better countercyclical policies does not exceed a tenth of a percent. He recognizes that the existence of rigidities requires the implementation of stabilization policies, but the potential for welfare gains is limited.

The equilibrium model is a theoretical benchmark against which the actual features of the economy must be set when evaluating policy effectiveness and, in particular, a given monetary setting. As these features – availability of information, absence of rigidities, and efficiency of the institutional and legal framework – approximate the assumptions underlying the equilibrium hypothesis, the propositions of the classical model hold. At the limit, the equilibrium model leads to a single world money, an ideal case pursued by many reformers and approached by the gold standard: As Milton Friedman remarked, "[T]he gold standard . . . came very close to being a unified currency" (1968b, 268). Conversely, as uncertainty rises and frictions increase, this model is removed to various degrees from applicability and the scope for policy action widens. Then the question of which model is relevant has no clear-cut answer, depending on the characteristics of the economy.[20] These, in turn, are indirectly affected by theory. Since the end of the 1970s, for instance, the sweeping changes in public policies, particularly monetary policy and market deregulation, were the product of the revival of the classical paradigm.

The role of economic policy generally stems from the incompleteness of information, a pervasive characteristic of economics, central to the topical effort to construct a new financial architecture. Yet one lesson of Bretton Woods is the difficulty of designing monetary arrangements at the drawing board. This applies even more to the current, radically new monetary environment that emerged from the spread of fiat money, in which the essential properties of commodity standards have vanished. Fixed parities, strict discipline in economic policy, stabilizing capital movements – all are remembrances of a bygone age. Reinstating them is hardly conceivable; lacking the ground rules underlying them, it would be like erecting a building without foundations.

Nowadays, increasingly differentiated patterns characterize and distinguish the monetary from the financial side of the international monetary system. While progress in payment technology makes the system more efficient, the sheer expansion and greater complexity of financial intermediation elicits new institutions, a typical feature of evolving monetary arrangements (Hicks 1967a,

---

[20] Accounting for the stability of the postwar U.S. economy relative to the interwar years, Robert Lucas credited both Keynesian and monetarist economists for supporting suitable demand management policies. This ecumenical conclusion rests on the assumption of significant but not quite complete information. (For an early criticism of the rational expectations hypothesis that highlights the incompleteness of information, see B. Friedman 1979.) Contrasting the static theory of general equilibrium of Patinkin's *Money, Interest, and Prices* with modern theory, Lucas remarks: "For us, today, value theory refers to models of dynamic economies subject to unpredictable shocks, populated by agents who are good at processing information and making choices over time. The macroeconomic research I have discussed today makes essential use of value theory in this modern sense: formulating explicit models, computing solutions, comparing their behavior quantitatively to observed time series and other data sets. As a result, we are able to form a much sharper quantitative view of the potential of changes in policy to improve peoples' lives than was possible a generation ago" (2003, 12).

Chapter 1). In a future perspective, the design of rules and provisions will reflect this dichotomy, tilting the balance toward financial issues. However, intervention in this field is impeded by the lack of a supranational political authority. National sovereignty starts in the realm of politics, of course; but in the monetary arena, it rests on an economic basis as well. As noted, the uniqueness of money inside a country is dictated by theory – that is, by the principles underlying an exchange as against a Walrasian economy. Also, on the macroeconomic plane the adjustment mechanism is enhanced within national borders by the fact that both the agents' information set and the policymaker's toolkit are more extensive. Hence, there is likely to be little willingness to part with substantial shares of sovereignty, so designing a comprehensive set of rules, like Bretton Woods, now seems quite utopian. In the new scenario, the need for other kinds of provisions will be based on different rationales, such as the solution to price level indeterminacy, that may not be immediately envisaged. In this state of flux, it is to the factors underlying the evolution of monetary arrangements – the advancement of economic theory, the occurrence of major shocks, and innovation in payment technology and in the financial industry – that we should again look at as the driving forces of the evolutionary process.

REFERENCES

Addis, Charles. [1923] 1981. Letter to Keynes, 21 December 1923. In Donald Moggridge, ed. *The Collected Writings of John Maynard Keynes*, Vol. 19. London: Macmillan, p. 163.

Addis, Charles. 1924a. Discussion on Monetary Reform. *Economic Journal* 34(June): 166–9.

Addis, Charles. [1924b] 1981. Letter to Keynes, 21 July 1924. In Donald Moggridge, ed. *The Collected Writings of John Maynard Keynes*, Vol. 19. London: Macmillan, pp. 268–9.

Alesina, Alberto, and Barro, Robert J. 2002. Currency Unions. *Quarterly Journal of Economics* 117(May): 409–36.

Allen, William R. 1993. Irving Fisher and the 100 percent Reserve Proposal. *Journal of Law and Economics* 36(October): 703–17.

Angell, James W. 1922. International Trade Under Inconvertible Paper. *Quarterly Journal of Economics* 36(May): 359–412.

Angell, James W. [1933] 1967. Monetary Control and General Business Stabilization. In *Economic Essays in Honour of Gustav Cassel. October 20th 1933*. London: Frank Cass, pp. 53–68.

Angell, James W. 1937. The General Objectives of Monetary Policy. In Arthur D. Gayer, ed. *The Lessons of Monetary Experience: Essays in Honor of Irving Fisher*. London: George Allen and Unwin, pp. 50–88.

Bayoumi, Tamim, Eichengreen, Barry, and Taylor, Mark P. 1996. Modern Perspectives on the Gold Standard: Introduction. In Tamim Bayoumi, Barry Eichengreen, and Mark P. Taylor, eds. *Modern Perspectives on the Gold Standard*. Cambridge: Cambridge University Press, pp. 3–16.

Beale, W. T. M., Jr., Kennedy, M. T., and Winn, Willis J. 1942. Commodity Reserve Currency: A Critique. *Journal of Political Economy* 50(August): 579–94.

Bellerby, J. R. 1924. The Monetary Policy of the Future. *Economic Journal* 34(June): 177–87.

References

Bernanke, Ben S. 1993. The World on a Cross of Gold: A Review of "Golden Fetters: The Gold Standard and the Great Depression, 1919–1939." *Journal of Monetary Economics* 31(April): 251–67.

Bernstein, Edward M. 1944. A Practical International Monetary Policy. *American Economic Review* 34(December): 771–84.

Bernstein, Edward M. 1945. Scarce Currencies and the International Monetary Fund. *Journal of Political Economy* 53(March): 1–14.

Bickerdike, C. F. 1920. The Instability of Foreign Exchange. *Economic Journal* 30(March): 118–22.

Bickerdike, C. F. 1922. Internal and External Purchasing Power of Paper Currencies. *Economic Journal* 32(March): 28–38.

Black, Fischer. 1970. Banking and Interest Rates in a World Without Money: The Effects of Uncontrolled Banking. *Journal of Bank Research* 1(3): 9–20.

Blaug, Mark. 1997. *Economic Theory in Retrospect.* Cambridge: Cambridge University Press.

Block, Fred L. 1977. *The Origins of International Economic Disorder: A Study of United States International Monetary Policy from World War II to the Present.* Berkeley: University of California Press.

Bloomfield, Arthur I. 1947. Discussion of "International Monetary Policy and the Search for Economic Stability" by Ragnar Nurkse. *American Economic Review: Papers and Proceedings* 37(May): 581–3.

Bloomfield, Arthur I. 1959. *Monetary Policy Under the International Gold Standard: 1880–1914.* New York: Federal Reserve Bank of New York.

Bordo, Michael D. 1984. The Gold Standard: The Traditional Approach. In Michael D. Bordo and Anna J. Schwartz, eds. *A Retrospective on the Classical Gold Standard, 1821–1931.* Chicago: University of Chicago Press, pp. 23–113.

Bordo, Michael D. 1993. The Bretton Woods International Monetary System: A Historical Overview. In Michael D. Bordo and Barry Eichengreen, eds. *A Retrospective on the Bretton Woods System: Lessons for International Monetary Reform.* Chicago: University of Chicago Press, pp. 3–98.

Bordo, Michael D., Choudhri, Ehsan U., and Schwartz, Anna J. 2002. Was Expansionary Monetary Policy Feasible During the Great Contraction? An Examination of the Gold Standard Constraint. *Explorations in Economic History* 39(January): 1–28.

Bordo, Michael D., and Eichengreen, Barry, eds. 1993. *A Retrospective on the Bretton Woods System: Lessons for International Monetary Reform.* Chicago: University of Chicago Press.

Bordo, Michael D., and Eichengreen, Barry. 1998. Implications of the Great Depression for the Development of the International Monetary System. In Michael D. Bordo, Claudia Goldin, and Eugene N. White, eds. *The Defining*

Moment: The Great Depression and the American Economy in the Twentieth Century. Chicago: University of Chicago Press, pp. 403–53.

Bordo, Michael D., Goldin, Claudia, and White, Eugene N., eds. 1998. *The Defining Moment: The Great Depression and the American Economy in the Twentieth Century.* Chicago: University of Chicago Press.

Bordo, Michael D., and Kydland, Finn E. 1995. The Gold Standard As a Rule: An Essay in Exploration. *Explorations in Economic History* 32(October): 423–64.

Bordo, Michael D., and Rockoff, Hugh. 1996. The Gold Standard as a "Good Housekeeping Seal of Approval." *Journal of Economic History* 56(June): 389–428.

Bordo, Michael D., and Schwartz, Anna J., eds. 1984. *A Retrospective on the Classical Gold Standard, 1821–1931.* Chicago: University of Chicago Press.

Boughton, James M. 2002. Why White, Not Keynes? Inventing the Post-War International Monetary System. In Arie Arnon and Warren Young, eds. *The Open Economy Macromodel: Past, Present and Future.* Boston: Kluwer, pp. 73–102.

Boughton, James M. 2004. New Light on Harry Dexter White. *Journal of the History of Economic Thought* 26(June): 179–95.

Bourneuf, Alice E. 1944. Professor Williams and the Fund. *American Economic Review* 34(December): 840–7.

Bourneuf, Alice E. 1945. Discussion of "The Commercial Policy Implications of the Fund and Bank" by William Fellner. *American Economic Review: Papers and Proceedings* 35(May): 289–94.

Brown, William A. 1941. Comments on Gold and the Monetary System. *American Economic Review: Papers and Proceedings* 30(February): 38–51.

Calomiris, Charles W., and Wheelock, David C. 1998. Was the Great Depression a Watershed for American Monetary Policy? In Michael D. Bordo, Claudia Goldin, and Eugene N. White, eds. *The Defining Moment: The Great Depression and the American Economy in the Twentieth Century.* Chicago: University of Chicago Press, pp. 23–65.

Cannan, Edwin. 1924. Discussion on Monetary Reform. *Economic Journal* 34(June): 155–62.

Cantillon, Richard. [1734] 1959. *Essai sur la Nature du Commerce en Général.* Reissued for the Royal Economic Society. London: Frank Cass.

Cassel, Gustav. 1922. *Money and Foreign Exchange after 1914.* London: Constable.

Cassel, Gustav. 1923. The Restoration of the Gold Standard. *Economica* 9(November): 171–85.

Cassel, Gustav. [1932a] 1967. *The Theory of Social Economy.* New York: Augustus M. Kelley.

References

Cassel, Gustav. 1932b. *The Crisis in the World's Monetary System*. Oxford: Clarendon Press.

Cassel, Gustav. [1936] 1966. *The Downfall of the Gold Standard*. New York: Augustus M. Kelley.

Cesarano, Filippo. 1983a. The Rational Expectations Hypothesis in Retrospect. *American Economic Review* 73(March): 198–203.

Cesarano, Filippo. 1983b. On the Role of the History of Economic Analysis. *History of Political Economy* 15(Spring): 63–82.

Cesarano, Filippo. 1990. Law and Galiani on Money and Monetary Systems. *History of Political Economy* 22(Summer): 321–40.

Cesarano, Filippo. 1995. The New Monetary Economics and the Theory of Money. *Journal of Economic Behavior and Organization* 26(May): 445–55.

Cesarano, Filippo. 1996. On the Effectiveness of Changes in Money Supply: The Puzzle of Mill's View. *History of Political Economy* 28(Fall): 459–73.

Cesarano, Filippo. 1997. Currency Areas and Equilibrium. *Open Economies Review* 8(January): 51–9.

Cesarano, Filippo. 1998a. Hume's Specie-Flow Mechanism and Classical Monetary Theory: An Alternative Interpretation. *Journal of International Economics* 45(June): 173–86.

Cesarano, Filippo. 1998b. Expectations and Monetary Policy: A Historical Perspective. *Manchester School* 66(September): 439–52.

Cesarano, Filippo. 1998c. Providing for the Optimum Quantity of Money. *Journal of Economic Studies* 25(6): 441–9.

Cesarano, Filippo. 1999a. Monetary Systems and Monetary Theory. *Kredit und Kapital* 32(2): 192–208.

Cesarano, Filippo. 1999b. Competitive Money Supply: The International Monetary System in Perspective. *Journal of Economic Studies* 26(3): 188–200.

Cesarano, Filippo. 2003a. Keynes's Revindication of Classical Monetary Theory. *History of Political Economy* 35(Fall): 491–519.

Cesarano, Filippo. 2003b. Defining Fundamental Disequilibrium: Keynes's Unheeded Contribution. *Journal of Economic Studies* 30(5): 474–92.

Choudhri, Ehsan U., and Kochin, Levis A. 1980. The Exchange Rate and the International Transmission of Business Cycle Disturbances. *Journal of Money, Credit and Banking* 12(November): 565–74.

Clark, John M. [1933] 1967. The Proposal for a Composite Commodity Currency. In *Economic Essays in Honour of Gustav Cassel, October 20th 1933*. London: Frank Cass, pp. 75–87.

Clarke, Stephen V. O. 1973. *The Reconstruction of the International Monetary System: The Attempts of 1922 and 1933*. Studies in International Finance 33. Princeton, NJ: International Finance Section.

References

Committee on Currency and Foreign Exchanges after the War (Cunliffe Committee). [1918] 1997. *First Interim Report*. Cd. 9182. London: HMSO, pp. 3–7, 11–2. Reprinted in Barry Eichengreen and Marc Flandreau, eds. *The Gold Standard in Theory and History*, 2nd ed. London: Routledge, pp. 231–45.

Committee on Finance and Industry (Macmillan Committee). 1931. *Report*. Cmd. 3897. London: HMSO.

Condliffe, J. B. 1944. Exchange Stabilization and International Trade. *Review of Economic Statistics* 26(November): 166–9.

Cooper, Richard N. [1982] 1987. The Gold Standard: Historical Facts and Future Prospects. In Richard N. Cooper, *The International Monetary System: Essays in World Economics*. Cambridge, MA: MIT Press.

Copernicus, Nicolas. [1526] 1864. *Monete Cudende Ratio*, edited by Louis Wolowski. Paris: Guillaumin.

Currie, Lauchlin B. 1934. The Failure of Monetary Policy to Prevent the Depression of 1929–32. *Journal of Political Economy* 42(April): 145–77.

Currie, Lauchlin B. [1936] 1967. Domestic Stability and the Mechanism of Trade Adjustment to International Capital Movements. In *Explorations in Economics: Notes and Essays Contributed in Honor of F. W. Taussig*. Freeport, NY: Books for Libraries Press, pp. 46–56.

Currie, Lauchlin B., Ellsworth, Paul T., and White, Harry D. [1932] 2002. Memorandum Prepared by L. B. Currie, P. T. Ellsworth, and H. D. White (Cambridge, Mass., 1932), ed. by David Laidler and Roger Sandilands, An Early Harvard Memorandum on Anti-Depression Policies: An Introductory Note. *History of Political Economy* 34(Fall): 533–52.

Davies, Glyn. 1994. *A History of Money: From Ancient Times to the Present Day*. Cardiff: University of Wales Press.

De Cecco, Marcello. 1979. Origins of the Post-War Payments System. *Cambridge Journal of Economics* 3(March): 49–61.

De Cecco, Marcello. 1984. *The International Gold Standard: Money and Empire*. London: Frances Pinter.

De Cecco, Marcello. 1987. Gold Standard. In John Eatwell, Murray Milgate, and Peter Newman, eds. *The New Palgrave: A Dictionary of Economics*, Vol. 2. London: Macmillan, pp. 539–45.

Despres, Emile, Kindleberger, Charles P., and Salant, Walter S. 1966. The Dollar and World Liquidity: A Minority View. *The Economist* 218(February 5): 526–9.

de Vegh, Imre. 1943. The International Clearing Union. *American Economic Review* 33(September): 534–56.

de Vegh, Imre. 1945. Peace Aims, Capital Requirements, and International Lending. *American Economic Review: Papers and Proceedings* 35(May): 253–61.

Dimand, Robert W. 2003. Irving Fisher on the International Transmission of Booms and Depressions Through Monetary Standards. *Journal of Money, Credit and Banking* 35(February): 49–90.

Durbin, Evan F. M. 1935. *The Problem of Credit Policy.* London: Chapman & Hall.

Eccles, Marriner S. 1937. Controlling Booms and Depressions. In Arthur D. Gayer, ed. *The Lessons of Monetary Experience: Essays in Honor of Irving Fisher.* London: George Allen and Unwin, pp. 3–22.

Eichengreen, Barry, ed. 1985. *The Gold Standard in Theory and History.* New York: Methuen.

Eichengreen, Barry. 1988. Did International Economic Forces Cause the Great Depression? *Contemporary Policy Issues* 6(April): 90–114.

Eichengreen, Barry. 1989. Hegemonic Stability Theories of the International Monetary System. In Richard N. Cooper, Barry Eichengreen, C. Randall Henning, Gerald Holtham, and Robert D. Putnam, eds. *Can Nations Agree? Issues in International Economic Cooperation.* Washington, DC: Brookings Institution, pp. 255–98.

Eichengreen, Barry. [1990] 1992. International Monetary Instability Between the Wars: Structural Flaws or Misguided Policies? In Yoshio Suzuki, Junichi Miyake, and Mitsuaki Okabe, eds. *The Evolution of the International Monetary System.* Tokyo: University of Tokyo Press, pp. 71–116. Reprinted in Barry Eichengreen, ed. *Monetary Regime Transformations.* Aldershot, England: Edward Elgar, pp. 355–400.

Eichengreen, Barry. 1992a. *Golden Fetters: The Gold Standard and the Great Depression, 1919–1939.* Oxford: Oxford University Press.

Eichengreen, Barry. 1992b, ed. *Monetary Regime Transformations.* Aldershot, England: Edward Elgar.

Eichengreen, Barry. 1994. *International Monetary Arrangements for the 21st Century.* Washington, DC: Brookings Institution.

Eichengreen, Barry. 1996. *Globalizing Capital: A History of the International Monetary System.* Princeton, NJ: Princeton University Press.

Eichengreen, Barry, and Flandreau, Marc, eds. 1997. *The Gold Standard in Theory and History,* 2nd ed. London: Routledge.

Einzig, Paul. 1930. Some New Features of Gold Movements. *Economic Journal* 40(March): 56–63.

Ellis, Howard S. 1942. The Problem of Exchange Systems in the Postwar World. *American Economic Review: Papers and Proceedings* 32(March): 195–205.

Ellis, Howard S. 1944. Can National and International Monetary Policies Be Reconciled? *American Economic Review: Papers and Proceedings* 34(March): 385–95.

Fama, Eugene F. 1980. Banking in the Theory of Finance. *Journal of Monetary Economics* 6(January): 39–57.

Fanno, Marco. 1923. *Inflazione monetaria e corso dei cambi*. Città di Castello: Società tipografica "Leonardo da Vinci."

Fanno, Marco. 1932. *Lezioni di economia politica. Parte speciale: La moneta e i sistemi monetari*. Padua, Italy: CEDAM.

Fanno, Marco. 1935. *I trasferimenti anormali dei capitali e le crisi*. Turin, Italy: Giulio Einaudi.

Fanno, Marco. 1939. *Normal and Abnormal International Capital Transfers*. Studies in Economic Dynamics 1. Minneapolis: University of Minnesota Press.

Feis, Herbert. 1942. Restoring Trade After the War: A Suggested Remedy for Old Defects. *Foreign Affairs* 20(February): 282–92.

Fellner, William. 1945. The Commercial Policy Implications of the Fund and Bank. *American Economic Review: Papers and Proceedings* 35(May): 262–71.

Fels, Rendigs. 1949. Gold and International Equilibrium. *American Economic Review* 39(December): 1281–3.

Fisher, Irving. [1911] 1963. *The Purchasing Power of Money: Its Determination and Relation to Credit, Interest and Crises*. New York: Augustus M. Kelley.

Fisher, Irving. 1913a. A Compensated Dollar. *Quarterly Journal of Economics* 27(February): 213–35.

Fisher, Irving. 1913b. What an International Conference on the High Cost of Living Could Do. ISI, 14th Session, 1913, Report 25. Voorburg, The Netherlands: International Statistical Institute.

Fisher, Irving. 1920. *Stabilizing the Dollar: A Plan to Stabilize the General Price Level Without Fixing Individual Prices*. New York: Macmillan.

Fisher, Irving. 1933. The Debt-Deflation Theory of Great Depressions. *Econometrica* 1(October): 337–57.

Fisher, Irving. [1934] 2003. Are Booms and Depressions Transmitted Internationally Through Monetary Standards? New Haven, CT: Irving Fisher. Reprinted in Robert W. Dimand, *Journal of Money, Credit and Banking* 35(February): 49–90.

Fisher, Irving. [1935] 1945. *100% Money*. New Haven, CT: City Printing Co.

Flanders, M. June. 1989. *International Monetary Economics, 1870–1960: Between the Classical and the New Classical*. Cambridge: Cambridge University Press.

Flandreau, Marc. 1997. Central Bank Cooperation in Historical Perspective: A Sceptical View. *Economic History Review* 50(November): 735–63.

Flandreau, Marc, Le Cacheux, Jacques, and Zumer, Frédéric. 1998. Stability Without a Pact? Lessons from the European Gold Standard, 1880–1914. *Economic Policy* 26(April): 117–62.

Frankel, Jeffrey A., and Rose, Andrew K. 1998. The Endogeneity of the Optimum Currency Area Criteria. *Economic Journal* 108(July): 1009–25.

Friedman, Benjamin M. 1979. Optimal Expectations and the Extreme Information Assumptions of "Rational Expectations" Macromodels. *Journal of Monetary Economics* 5(January): 23–41.

Friedman, Milton. 1953a. The Case for Flexible Exchange Rates. In Milton Friedman, *Essays in Positive Economics*. Chicago: University of Chicago Press, pp. 157–203.

Friedman, Milton. [1953b] 1968. Why the Dollar Shortage? *The Freeman* 4(6): 201–3. Reprinted in Milton Friedman, *Dollars and Deficits: Inflation, Monetary Policy and the Balance of Payments*. Englewood Cliffs, NJ: Prentice-Hall, pp. 211–7.

Friedman, Milton. [1954] 1968. Why the American Economy is Depression-Proof. *Nationalekonomiska Föreningens Förhandlingar* (3): 55–77. Reprinted in Milton Friedman, *Dollars and Deficits: Inflation, Monetary Policy and the Balance of Payments*. Englewood Cliffs, NJ: Prentice-Hall, pp. 72–96.

Friedman, Milton. 1960. *A Program for Monetary Stability*. New York: Fordham University Press.

Friedman, Milton. [1961] 1968. Real and Pseudo Gold Standards. *Journal of Law and Economics* 4(October): 66–79. Reprinted in Milton Friedman, *Dollars and Deficits: Inflation, Monetary Policy and the Balance of Payments*. Englewood Cliffs, NJ: Prentice-Hall, pp. 247–65.

Friedman, Milton. [1968a] 1969. The Role of Monetary Policy. *American Economic Review* 58(March): 1–17. Reprinted in Milton Friedman, *The Optimum Quantity of Money and Other Essays*. Chicago: Aldine.

Friedman, Milton. 1968b. The Political Economy of International Monetary Arrangements. In Milton Friedman, *Dollars and Deficits: Inflation, Monetary Policy and the Balance of Payments*. Englewood Cliffs, NJ: Prentice-Hall, pp. 266–79.

Friedman, Milton. 1969a. The Optimum Quantity of Money. In Milton Friedman, *The Optimum Quantity of Money and Other Essays*. Chicago: Aldine, pp. 1–50.

Friedman, Milton. 1969b. *The Optimum Quantity of Money and Other Essays*. Chicago: Aldine.

Friedman, Milton. 1976. Comments on "Long-Run Effects of Fiscal and Monetary Policy on Aggregate Demand" by James Tobin and Willem Buiter. In Jerome L. Stein, ed. *Monetarism*. Amsterdam: North-Holland, pp. 310–7.

References

Friedman, Milton. 1984. Comment on "The Success of Purchasing-Power Parity: Historical Evidence and Its Implications for Macroeconomics" by Donald N. McCloskey and J. Richard Zecher. In Michael D. Bordo and Anna J. Schwartz, eds. *A Retrospective on the Classical Gold Standard, 1821–1931*. Chicago: University of Chicago Press, pp. 157–62.

Friedman, Milton. 1986. The Resource Cost of Irredeemable Paper Money. *Journal of Political Economy* 94(June): 642–7.

Friedman, Milton. 1992. *Money Mischief*. New York: Harcourt Brace Jovanovich.

Friedman, Milton. 1997. John Maynard Keynes. *Federal Reserve Bank of Richmond Economic Quarterly* 83(Spring): 2–23.

Friedman, Milton. 2001. Friedman on Friedman. *Rivista di Storia Economica* 17(April): 127–30.

Friedman, Milton, and Schwartz, Anna J. 1963. *A Monetary History of the United States, 1867–1960*. Princeton, NJ: Princeton University Press.

Friedman, Milton, and Schwartz, Anna J. 1986. Has Government Any Role in Money? *Journal of Monetary Economics* 17(January): 37–62.

Funk, Walther. 1940. *Wirtschaftliche Neuordnung Europas*. Berlin: M. Müller und Sohn.

Galiani, Ferdinando. [1751] 1977. *On Money*. Translated by Peter R. Toscano. Ann Arbor, MI: University Microfilms International.

Gallarotti, Giulio M. 1995. *The Anatomy of an International Monetary Regime: The Classical Gold Standard*. Oxford: Oxford University Press.

Gardner, Richard N. 1969. *Sterling-Dollar Diplomacy: The Origins and the Prospects of Our International Economic Order*, 2nd ed. New York: McGraw-Hill.

Gardner, Walter R. 1945. The Future International Position of the United States as Effected by the Fund and Bank. *American Economic Review: Papers and Proceedings* 35(May): 272–88.

Gayer, Arthur D., ed. 1937. *The Lessons of Monetary Experience: Essays in Honor of Irving Fisher*. London: George Allen and Unwin.

Giovannini, Alberto. 1993. Bretton Woods and Its Precursors: Rules Versus Discretion in the History of International Monetary Regimes. In Michael D. Bordo and Barry Eichengreen, eds. *A Retrospective on the Bretton Woods System: Lessons for International Monetary Reform*. Chicago: University of Chicago Press, pp. 109–47.

Gold, Joseph. 1981. *The Multilateral System of Payments: Keynes, Convertibility, and the International Monetary Fund's Articles of Agreement*. Washington, DC: International Monetary Fund.

Graham, Benjamin. 1937. *Storage and Stability: A Modern Ever-Normal Granary*. New York: McGraw-Hill.

Graham, Benjamin. 1943. The Critique of Commodity-Reserve Currency: A Point-by-Point Reply. *Journal of Political Economy* 51(February): 66–9.

Graham, Benjamin. 1944. *World Commodities and World Currency*. New York: McGraw-Hill.

Graham, Benjamin. 1947. Money As Pure Commodity. *American Economic Review: Papers and Proceedings* 37(May): 304–7.

Graham, Benjamin, and Hirsch, Julius. 1952. *Stockpiles for Stability: Buffer Stocks and International Monetary Policy*. Memorandum Presented to the Mexico City Conference of IMF and BRD, September 2. New York: Committee for Economic Stability.

Graham, Frank D. 1940a. Achilles' Heels in Monetary Standards. *American Economic Review* 30(March): 16–32.

Graham, Frank D. 1940b. The Primary Functions of Money and Their Consummation in Monetary Policy. *American Economic Review: Papers and Proceedings* 30(March): 1–16.

Graham, Frank D. 1943a. Commodity-Reserve Currency: A Criticism of the Critique. *Journal of Political Economy* 51(February): 70–5.

Graham, Frank D. 1943b. *Fundamentals of International Monetary Policy*. Essays in International Finance 2. Princeton, NJ: International Finance Section.

Graham, Frank D. 1944a. Discussion of "Can National and International Monetary Policies Be Reconciled?" by Howard S. Ellis. *American Economic Review: Papers and Proceedings* 34(March): 399–401.

Graham, Frank D. 1944b. Keynes vs. Hayek on a Commodity Reserve Currency. *Economic Journal* 54(December): 422–9.

Graham, Frank D. 1949. *The Cause and Cure of "Dollar Shortage."* Essays in International Finance 10. Princeton, NJ: International Finance Section.

Greenfield, Robert L., and Yeager, Leland B. 1983. A Laissez-Faire Approach to Monetary Stability. *Journal of Money, Credit and Banking* 15(August): 302–15.

Gregory, Theodore E. 1925. What Can Central Banks Really Do? *American Economic Review* 15(March): 53–9.

Gregory, Theodore E. 1931. The Economic Significance of "Gold Maldistribution." *Manchester School of Economic and Social Studies* 2(2): 77–85.

Gregory, Theodore E. 1934. *The Gold Standard and Its Future*. London: Methuen.

Grubel, Herbert G. 1969. *The International Monetary System*. Harmondsworth, England: Penguin Books.

Haberler, Gottfried. 1944. Some Comments on Professor Hansen's Note. *Review of Economic Statistics* 26(November): 191–3.

Haberler, Gottfried. 1947. Comments on "National Central Banking and the International Economy" by Robert Triffin. In *International Monetary*

References

Policies. Postwar Economic Studies 7. Washington, DC: Board of Governors of the Federal Reserve System, pp. 82–102.

Haines, Walther W. 1943. Keynes, White, and History. *Quarterly Journal of Economics* 58(November): 120–33.

Hall, Robert E. 1982. Explorations in the Gold Standard and Related Policies for Stabilizing the Dollar. In Robert E. Hall, ed. *Inflation: Causes and Effects.* Chicago: University of Chicago Press, pp. 111–22.

Hall, Robert E. 1997. Irving Fisher's Self-Stabilizing Money. *American Economic Review: Papers and Proceedings* 87(May): 436–8.

Hallwood, Paul C., MacDonald, Ronald, and Marsh, Ian W. 1996. Credibility and Fundamentals: Were the Classical and Interwar Gold Standards Well-Behaved Target Zones? In Tamim Bayoumi, Barry Eichengreen, and Mark P. Taylor, eds. *Modern Perspectives on the Gold Standard.* Cambridge: Cambridge University Press, pp. 129–61.

Halm, George N. 1944. The International Monetary Fund. *Review of Economic Statistics* 26(November): 170–5.

Hamada, Koichi. 1977. On the Political Economy of Monetary Integration: A Public Economics Approach. In Robert Z. Aliber, ed. *The Political Economy of Monetary Reform.* London: Macmillan, pp. 13–31.

Hamilton, James D. 1987. Monetary Factors in the Great Depression. *Journal of Monetary Economics* 19(March): 145–69.

Hansen, Alvin H. [1933] 1967. The Maintenance of Purchasing Power. In *Economic Essays in Honour of Gustav Cassel, October 20th 1933.* London: Frank Cass, pp. 247–55.

Hansen, Alvin H. 1937a. The Situation of Gold Today in Relation to World Currencies. *American Economic Review: Papers and Proceedings* 27(March): 130–40.

Hansen, Alvin H. 1937b. Monetary Policy in the Upswing. In Arthur D. Gayer, ed. *The Lessons of Monetary Experience: Essays in Honor of Irving Fisher.* London: George Allen and Unwin, pp. 89–98.

Hansen, Alvin H. 1944. A Brief Note on "Fundamental Disequilibrium." *Review of Economic Statistics* 26(November): 182–4.

Harrod, Roy F. 1951. *The Life of John Maynard Keynes.* London: Macmillan.

Hart, Albert G., Kaldor, Nicholas, and Tinbergen, Jan. 1964. *The Case for an International Commodity Reserve Currency.* Geneva: United Nations Conference on Trade and Development, 17 February 1964. Reprinted in Nicholas Kaldor, *Essays on Economic Policy,* Vol. 2. London: Gerald Duckworth, pp. 131–77.

Hawtrey, Ralph G. 1919. The Gold Standard. *Economic Journal* 29(December): 428–42.

Hawtrey, Ralph G. 1922. The Genoa Resolutions on Currency. *Economic Journal* 32(September): 290–304.

References

Hawtrey, Ralph G. 1924. Discussion on Monetary Reform. *Economic Journal* 34(June): 162–6.

Hawtrey, Ralph G. 1929a. London and the Trade Cycle. *American Economic Review: Papers and Proceedings* 19(March): 69–77.

Hawtrey, Ralph G. 1929b. Money. In *The Encyclopaedia Britannica*, 14th ed., Vol. 15. New York: Encyclopaedia Britannica, pp. 692–9.

Hawtrey, Ralph G. [1932] 1970. *The Art of Central Banking*. London: Frank Cass.

Hawtrey, Ralph G. 1937. The Credit Deadlock. In Arthur D. Gayer, ed. *The Lessons of Monetary Experience: Essays in Honor of Irving Fisher*. London: George Allen and Unwin, pp. 129–44.

Hawtrey, Ralph G. 1938. *A Century of Bank Rate*. London: Longmans, Green.

Hawtrey, Ralph G. 1944. *Economic Destiny*. London: Longmans, Green.

Hawtrey, Ralph G. 1947. *The Gold Standard in Theory and Practice*, 5th ed. London: Longmans, Green.

Hawtrey, Ralph G. 1950. *Currency and Credit*, 4th ed. London: Longmans, Green.

Hayek, Friedrich A. von. [1929] 1966. *Monetary Theory and the Trade Cycle*. Translated by Nicholas Kaldor and Honor M. Croome. New York: Augustus M. Kelley.

Hayek, Friedrich A. von. [1931] 1967. *Prices and Production*, 2nd rev. ed., 1935. New York: Augustus M. Kelley.

Hayek, Friedrich A. von. [1932] 1984. The Fate of the Gold Standard. In Friedrich A. von Hayek, *Money, Capital and Fluctuations: Early Essays*, ed. by Roy McCloughry. London: Routledge & Kegan Paul.

Hayek, Friedrich A. von. [1933] 1984. On "Neutral Money." In Friedrich A. von Hayek, *Money, Capital and Fluctuations: Early Essays*, ed. by Roy McCloughry. London: Routledge & Kegan Paul.

Hayek, Friedrich A. von. [1937] 1939. *Monetary Nationalism and International Stability*, 2nd ed. London: Longmans, Green.

Hayek, Friedrich A. von. 1943. A Commodity Reserve Currency. *Economic Journal* 53(June–September): 176–84.

Hayek, Friedrich A. von. 1984. *Money, Capital and Fluctuations: Early Essays*, ed. by Roy McCloughry. London: Routledge & Kegan Paul.

Hicks, John. 1967a. *Critical Essays in Monetary Theory*. Oxford: Oxford University Press.

Hicks, John. 1967b. Monetary Theory and History – An Attempt at Perspective. In John Hicks, *Critical Essays in Monetary Theory*. Oxford: Oxford University Press, pp. 155–73.

Hicks, John. 1969. *A Theory of Economic History*. Oxford: Oxford University Press.

References

Horsefield, J. Keith. 1969a. *The International Monetary Fund, 1945–1965: Twenty Years of International Monetary Cooperation*, Vol. 1, *Chronicle*. Washington, DC: International Monetary Fund.

Horsefield, J. Keith. 1969b. *The International Monetary Fund, 1945–1965: Twenty Years of International Monetary Cooperation*, Vol. 3, *Documents*. Washington, DC: International Monetary Fund.

Huffman, Wallace E., and Lothian, James R. 1984. The Gold Standard and the Transmission of Business Cycles, 1833–1932. In Michael D. Bordo and Anna J. Schwartz, eds. *A Retrospective on the Classical Gold Standard, 1821–1931*. Chicago: University of Chicago Press, pp. 455–507.

Hume, David. [1750] 1970. Letter to Oswald, 1 November 1750. Reprinted in David Hume, *Writings on Economics*, ed. by Eugene Rotwein. Madison: University of Wisconsin Press, pp. 197–9.

Hume, David. [1752a] 1970. Of Money. Reprinted in David Hume, *Writings on Economics*, ed. by Eugene Rotwein. Madison: University of Wisconsin Press, pp. 33–46.

Hume, David. [1752b] 1970. Of the Balance of Trade. Reprinted in David Hume, *Writings on Economics*, ed. by Eugene Rotwein. Madison: University of Wisconsin Press, pp. 60–77.

Hume, David. 1970. *Writings on Economics*, ed. by Eugene Rotwein. Madison: University of Wisconsin Press.

Ikenberry, John G. 1993. The Political Origins of Bretton Woods. In Michael D. Bordo and Barry Eichengreen, eds. *A Retrospective on the Bretton Woods System: Lessons for International Monetary Reform*. Chicago: University of Chicago Press, pp. 155–82.

James, Harold. 1996. *International Monetary Cooperation Since Bretton Woods*. Washington, DC and Oxford: International Monetary Fund and Oxford University Press.

Jevons, Stanley W. [1875] 1878. *Money and the Mechanism of Exchange*, 4th ed. London: Kegan Paul.

Jevons, Stanley W. 1884. *Investigations in Currency and Finance*. London: Macmillan.

Jones, J. H. 1933. The Gold Standard. *Economic Journal* 43(December): 551–74.

Jones, Robert A. 1976. The Origin and Development of Media of Exchange. *Journal of Political Economy* 84(August): 757–75.

Kahn, Richard F. 1976. Historical Origins of the International Monetary Fund. In A. P. Thirlwall, ed. *Keynes and International Monetary Relations: The Second Keynes Seminar Held at the University of Kent at Canterbury 1974*. London: Macmillan, pp. 3–35.

Kemmerer, Edwin W. 1920. *High Prices and Deflation*. Princeton, NJ: Princeton University Press.

Kemmerer, Edwin W. 1932. Gold and the Gold Standard. *Proceedings of the American Philosophical Society* 71: 85–104.

Kemmerer, Edwin W. [1933] 1967. The Gold Exchange Standard. In *Economic Essays in Honour of Gustav Cassel, October 20th 1933*. London: Frank Cass, pp. 311–26.

Kemmerer, Edwin W. 1944. *Gold and the Gold Standard: The Story of Gold Money: Past, Present and Future*. New York: McGraw-Hill.

Keynes, John M. 1923. *A Tract on Monetary Reform*. London: Macmillan.

Keynes, John M. 1924a. Discussion on Monetary Reform. *Economic Journal* 34(June): 169–76.

Keynes, John M. 1924b. Letter to Addis, 25 July 1924. Reprinted in Donald Moggridge, ed. *The Collected Writings of John Maynard Keynes*, Vol. 19. London: Macmillan, pp. 270–2.

Keynes, John M. [1925a] 1972. The Return Towards Gold. Reprinted in *The Collected Writings of John Maynard Keynes*, Vol. 9. London: Macmillan, pp. 192–200.

Keynes, John M. [1925b] 1972. *The Economic Consequences of Mr Churchill*. Reprinted in *The Collected Writings of John Maynard Keynes*, Vol. 9. London: Macmillan, pp. 207–30.

Keynes, John M. [1929] 1981. Is There Enough Gold? The League Of Nations Inquiry. Reprinted in Donald Moggridge, ed. *The Collected Writings of John Maynard Keynes*, Vol. 19. London: Macmillan, pp. 775–80.

Keynes, John M. 1930. *A Treatise on Money*. London: Macmillan.

Keynes, John M. [1931a] 1972. The End of the Gold Standard (27 September 1931). Reprinted in *The Collected Writings of John Maynard Keynes*, Vol. 9. London: Macmillan, pp. 245–9.

Keynes, John M. [1931b] 1989. For What Objects Do Central Banks Hold Gold? In The Royal Institute of International Affairs, *The International Gold Problem*. Oxford: Oxford University Press, pp. 18, 167, 186–90. Reprinted in Donald Moggridge, ed. *The Collected Writings of John Maynard Keynes*, Vol. 30. London: Macmillan, pp. 12–8.

Keynes, John M. [1933a] 1972. *The Means to Prosperity*. Reprinted in *The Collected Writings of John Maynard Keynes*, Vol. 9. London: Macmillan, pp. 335–66.

Keynes, John M. [1933b] 1982. Letter to *The Economist*, 20 March 1933. Reprinted in Donald Moggridge, ed. *The Collected Writings of John Maynard Keynes*, Vol. 21. London: Macmillan, p. 186.

Keynes, John M. [1934] 1973. Poverty in Plenty: Is the Economic System Self-Adjusting? Reprinted in Donald Moggridge, ed. *The Collected Writings of John Maynard Keynes*, Vol. 13. London: Macmillan, pp. 485–92.

References

Keynes, John M. [1935] 1982. The Future of the Foreign Exchanges. Reprinted in Donald Moggridge, ed. *The Collected Writings of John Maynard Keynes*, Vol. 21. London: Macmillan, pp. 360–9.

Keynes, John M. [1936] 1964. *The General Theory of Employment, Interest and Money*. London: Macmillan.

Keynes, John M. 1938. The Policy of Government Storage of Foodstuffs and Raw Materials. *Economic Journal* 48(September): 449–60.

Keynes, John M. 1943. The Objective of International Price Stability. *Economic Journal* 53(June–September): 185–7.

Keynes, John M. 1944. Note on "Keynes vs. Hayek on a Commodity Reserve Currency" by Frank D. Graham. *Economic Journal* 54(December): 429–30.

Keynes, John M. 1946. The Balance of Payments of the United States. *Economic Journal* 56(June): 172–87.

Keynes, John M. 1980a. *Activities 1940–1944: Shaping the Post-War World: The Clearing Union*, ed. by Donald Moggridge. *The Collected Writings of John Maynard Keynes*, Vol. 25. London: Macmillan.

Keynes, John M. 1980b. *Activities 1941–1946: Shaping the Post-War World: Bretton Woods and Reparations*, ed. by Donald Moggridge. *The Collected Writings of John Maynard Keynes*, Vol. 26. London: Macmillan.

Kindleberger, Charles P. 1943. International Monetary Stabilization. In Seymour E. Harris, ed. *Postwar Economic Problems*. New York: McGraw-Hill, pp. 375–95.

Kindleberger, Charles P. 1973. *The World in Depression, 1929–1939*. London: Allen Lane.

Klein, Benjamin. 1974. The Competitive Supply of Money. *Journal of Money, Credit and Banking* 6(November): 423–53.

Krugman, Paul R. 1984. The International Role of the Dollar: Theory and Prospect. In John F. O. Bilson and Richard C. Marston, eds. *Exchange Rate Theory and Practice*. Chicago: University of Chicago Press. Reprinted in Paul R. Krugman, *Currencies and Crises*. Cambridge, MA: MIT Press, 1992, pp. 165–83.

Krugman, Paul R. 1993. *What Do We Need to Know About the International Monetary System?* Essays in International Finance 193. Princeton, NJ: International Finance Section.

Kuhn, Thomas S. 1970. *The Structure of Scientific Revolutions*, 2nd ed. Chicago: University of Chicago Press.

Laidler, David. 1991. *The Golden Age of the Quantity Theory: The Development of Neoclassical Monetary Economics, 1870–1914*. Hemel Hempstead, England: Philip Allan.

Laidler, David. 1993. Hawtrey, Harvard, and the Origins of the Chicago Tradition. *Journal of Political Economy* 101(December): 1068–103.

References

Laidler, David. 1999. *Fabricating the Keynesian Revolution: Studies of the Inter-war Literature on Money, the Cycle, and Unemployment.* Cambridge: Cambridge University Press.

Laidler, David. 2002. Rules, Discretion and Financial Crises in Classical and Neoclassical Monetary Economics. *Economic Issues* 7(September): 11–33.

Laidler, David, and Sandilands, Roger. 2002. An Early Harvard Memorandum on Anti-Depression Policies: An Introductory Note. *History of Political Economy* 34(Fall): 515–32.

Lastrapes, William D., and Selgin, George. 1997. The Check Tax: Fiscal Folly and the Great Monetary Contraction. *Journal of Economic History* 57(December): 859–78.

Law, John. [1705] 1966. *Money and Trade Considered with a Proposal for Supplying the Nation with Money.* New York: Augustus M. Kelley.

Layton, Walter T. 1925. British Opinion on the Gold Standard. *Quarterly Journal of Economics* 39(February): 184–95.

Lerner, Abba P. 1947. Discussion of "International Monetary Policy and the Search for Economic Stability" by Ragnar Nurkse. *American Economic Review: Papers and Proceedings* 37(May): 592–4.

Lester, Richard A. 1939. *Monetary Experiments: Early American and Recent Scandinavian Efforts to Overcome Depressions.* Princeton, NJ: Princeton University Press.

Lindahl, Erik. 1937. International Economic Reconstruction Realized Through Rational Management of Free Currencies. In Arthur D. Gayer, ed. *The Lessons of Monetary Experience: Essays in Honor of Irving Fisher.* London: George Allen and Unwin, pp. 309–17.

Lucas, Robert E. 2003. Macroeconomic Priorities. *American Economic Review* 93(March): 1–14.

Lüke, Rolf E. 1985. The Schacht and the Keynes Plans. *Banca Nazionale del Lavoro Quarterly Review* No. 152: 65–76.

Lutz, Friedrich A. 1943. *The Keynes and White Proposals.* Essays in International Finance 1. Princeton, NJ: International Finance Section.

Marshall, Alfred. 1923. *Money, Credit and Commerce.* London: Macmillan.

McCloskey, Donald N., and Zecher, Richard J. 1976. How the Gold Standard Worked, 1880–1913. In Jacob A. Frenkel and Harry G. Johnson, eds. *The Monetary Approach to the Balance of Payments.* London: George Allen and Unwin, pp. 357–85.

McCloskey, Donald N., and Zecher, Richard J. 1984. The Success of Purchasing Power Parity: Historical Evidence and Its Implications for Macroeconomics. In Michael D. Bordo and Anna J. Schwartz, eds. *A Retrospective on the Classical Gold Standard, 1821–1931.* Chicago: University of Chicago Press, pp. 121–50.

McKinnon, Ronald I. 1993. The Rules of the Game: International Money in Historical Perspective. *Journal of Economic Literature* 31(March): 1–44.

Meltzer, Allan H. 1989. Keynes on Monetary Reform and International Economic Order. In Forrest Capie and Geoffrey E. Wood, eds. *Monetary Economics in the 1980s*. London: Macmillan, pp. 101–50.

Menger, Carl. [1871] 1981. *Principles of Economics*. Translated by James Dingwall and Bert F. Hoselitz; with an Introduction by Friedrich A. Hayek. New York: New York University Press.

Menger, Carl. 1892. On the Origin of Money. *Economic Journal* 2(June): 239–55.

Metzler, Lloyd A. 1948. The Theory of International Trade. In Howard S. Ellis, ed. *A Survey of Contemporary Economics*. Philadelphia: Blakiston, pp. 210–54.

Mikesell, Raymond F. 1947. The Role of the International Monetary Agreements in a World of Planned Economies. *Journal of Political Economy* 55(December): 497–512.

Mikesell, Raymond F. 1949. The International Monetary Fund. *Journal of Political Economy* 57(October): 395–412.

Mikesell, Raymond F. 1994. *The Bretton Woods Debates: A Memoir*. Essays in International Finance 192. Princeton, NJ: International Finance Section.

Mill, John S. 1844. *Essays on Some Unsettled Questions in Political Economy*. London: John W. Parker.

Mill, John S. [1848] 1987. *Principles of Political Economy*, ed. by William Ashley. New York: Augustus M. Kelley.

Mises, Ludwig von. [1912] 1980. *The Theory of Money and Credit*, 2nd American ed. Indianapolis: Liberty Classics.

Mises, Ludwig von. [1928] 1994. Monetary Stabilization and Cyclical Policy. Reprinted in Israel M. Kirzner, ed. *Classics in Austrian Economics: A Sampling in the History of a Tradition*, Vol. 3. London: William Pickering, pp. 33–111.

Mises, Ludwig von. 1949. *Human Action: A Treatise on Economics*. London: William Hodge.

Mlynarski, Feliks. 1929. *Gold and Central Banks*. New York: Macmillan.

Mlynarski, Feliks. 1931. *The Functioning of the Gold Standard*. Geneva: League of Nations.

Mlynarski, Feliks. 1936a. Memorandum on the Production and Distribution of Gold. In Carnegie Endowment–International Chamber of Commerce, *The Problems of Monetary Stabilization*. Paris: International Chamber of Commerce, pp. 318–31.

Mlynarski, Feliks. 1936b. Memorandum on the Cooperation of Central Banks. In Carnegie Endowment–International Chamber of Commerce, *The*

Problems of Monetary Stabilization. Paris: International Chamber of Commerce, pp. 332–45.

Mlynarski, Feliks. 1937. Proportionalism and Stabilization Policy. In Arthur D. Gayer, ed. *The Lessons of Monetary Experience: Essays in Honor of Irving Fisher.* London: George Allen and Unwin, pp. 269–308.

Moggridge, Donald E. 1972. *British Monetary Policy 1924–1931: The Norman Conquest of $4.86.* Cambridge: Cambridge University Press.

Moggridge, Donald E. 1986. Keynes and the International Monetary System, 1909–46. In Jon S. Cohen and G. C. Harcourt, eds. *International Monetary Problems and Supply-Side Economics: Essays in Honour of Lorie Tarshis.* London: Macmillan, pp. 56–83.

Moggridge, Donald E. 2001. "Maynard would not have wished"? Second-Guessing the Author of "The Balance of Payments of the United States." *History of Political Economy* 33(Winter): 815–24.

Mundell, Robert A. 1961. A Theory of Optimum Currency Areas. *American Economic Review* 51(September): 657–65.

Mundell, Robert A. 1962. The Appropriate Use of Monetary and Fiscal Policy for Internal and External Stability. *International Monetary Fund Staff Papers* 9(March): 70–7.

Mundell, Robert A. 1968. The Redundancy Problem and the World Price Level. In Robert A. Mundell, *International Economics.* New York: Macmillan, pp. 195–8.

Mundell, Robert A. 1972. The Future of the International Financial System. In A. L. Keith Acheson, John F. Chant, and Martin F. J. Prachowny, eds. *Bretton Woods Revisited.* London: Macmillan, pp. 91–104.

Mundell, Robert A. 1995. Prospects for the International Monetary System and Its Institutions. In Hans Genberg, ed. *The International Monetary System: Its Institutions and its Future.* Berlin: Springer, pp. 21–46.

Niehans, Jürg. 1976. How to Fill an Empty Shell. *American Economic Review: Papers and Proceedings* 66(May): 177–83.

Niehans, Jürg. 1978. *The Theory of Money.* Baltimore: Johns Hopkins University Press.

Niehans, Jürg. 1984. *International Monetary Economics.* Baltimore: Johns Hopkins University Press.

Nurkse, Ragnar. 1944. *International Currency Experience: Lessons of the Inter-War Period.* Geneva: League of Nations.

Nurkse, Ragnar. 1947. International Monetary Policy and the Search for Economic Stability. *American Economic Review: Papers and Proceedings* 37(May): 569–80.

Obstfeld, Maurice, and Rogoff, Kenneth. 1995. The Mirage of Fixed Exchange Rates. *Journal of Economic Perspectives* 9(Fall): 73–96.

References

Ohlin, Bertil. 1937. Mechanisms and Objectives of Exchange Control. *American Economic Review: Papers and Proceedings* 27(March): 141–50.

Oliver, Robert W. 1975. *International Economic Co-operation and the World Bank*. London: Macmillan.

Opie, Redvers. 1944. Discussion of "Can National and International Monetary Policies Be Reconciled?" by Howard S. Ellis. *American Economic Review: Papers and Proceedings* 34(March): 396–9.

Oswald of Dunnikier, James. [1750] 1970. Letter to Hume, 10 October 1750. In David Hume, *Writings on Economics*, ed. by Eugene Rotwein. Madison: University of Wisconsin Press, pp. 190–6.

Pantaleoni, Maffeo. 1898. Dei criteri che debbono informare la storia delle dottrine economiche. *Giornale degli Economisti* 17(November): 407–31.

Patinkin, Don. 1961. Financial Intermediaries and the Logical Structure of Monetary Theory. *American Economic Review* 51(March): 95–116.

Phillips, Ronnie J. 1995. *The Chicago Plan and New Deal Banking Reform*. Armonk, NY: M. E. Sharpe.

Pigou, Arthur C. 1917–18. The Value of Money. *Quarterly Journal of Economics* 32(November): 38–65.

Pigou, Arthur C. 1922. The Foreign Exchanges. *Quarterly Journal of Economics* 37(November): 52–74.

Pigou, Arthur C. 1927. *Industrial Fluctuations*. London: Macmillan.

Puhl, E. 1940. Europäische Währungs- und Kreditordnung. *Die Deutsche Volkswirtschaft* 9(Oktober): 946–50.

Redish, Angela. 1990. The Evolution of the Gold Standard in England. *Journal of Economic History* 50(December): 789–805.

Redish, Angela. 1993. Anchors Aweigh: The Transition from Commodity Money to Fiat Money in Western Economies. *Canadian Journal of Economics* 26(November): 777–95.

Redmond, John. [1992] 1996. The Gold Standard Between the Wars. In Stephen N. Broadberry and Nicholas F. R. Crafts, eds. *Britain in the International Economy*. Cambridge: Cambridge University Press, pp. 346–68. Reprinted in Mark Thomas, ed. *The Disintegration of the World Economy Between the World Wars*, Vol. 1. Cheltenham, England: Edward Elgar, pp. 294–318.

Rist, Charles. 1934. Gold and the End of the Depression. *Foreign Affairs* 12(January): 244–59.

Robertson, Dennis H. [1922] 1970. *Money*, 4th rev. ed. London: James Nisbet.

Robertson, Dennis H. [1928] 1940. Theories of Banking Policy. *Economica* 8(June): 131–46. Reprinted in Dennis H. Robertson, *Essays in Monetary Theory*. London: Staples Press, pp. 39–59.

Robertson, Dennis H. 1931. How Do We Want Gold to Behave? In *The International Gold Problem: Collected Papers*. Royal Institute of International Affairs, 1929–1931. Oxford: Oxford University Press, pp. 18–46.

Robertson, Dennis H. 1943. The Post-War Monetary Plans. *Economic Journal* 53(December): 352–60.

Robinson, Joan. 1943. The International Currency Proposals. *Economic Journal* 53(June–September): 161–75.

Rogers, James H. 1931. *America Weighs Her Gold*. New Haven, CT: Yale University Press.

Rogers, James H. 1932. Gold, International Credits and Depression. *Journal of the American Statistical Association* 27(September): 237–50.

Rogers, James H. 1937. Monetary Initiative in a Traditional World. In Arthur D. Gayer, ed. *The Lessons of Monetary Experience: Essays in Honor of Irving Fisher*. London: George Allen and Unwin, pp. 99–116.

Rosen, Sherwin. 1997. Austrian and Neoclassical Economics: Any Gains from Trade? *Journal of Economic Perspectives* 11(Fall): 139–52.

Rueff, Jacques, and Hirsch, Fred. 1965. *The Role and the Rule of Gold: An Argument*. Essays in International Finance 47. Princeton, NJ: International Finance Section.

Samuelson, Paul A. 1980. A Corrected Version of Hume's Equilibrating Mechanisms for International Trade. In John S. Chipman and Charles P. Kindleberger, eds. *Flexible Exchange Rates and the Balance of Payments: Essays in Memory of E. Sohmen*. Amsterdam: North-Holland, pp. 141–58.

Samuelson, Paul A. 2001. Economic History and Mainstream Economic Analysis. *Rivista di Storia Economica* 17(agosto): 271–7.

Sargent, Thomas J. 1999. A Primer on Monetary and Fiscal Policy. *Journal of Banking and Finance* 23(10): 1463–82.

Sayers, Richard S. [1960] 1992. The Return to Gold, 1925. In Leslie S. Pressnell, ed. *Studies in the Industrial Revolution*. London: Athlone Press, pp. 85–98. Reprinted in Barry Eichengreen, ed. *Monetary Regime Transformations*. Aldershot, England: Edward Elgar, pp. 282–95.

Schumacher, E. F. 1943. The New Currency Plans. *Bulletin, Institute of Statistics, Oxford* 5(August): 8–29.

Schumacher, E. F., and Balogh, Thomas. 1944. An International Monetary Fund. *Bulletin, Institute of Statistics, Oxford* 6(April): 81–93.

Schumpeter, Joseph A. 1954. *History of Economic Analysis*. Oxford: Oxford University Press.

Shields, Murray, ed. 1944. *International Financial Stabilization: A Symposium*. New York: Irving Trust.

Simons, Henry C. [1936] 1948. Rules Versus Authorities in Monetary Policy. *Journal of Political Economy* 44(February): 1–30. Reprinted in Henry C.

Simons, *Economic Policy for a Free Society*. Chicago: University of Chicago Press, pp. 160–83.

Simons, Henry C. 1945. Discussion of "Peace Aim, Capital Requirements, and International Lending" by Imre de Vegh. *American Economic Review: Papers and Proceedings* 35(May): 294–6.

Snyder, Carl. 1923. The Stabilization of Gold: A Plan. *American Economic Review* 13(June): 276–85.

Stafford, Jack. 1931. The Abandonment of the Gold Standard. *Manchester School of Economic and Social Studies* 2(2): 92–9.

Steindl, Frank G. 1991. The Monetary Economics of Lauchlin Currie. *Journal of Monetary Economics* 27(June): 445–61.

Steindl, Frank G. 1995. *Monetary Interpretations of the Great Depression*. Ann Arbor: University of Michigan Press.

Steindl, Frank G. 1997. Was Fisher a Practicing Quantity Theorist? *Journal of the History of Economic Thought* 19(Fall): 241–60.

Sumner, Scott. 1997. News, Financial Markets, and the Collapse of the Gold Standard: 1931–1932. In Alexander J. Field, ed. *Research in Economic History*, Vol. 17. Greenwich, CT: JAI Press, pp. 39–84.

Temin, Peter. 1989. *Lessons from the Great Depression*. Cambridge, MA: MIT Press.

Temin, Peter, and Wigmore, Barrie A. [1990] 1992. The End of One Big Deflation. *Explorations in Economic History* 27(October): 483–502. Reprinted in Barry Eichengreen, ed. *Monetary Regime Transformations*. Aldershot, England: Edward Elgar, pp. 335–54.

Thomas, Mark, ed. 1996. *The Disintegration of the World Economy Between the World Wars*. Cheltenham, England: Edward Elgar.

Thornton, Henry. 1802. *An Enquiry into the Nature and Effects of the Paper Credit of Great Britain*. London: J. Hatchard.

Tobin, James. 1976. Reply: Is Friedman a Monetarist? In Jerome L. Stein, ed. *Monetarism*. Amsterdam: North-Holland, pp. 332–6.

Triffin, Robert. 1947a. National Central Banking and the International Economy. In *International Monetary Policies*, Postwar Economic Studies 7. Washington: Board of Governors of the Federal Reserve System, pp. 46–81.

Triffin, Robert. 1947b. International Versus Domestic Money. *American Economic Review: Papers and Proceedings* 37(May): 322–4.

Triffin, Robert. 1960. *Gold and the Dollar Crisis: The Future of Convertibility*. New Haven, CT: Yale University Press.

Triffin, Robert. [1964] 1997. The Myth and Realities of the So-Called Gold Standard. In Robert Triffin, *The Evolution of the International Monetary System: Historical Reappraisal and Future Perspectives*. Princeton, NJ: Princeton University Press, pp. 2–20. Reprinted in Barry Eichengreen and Marc Flandreau, eds. *The Gold Standard in Theory and History*, 2nd ed. London: Routledge, pp. 140–60.

Tullio, Giuseppe, and Wolters, Jürgen. 1996. Was London the Conductor of the International Orchestra or Just the Triangle Player? An Empirical Analysis of Asymmetries in Interest Rate Behaviour During the Classical Gold Standard, 1876–1913. *Scottish Journal of Political Economy* 43(September): 419–43.

Tullock, Gordon. 1957. Paper Money – A Cycle in Cathay. *Economic History Review* 9(April): 393–407.

Van Dormael, Armand. 1978. *Bretton Woods: Birth of a Monetary System*. London: Macmillan.

Verrijn Stuart, C. A. 1923. Metallic and Non-Metallic Standards of Money. *Economic Journal* 33(June): 143–54.

Viner, Jacob. 1932. International Aspects of the Gold Standard. In Quincy Wright, ed. *Gold and Monetary Stabilization*. Chicago: University of Chicago Press, pp. 3–39.

Viner, Jacob. [1943] 1951. Two Plans for International Monetary Stabilization. *Yale Review* 33(September). Reprinted in Jacob Viner, *International Economics*. Glencoe, IL: Free Press, pp. 192–215.

Viner, Jacob. [1944] 1951. The Bretton Woods Agreements. In Murray Shields, ed. *International Financial Stabilization: A Symposium*. New York: Irving Trust, pp. 53–68. Reprinted in Jacob Viner, *International Economics*. Glencoe, IL: Free Press, pp. 232–46.

Viner, Jacob. [1947a] 1951. International Economic Coöperation. In *The United States in the Post-War World*. Ann Arbor, MI: University of Michigan Press. Reprinted in Jacob Viner, *International Economics*. Glencoe, IL: Free Press, pp. 282–99.

Viner, Jacob. 1947b. International Finance in the Postwar World. *Journal of Political Economy* 55(April): 97–107.

Viner, Jacob. 1951. *International Economics*. Glencoe, IL: Free Press.

Vines, David. 2003. John Maynard Keynes 1937–1946: The Creation of International Macroeconomics. *Economic Journal* 113(June): F338–61.

Waterman, A. M. C. 1988. Hume, Malthus, and the Stability of Equilibrium. *History of Political Economy* 20(Spring): 85–94.

Whale, P. B. [1937] 1997. The Working of the Prewar Gold Standard. *Economica, New Series* 4(February): 18–32. Reprinted in Barry Eichengreen and Marc Flandreau, eds. *The Gold Standard in Theory and History*, 2nd ed. London: Routledge, pp. 44–56.

White, Harry D. 1933. *The French International Accounts, 1890–1913*. Cambridge, MA: Harvard University Press.

White, Harry D. 1943. Postwar Currency Stabilization. *American Economic Review: Papers and Proceedings* 33(March): 382–92.

White, Harry D. 1945. The Monetary Fund: Some Criticisms Examined. *Foreign Affairs* 23(January): 195–210.

Wicksell, Knut. [1898] 1965. *Interest and Prices: A Study of the Causes Regulating the Value of Money*. New York: Augustus M. Kelley.

Wicksell, Knut. [1906] 1946. *Lectures on Political Economy*, Vol. 2: *Money*. London: Routledge.

Williams, David. 1963. The 1931 Financial Crisis. *Yorkshire Bulletin of Economic and Social Research* 15(November): 92–110. Reprinted in Mark Thomas, ed. *The Disintegration of the World Economy Between the World Wars*, Vol. 2. Cheltenham, England: Edward Elgar.

Williams, John H. 1935. Monetary Stabilization from an International Point of View. *American Economic Review: Papers and Proceedings* 25(March): 156–63.

Williams, John H. 1937. International Monetary Organization and Policy. In Arthur D. Gayer, ed. *The Lessons of Monetary Experience: Essays in Honor of Irving Fisher*. London: George Allen and Unwin, pp. 23–49.

Williamson, John. 1977. *The Failure of World Monetary Reform, 1971–74*. New York: New York University Press.

Williamson, John. 1983. Keynes and the International Economic Order. In David Worswick and James Trevithick, eds. *Keynes and the Modern World*. Cambridge: Cambridge University Press, pp. 87–113.

Williamson, John. 1985. On the System in Bretton Woods. *American Economic Review: Papers and Proceedings* 75(May): 74–9.

Winn, Willis J. 1943. Commodity-Reserve Currency: A Rejoinder. *Journal of Political Economy* 51(April): 175–7.

Wood, Elmer. 1947. Discussion of "International Monetary Policy and the Search for Economic Stability" by Ragnar Nurkse. *American Economic Review: Papers and Proceedings* 37(May): 583–7.

Yeager, Leland B. 1988. The Austrian School on Money and Gold. *Journal of Economic Studies* 15(3/4): 92–105.

Young, Allyn A. 1923. The Trend of Prices. *American Economic Review: Papers and Proceedings* 13(March): 5–14.

Young, Allyn A. [1929] 1999. Downward Price Trend Probable, Due to Hoarding of Gold by Central Banks. *The Annalist* 33(January 18): 96–7. Reprinted in Perry G. Mehrling and Roger J. Sandilands, eds. *Money and Growth: Selected Papers of Allyn Abbott Young*. London: Routledge, pp. 369–73.

AUTHOR INDEX

Author Index

SUBJECT INDEX